JUST TEN OF SONNY BLOCH'S MONEY-MAKING IDEAS FOR YOU

1. Invest in the best-kept secret in real estate.

2. Turn raw land into a money machine.

3. Start sleeping in your bank, if you don't already.

4. Put other people's money and time to work for you.

5. Buy in real estate's bargain basement: foreclosure and tax sales.

6. Learn the first secret to success in buying land.

7. Play to win at the auction game.

8. Follow the Golden Rule . . . of mortgage buying.

9. Get great property deals from a relative: Uncle Sam.

10. Become an "angel"—no wings necessary!

PLUS 161 OTHER GREAT WAYS TO PROFIT IN REAL ESTATE

BANTAM BUSINESS BOOKS

SONNY BLOCH'S 171 WAYS TO MAKE MONEY IN REAL ESTATE

SONNY BLOCH

AND

GRACE LICHTENSTEIN

BANTAM BOOKS

NEW YORK · TORONTO · LONDON · SYDNEY · AUCKLAND

*This edition contains the complete text
of the original hardcover edition.*
NOT ONE WORD HAS BEEN OMITTED.

SONNY BLOCH'S 171 WAYS TO MAKE MONEY IN REAL ESTATE
*A Bantam Book / published by arrangement with
Prentice Hall Press*

PRINTING HISTORY
Prentice Hall Press edition published 1989
Bantam trade edition / March 1991

All rights reserved.
Copyright © 1989 by Sonny Bloch and Grace Lichtenstein.
Cover photo copyright © 1991 by John Neubauer.
Cover type and design copyright © 1991 by One Plus One Studio.
Library of Congress Catalog Card Number: 89-33228.
*No part of this book may be reproduced or transmitted
in any form or by any means, electronic or mechanical, including
photocopying, recording, or by any information storage
and retrieval system, without permission in writing from the publisher.*
For information address:
Prentice Hall Press,
15 Columbus Circle, New York, New York 10023.

ISBN 0-553-35253-9

Published simultaneously in the United States and Canada

Bantam Books are published by Bantam Books, a division of Bantam Doubleday Dell Publishing Group, Inc. Its trademark, consisting of the words "Bantam Books" and the portrayal of a rooster, is Registered in U.S. Patent and Trademark Office and in other countries. Marca Registrada. Bantam Books, 666 Fifth Avenue, New York, New York 10103.

PRINTED IN THE UNITED STATES OF AMERICA

RRH   0 9 8 7 6 5 4 3 2 1

ACKNOWLEDGMENTS

A book begins with an idea, so to you my radio-listening friends and television viewers, thanks for the thousands of calls and letters that are the source of the ideas in this book. The 171 ways to make money in real estate are the ones you most frequently ask about.

I dedicate this book to my enthusiastic audience and to my team of family members, colleagues, and experts including Mom and Dad, Stuart, Ivan, and Harriett, Harry Frieland, Carl Jenny, Paul Kamke, Wayne Phillips, Don and Paul Zoch, the Stanger Organization, Bill Whiting, Jay Dryer, Nick Koon, and Jimmy Napier. Thanks also to my production teams: Mike Castello, Julia Heath, Milford Edwards, Mike Laboy, and Paul Howard Bloch (radio), plus Gale B. Nemec, Jamie Maurey, Tony Piazza, and Nadia Moritz for keeping the shows together while I was writing this book.

—Sonny Bloch

I owe a deep and abiding debt of gratitude to my writers' group—Ann Banks, Gwenda Blair, Catherine Breslin, Carol Brightman, Jane Ciabattari, Robin Reisig, and Marilyn Webb—and to Laurie, Steve, and Lou for sustaining me throughout the year.

Special thanks to Stanley I. Aber for reading and critiquing various chapters; Janice Goodman for thoughtful legal counsel; Sandra Kane and Pamela Cox for facilitating exchange of materials; Stevie Phillips and all my friends in Aspen and Snowmass Village for companionship in the per-

fect writing environment; Ann Weissman for keeping me fit; and Gustav
Mahler and Etta James for musical inspiration.

—Grace Lichtenstein

Both authors wish to thank our agent, Nate Horrow, and Paul Aron, who
is a caring, patient, and good-humored editor.

CONTENTS

FOREWORD

This book is a practical, straightforward guide to help you reap the profits that are available to everyone in the field of real estate. You can use it as a companion to, and continuation of, our first book, *Inside Real Estate: The Complete Guide to Buying and Selling Your Home, Co-op, or Condominium,* but it covers fresh and different ground.

The first book was aimed directly at the *first-time home buyer or seller.* The book you are reading now, on the other hand, is aimed at the *novice investor*—the person who is beginning to buy real estate in order to make money, whether or not that person owns a home.

As I always stress on my nationwide radio call-in show on real estate, at public seminars, and on television, I do have certain principles that apply to both the home buyer/seller as well as the investor. Two principles are so important that even though they were discussed in detail in *Inside Real Estate,* I want to begin by emphasizing them again.

First, anyone getting into the real estate game should assemble a trusted group of experts for his or her team, starting with an attorney and a certified public accountant. Second, no matter what has been discussed in any real estate deal, the only items that count are those that you get in writing. Keep these paramount principles in mind as you go through the following investment ideas.

Wondering about the number 171 in the title? It is not a gimmick. In each of the twenty chapters that follow, I outline specific tips that will earn you more money and improve your margin of profit in real estate—from the simplest (always try to buy investment property at 20 percent or more below market price) to the most complex (make certain you are included as a loss payee on insurance when buying second mortgages). You can find a review of each of the 171 ways, chapter by chapter, at the end of the book.

For me, real estate is the most fascinating game in the world, because the potential for increasing your wealth is unlimited, yet anybody with a dream and a taste for hard work can play. Ready to join? Chapter 1 tells you about the basic rules of the game and helps you explore the many avenues you can take on the road to winning. Chapters 2 through 19 describe different strategies. Chapter 20 explains how to maximize your gains by making federal tax laws work on your behalf.

Out of 171 ways to make money investing in real estate, I know you can find many that make sense for you.

PART ONE

ACTIVE INVESTING

1

How to Jump from Being a Successful Real Estate Consumer to Being a Successful Real Estate Investor

The time is always ripe for investing in real estate. However, now more than ever before, small investors, through real estate, seek tried and true income-producing returns on their money.

Especially in an uncertain economy, with gyrating stock prices, creeping inflation, a fluctuating money supply, and wavering interest rates, the smart ones turn to real estate as a safe, sane, profitable haven for their extra dollars.

Why real estate? Because it is an essential part of our lives, like food and clothing. Housing—affordable residential housing, not luxury homes or commercial space—is recession-proof. There is always a market for it.

There is a market, too, for new investors such as yourself. The bad news is, it takes plenty of work. I know, because I have spent a good portion of my working life investing in real estate. The good news is, you don't need to be wealthy to begin your investing career.

WHAT THIS BOOK WILL DO FOR YOU

As I did in our first book, *Inside Real Estate,* I will demystify the world of real estate. I will simplify investing for first-time investors or novice investors who feel the need to know more about what they are doing.

This book will explain to you what options are available to you, the small investor. It will lead you step by step through each investment opportunity—from your first rental house through raw land, tax sales, auctions, government loans . . . and, for very busy or lazy investors, through passive investments such as limited partnerships and real estate investment trusts (REITs).

At this point perhaps you are protesting, "I'm small potatoes, not Donald Trump! I'm an average person with only an amateur background in real estate."

Everyone who invests in real estate deals with the "fear factor," even the professionals. It is the feeling you have the first time you jump into a swimming pool, the first time you fly in an airplane, the first time you make love. You know others have done it successfully, yet you still need some kind of convincing to hurdle that first fence.

You are probably reading this book because you have dreamed about making money in real estate. You want to get involved but are not quite sure where to start. Maybe you were once burned in a deal, or lost a bundle in the stock market or with mutual funds. So you are understandably nervous about jumping into this pool.

My philosophy is that you can build wealth without mortgaging your financial health. That's why, as in *Inside Real Estate,* I will help you first establish your *comfort zones*—the parameters of money, time, and risk that allow you to make a profit and still sleep at night.

Believe me—you can, in your own small way, be just as smart as the big boys. It's not as complicated as you might think. And in a market where you are cash-light and knowledge-heavy, you can do nicely indeed.

You do not even need to be a home or apartment owner to be a real estate investor. Many successful investors live in a rental property and own millions of dollars worth of investment property. For instance, if you have a rent-controlled or stabilized apartment on Park Avenue in New York City, it would be foolish for you to move out. You can get more bang for your buck investing in other areas.

AFFORDABLE = PROFITABLE

A phrase you will see repeated often here is "affordable housing." Real estate is not a beauty contest. It is a numbers game. If the numbers work for you, you can be a winner.

Here is an example. Say you own a $300,000 3-bedroom, 2-bath house in Birmingham, Michigan. It might bring you $2,000 a month in rent. With a 10 percent down payment, your mortgage payment (principal, interest, taxes, insurance) would be approximately $2,700 a month.

That means you have a monthly negative cash flow in the range of $700. In other words, you lose money every thirty days! This property might be lovely, but it is a lousy investment. Certainly it is fun to drive by the place and have your friends admire it. Unfortunately, it can drive you to the poorhouse. Uninformed real estate amateurs buy such houses all the time, simply because they are gorgeous and prestigious.

On the other hand, if you drive fifteen minutes away, you could buy a nice 3-bedroom, 2-bath residence in Pontiac, Michigan, for $40,000, with the same 10 percent down. Your monthly mortgage payment would be $360 a month, while you could collect a monthly rental of $450. You wind up with a healthy $90 per month positive cash flow—extra money.

That's not the end of the example. The fancy Birmingham house costs you $30,000 up front as a down payment, while the Pontiac house costs only $4,000. The Pontiac house gives you $960 a year cash return on your cash investment—24 percent—plus the additional money that goes into your pocket in the form of income tax deductions for interest on the mortgage and depreciation on the house itself. Finally, assuming the Pontiac house appreciates—grows in value—by just 5 percent a year, you make an additional $2,000 annually.

Thus you get $2,960 per year total return on a $4,000 investment—a whopping 74 percent! There is no better way for the small investor to build wealth.

This is a simple example to illustrate why "affordable housing" is the key theme running through these pages. Time after time, the purchase of affordable housing, rather than good-looking or overpriced fancy housing, creates the success stories that people relate to me on the air and in person. The best thing about affordable housing is that it is within your reach.

The reason I downplay "beauty contest winners" is not because I don't like handsome properties. I appreciate mansions and million-dollar Park Avenue apartments as much as the next guy. I love to live in palatial digs.

But as an investor, I am not buying a place in which to live. I am buying a place through which I can make money, so I can buy the nicer home for myself. This requires a subtle but sincere shift in attitude, a new viewpoint. You now must shop for investment properties with an investor's eye for value, rather than a consumer's eye for personal appeal.

Read on. To begin with, I will supply you with the background you need when Uncle Joe says, "Boy, have I got a deal for you!" I will show you how to find money you did not know you had. You will learn the meaning of phrases like *appreciation, positive cash flow, OPM, front end load, payback agreement, cash-on-cash, general partner,* and so on.

I will open your eyes to the remarkable variety of investment real estate. You will learn how to get rental income directly from the government under Section 8 programs, how to bid on auction properties, how to get involved in a partnership venture.

Once you decide what kind of investment real estate is best for you, I will show you, step by step, how to concentrate on that area. I will describe how to hunt for your best investment, buy it at the right price, finance it, manage it, and sell it.

WHAT NOT TO EXPECT

What *won't* this book do for you? It will not show you an easy way to gamble on a property and win big. Real estate investing is not a race track, a lottery, or a craps table. It is a thoughtful, concentrated process that requires your time as well as your dreams.

I won't tell you how to get rich quick. I *will* show you how to make money the smart way.

I will not tell you about esoteric techniques or strategies, only about proven techniques already being used widely and successfully.

I will not show you how to steal property from unfortunate people. Nor will I let you in on the secrets of swindling or double-dealing.

Ours is a ''win-win'' game. This book will demonstrate that you can make a profit with both seller and buyer satisfied.

Before deciding to write *Inside Real Estate,* I spent six years as a consumer advocate giving free information to the public on radio and television. I built my reputation on down-to-earth, reasonable, constructive help—on ideas that you can trust.

Trust is the key to the advice in this book as well. It is based on my thirty years of personal experience in the real estate business, plus those questions most frequently asked by my radio, television, and seminar audiences.

BLOCH BY BLOCH

A bit of personal history is in order here. I am a licensed real estate broker, a former title-company president, a builder, and an owner. Moreover, I am a third-generation real estate investor.

Grandfather Harry Bloch arrived in northern Wisconsin from the old country early in the century. He was in the dry goods business, but when some farmers were unable to purchase what he had to sell, he bartered his goods for land. Land in northern Wisconsin was incredibly cheap then— as low as 25 to 30 cents an acre. My grandfather then sold the lumber from the land to lumber companies. What lumber was left standing, he used to build homes. Thus, the Bloch family got into the property business first, then the banking business.

My uncles and father, too, became involved in the lumber and real estate business. Conversation around the dinner table in our family was usually about real estate deals, and so my brothers, my sister, and I were introduced to the profession as youngsters.

My first real estate experience outside the family occurred when I was a young traveling singer and musician. Taking advantage of rumors, I began investing in acreage in a little town called Kissimee, Florida. If you look up my name in the Osceola County Courthouse records, you will discover that in 1962–63, I was buying and selling land in a most advantageous location: You know it now as the site of Disney World.

The fourth generation is busy following in the family footsteps. My oldest son is now buying and syndicating apartment houses and trailer parks in central Florida.

Unlike the "snake oil" salesman whose aim is to have you purchase his $300 set of cassettes, I have no ulterior motives. Now that you have borrowed this book from your library or plunked down $19.95 for it, my goal is to make the principles of real estate investing understandable. Once you read through the book, you can telephone me toll free on my nationwide radio show to ask further questions. The number is (800) 356-5566. Office hours are 3 P.M. to 7 P.M. Eastern time, Monday through Friday, or 10 A.M. to 1 P.M. Eastern time on Sundays.

A RISK WORTH TAKING

Real estate investing is not without risk, of course. But there are certain risks you should avoid—such as getting involved in a deal without an attorney, not analyzing a deal thoroughly, or buying a property that has secret restrictions. As long as you do your homework, you reduce your risks.

Each chapter contains charts, questionnaires, and worksheets to help you do that homework. I am a stern but fair teacher, so I expect you to fill out the worksheets, answer the questions, and keep a calculator handy to do the arithmetic as if you were studying for an A in your most important high school or college course. The more you know about this business, the less risky it becomes.

The major risk is . . . you.

If you are not willing to take the time and energy to research your investments, to complete your homework assignments, and to go through the records, you put yourself at risk.

The one promise I can make is that if you do your homework properly, the risk in real estate is quite low, barring catastrophes you can never predict, from a hurricane to the closing of a town's major industry. Furthermore, real estate is cyclical. The market for it never stays depressed; it always comes back. The recent resurgence of real estate in areas from Providence, Rhode Island, to Detroit, Michigan, is clear evidence of this.

During the ten-year period from 1978 through 1987, real estate's best performance was an 18.3 percent gain, its worst a 6.8 percent gain. Never has real estate dropped 22 percent in one day, as the stock market did in October, 1987.

Real estate is much less risky than the stock market, less risky than oil, less risky than gold or silver—and you can live in it.

YOU DON'T NEED A BARREL OF MONEY

The basic thrust of this book is to show you how to keep the money you make . . . and make the money that you keep make *more* money for you.

A great attraction of real estate is that the money you use to get started as an investor is *not* money you need to live on while you are putting deals together. It is either other people's money, credit, or money put aside for nonessentials.

If you do have savings, or other investments that can be sold for cash, your money goes a long way, since in real estate, a little controls a lot. You can buy 100 percent of a piece of property with only 10 percent down. That is the definition of *leverage,* a word you hear often in real estate conversation.

Let's say that you buy a $100,000 property in an area where the average annual increase in property value is 10 percent (that is the national average). By putting 10 percent, or $10,000, down, you own and control the property.

Then there is the *A* word, perhaps the most important term in the real estate field: *appreciation*. Because of the annual growth in its value, the property earns you a 100 percent tax-free return on your $10,000 investment every year. That is what "appreciation" means.

Put another way, the first year the property is worth $110,000. You invested $10,000. Therefore, you make $10,000 on paper on your $10,000 investment, which is a 100 percent return on your cash investment.

Appreciation—the annual growth in the worth of your property—is the reason I call real estate the "ultimate tax-free wealth builder."

Appreciation is one of two goals in your quest for long-term real estate success. The other is *flat* or *positive cash flow.* This will be discussed fully in a later chapter. However, the basic idea is to bring in as much as you are paying out, or more. Since your $10,000 down on the theoretical property leaves you with a $90,000 mortgage, you should be sure of getting a minimum of 1 percent of the mortgage—or $900—per month in rent, to cover principal, interest, taxes, and insurance.

Over the years, your rental income will increase, but your mortgage payments will not. When this happens, your cash flow becomes greater than your expenses—positive rather than flat.

Therefore, the worst that can happen with this property is an appreciation of $10,000 per year on a $100,000 house, while someone else makes your mortgage payments and thus increases your equity, and *you* benefit from the tax write-off of the interest on the mortgage plus depreciation (a gift from Uncle Sam that will also be explained later.)

IS NOW THE TIME TO ENTER THE REAL ESTATE WORLD?

Some people are better off as passive, not active, investors. Chapter 2 will help you determine your best role. Once you are convinced that real estate investing can work for you, the next question might be, when is the right time?

"There is never a bad time to buy real estate." I have told my audiences that a thousand times, and it is not a Pollyanna attitude. It is *always* a good time, provided you know what moves to make in the particular marketplace you are in.

For instance, in a down market such as Houston, a smart move would be to buy repossessed property from a bank at 30 to 40 percent below market value, with that bank financing your purchase at a low interest rate. You would then rent the property to a low-income tenant whose rent is paid by the Federal Government under Section 8 terms.

The other side of the coin would be a hot market such as San Francisco. A smart move in this case would be to buy from a motivated seller— someone in foreclosure, or behind on taxes. Disciplined aggressiveness pays off here as you go strictly for distressed property, which can be found in the midst of every boom.

Contrary to what some lay people think, you do not need to time your real estate deals to peaks or valleys in interest rates, the stock market, or inflation.

If you enter the real estate game in a period when interest rates are fluctuating, you *should* make sure that you get either a *fixed rate mortgage* or a *convertible adjustable rate mortgage*. With a fixed, the interest rate remains the same over the life of the mortgage, usually fifteen or thirty years. With a convertible ARM, the interest rate may change every few years, but you have the option of converting it to a fixed mortgage.

Once interest rates climb past 12 percent, or when interest rates go beyond the point where you can have a flat cash flow, you need to negotiate with the seller for owner-financing of a property. This means the seller becomes your banker, perhaps even taking a note in place of a down payment. Why would a seller agree to this? Because that owner cannot afford to sit with an empty piece of property, and the interest you pay the owner will yield much more than a CD or savings account.

What about starting your real estate portfolio when stock prices are bouncing around like corks in the ocean? This is precisely the situation in which wary market players pull some money out of stocks and bonds, and go into real estate. It is an especially good time to reinvest that money in passive real estate, since products such as limited partnerships tend to be undervalued.

Otherwise, there is hardly any connection between the movement of the Dow Jones Index and real estate markets. (During a bull market real estate prices do jump in places such as New York City, where people working in the financial field drive those prices up. During a bear market, those same residences become available at distressed prices. That small, though significant, pocket of the country is an exception, not the rule.)

I mentioned before that real estate is recession-proof. It is also inflation-proof.

As a general rule, real estate is 3 to 5 points ahead of inflation. So if inflation reaches 6 percent a year, real estate is escalating at 9 or 10 percent a year. As long as the appreciation of real estate stays ahead of inflation, which eats away at your dollars, your property is a great hedge against inflation.

In other words, while your dollars sit in a bank or money market fund losing value, real estate makes up the difference by increasing in value.

The message is clear: It always pays to park your safe dollars in real estate, not in a stagnant bank account or a risky Wall Street investment.

Ready for your first moves?

Move 1—find out what your comfort zone is for the various types of real estate investments. The next chapter gives you a quick overview, and a test that shows whether you are more suited to an active or a passive investment.

Move 2—either fill in the blanks on my simplified 15-minute chart below to analyze a deal you may already be studying . . . or be ready to answer the questionnaire so you know what basic information you will need once you find that potential deal.

Keep the questionnaire and worksheet with you (I don't mind if you make a set of photocopies!) and consult them when you begin to shop for properties. No matter whether you buy a house or apartment, whether you deal with a broker, an auctioneer, a government agency, or an owner, the questionnaire and worksheet will keep you on the profit-making track.

THE BIG 8 QUESTIONS:
ANALYZING YOUR FIRST DEAL

1. Since you should always buy wholesale (10 percent or more below market value), is the purchase price of the property at market value or lower?
2. If the purchase price is too high, is the seller motivated enough so you can negotiate a lower price?
3. Is the property in a move-in condition? If not, how much will it cost out of pocket to bring it up to that standard?
4. What does insurance cost for similar properties in this neighborhood?
5. What are the annual taxes on such property?
6. If you do not plan to manage the property yourself, what is the availability of good property managers?
7. How strong or weak is the demand for rentals in the neighborhood, as indicated by local real estate brokers, classified ads, and your own detective work?
8. Is government-subsidized (such as Section 8) housing being rented in the area, and if so, are governmental agencies open to new landlords such as yourself?

SONNY BLOCH'S 15-MINUTE RENTAL PROPERTY DIAGNOSIS

EQUITY POSITION

A. Price of house or apartment unit $ _____

B. Down payment $ _____

C. Closing costs* $ _____

D. Cleanup or fix-up costs $ _____

E. Total cash invested (B + C + D) $ _____

F. Market value $ _____

G. New mortgages needed for purchase $ _____

H. Equity after closing (G minus F) $ _____

YEARLY CASH-ON-CASH RETURN

I. Monthly rent × 11 (1 month vacancy cushion) $ _____

J. Management fee, maintenance, utilities × 12
(all optional) $ _____

K. Principal, interest, taxes, insurance × 12 $ _____

L. Cash return (I minus J and K) $ _____

M. % of cash return: Figure by determining what % L is
of E   _____ %

PLUS APPRECIATION, THE ULTIMATE
TAX-FREE WEALTH BUILDER

Market value (F) × 5% per year. $_____ year 1

$_____ year 2

$_____ year 3

$_____ year 4

$_____ year 5

Or, Market value (F) × 10% per year $_____ year 1

$_____ year 2

$_____ year 3

$_____ year 4

$_____ year 5

Do This Formula Yearly:
  Market value (F) + appreciation $_____

  Minus existing mortgage principal balance (G) $_____

  Equals current Equity $_____

Do a 5-year projection and watch your wealth grow!

*Closing costs should include inspection, legal fees, points paid on down payment, and/or mortgage, title insurance.

2

Movers, Shakers, Makers, Flippers, Angels, Bakers —How to Find Your Comfort Zone

Active investors are entrepreneurs. Truly active ones—call them the *movers*—are ready to spend their time . . . perhaps money . . . and certainly their sweat to make a real estate deal happen. Do you fit this category?

On the other hand, a second kind of active investor—the *shaker*—is able to find the deals but would rather get other investors to put up the cash. This is called using OPM, or *Other People's Money.* Does this kind of investor sound like you?

The third category of active investors is the *makers.* They find and make deals, and they put in their own money, but they do not want to get midnight phone calls from tenants. Nor are they willing or able to risk scraped knuckles or paint under their fingernails to fix up property. They are nonmanagers and active, yet silent, landlords. Do you have the dollars, but need OPT *(Other People's Time)* to make real estate dreams come true?

In the next category are the *flippers.* No, these are not dolphins but semiactive investors. They do not hold onto a newly purchased property, but "flip" it—sell it for an immediate profit. This is the old "buy low, sell high" attitude that has made many investors wealthy.

Do you want to generate a larger amount of cash (even though you must pay taxes on it) in order to have a heftier reserve fund for the down payment and/or repairs on your next purchase? You should start out as a flipper.

Yet another group of semiactive investors is the *angels.* They put up the money for deals found and made by others who become their partners.

The deal-making partners manage the property for investing angels. Eventually they split the profits, after paying the deal-making partners a management fee. Are you a potential angel?

Finally, there are the *bakers*—folks who put their dough in the real estate oven and watch it rise. These are people eager to reap the benefits of real estate. They have money . . . but neither the time nor the inclination to get truly involved with property. They would rather buy into registered financial products, such as limited partnerships or trusts, or mutual funds dealing with real estate. These are *passive* investors.

How can you know whether you should invest at all in property, or which type of investor—mover, shaker, maker, flipper, angel, baker—you are?

I can answer the question backwards: *Do not* invest in real estate if you expect to become rich overnight.

Do invest if you want your money to work harder for you than it does in a Certificate of Deposit or a money market fund. That kind of money works for the bank, which turns around and puts that money into higher-yielding investments, such as real estate mortgages. Your money market fund or CD brings you 4 to 6 percent after taxes, yet bankers charge others 10 percent and up for a mortgage.

Do invest in real estate if you are serious about your financial future and security . . . if you are willing to put in the time and energy required in viewing many properties (or directing others to do it for you), as well as handling your portfolio . . . if you enjoy making the kind of offers you will learn about here . . . if you are good at interacting with other people.

To determine whether you would do best as an active, semiactive, or passive investor, you need to establish your investing *comfort zone*.

Perhaps you knew the moment you picked up this book what your comfort zone was. If you have not made up your mind, check the investment comfort zone chart on page 17, and spend a few minutes with me zoning in on your investor profile.

ATTENTION, PLEASE!

Active investments require your attention, not twenty-four hours a day, but on a regular, intermittent basis. Active investors check their properties regularly, whether they are single family houses, commercial space, even raw land. They must look after the property's physical condition, consult with tenants and managers, collect rent, and pay taxes, insurance, and management fees.

In almost every case, a truly active investor is a landlord. The conventional, visible landlord has an ongoing relationship with his or her tenants. Talk about attention!

As a landlord, you will have to make yourself available to local inspectors, repair personnel, tax people, and prospective tenants. The reward for this effort is that you keep a larger share of the profits on your property.

However, there is an intermediate category of active investor who is a silent, invisible landlord. In such a case, you hire a professional management company, for a fixed monthly fee, to take over the landlording jobs from you. You give up some profit in exchange for time and peace of mind.

If you find the right management company, it is worth paying ten cents out of every dollar in order to free yourself from unwanted duties. A good management firm helps you avoid tenant calls in the middle of the night, deflects complaints about items like faulty wiring or plumbing, directs the workmen who come to fix such things so that they do it right and within specific time limits, and handles disputes between tenants about one another's behavior.

There are many excellent management companies in every community . . . as well as careless or inefficient ones. Later on, chapter 13 and its checklist will help you evaluate those available to you.

Once you insulate yourself from being a hands-on active investor and become instead a silent landlord, you can concentrate more on finding new deals, not to mention retaining your sanity.

The buy-and-flip procedure mentioned earlier, a semiactive investment strategy, frees you from even invisible landlording. You qualify as a flipper if you are good at finding below-market-value property, but want immediate income rather than long-term appreciation. This strategy works well for unusually good bargain properties bought at tax sales or after foreclosures, at auction, and via estate sales or "distress" situations (divorces, sudden job transfers, and so on).

RELPS, REITS, AND
OTHER PASSIVE REWARDS

Under the umbrella of *passive investments* come such products as real estate investment trusts, real estate limited partnerships, tax certificates, and mortgages.

A *Real Estate Limited Partnership* (RELP) refers to a partial share of ownership along with others in a collection of properties—residential, industrial, or commercial, or a mixture of these.

How much you can make depends on the structure and length of the particular partnership. It can last anywhere from five to ten years. The return might vary from as low as 8 percent to as high as 22 percent. A RELP can be a private investment or a public one; the latter is registered as a security.

A *Real Estate Investment Trust* (REIT) is a more liquid investment. You purchase stock in a REIT as you would a company: REITs are traded on public exchanges such as the New York and American Stock Exchanges. Thus you can buy shares on a Monday, then cash them in on Tuesday.

For the past ten years, REITs have returned from 7 percent to 18 percent annually.

A *tax certificate* is probably one of the most lucrative items, as well as one of the best-kept secrets, in the real estate game. It is a document issued by a state or local government on someone else's property for non-payment of taxes.

Tax certificates guarantee you a very high rate of return on your investment—from 8 percent to 50 percent a year, depending on the municipality. You might hold a tax certificate for one to three years, earning your percentage each year. Almost all delinquent taxpayers buy the certificates back from you before the specified term ends, but they must pay you the principal plus interest.

Should the delinquent taxpayer fail to buy the certificate back, you may convert the document into a real estate investment by purchasing the actual property for anywhere from 10 to 30 cents on the dollar. Rarely do people fail to redeem certificates for small amounts—$600 on a $60,000 house, for example. From time to time, however, it happens.

A *mortgage* can bring you a return of approximately 12 to 25 percent per year, depending upon how deep the discount is when you buy it, and what the lifetime of the mortgage is (generally from two to thirty years).

There is a thriving market for first and second mortgages that you buy from mortgage holders (banks and other lenders) who want to cash out.

YOUR INVESTMENT COMFORT ZONE— ARE YOU ACTIVE OR PASSIVE?

Okay, it's time to decide on your comfort zone. Respond honestly to the following questionnaire:

1. Would you be upset if someone called you in the middle of the night to fix a toilet?

Very upset (0 points)
Somewhat upset (5 points)
Mildly upset (10 points)

2. Do you enjoy interacting on the phone and in person with other people?

No, I'm too shy/nervous/impatient (0 points)
Sure, but not in the middle of the night (5 points)
I am at my best with people, rather than with data (10 points)

3. Do you mind going into a neighborhood that is not as nice as the one you live in to collect rent?

Yes, it would bother me (0 points)
I would do it if I had to (5 points)
No, I don't mind (10 points)

4. Are you willing to give up just about every weekend and some weeknights for the next six months to find a deal?

No, I'm overextended in terms of my time (0 points)
Perhaps, but I know I get discouraged easily (5 points)
Absolutely (10 points)

5. Are you ready to interview prospective tenants, ask them questions about their previous two or three landlords, and follow up with calls to their references, so you don't wind up with people who later will have to be evicted?

No, I don't have the time or inclination (0 points)
Yes, provided I don't spend long hours doing it (5 points)
Yes, I'm ready and can free up plenty of time (10 points)

6. Can you see yourself dealing with plumbers, painters, electricians, and carpenters?

Not really (0 points)
Yes, I can see trying this (5 points)
Yes, I am confident in this area (10 points)

7. How energetic are you at handling necessary paperwork and working alongside a CPA on such things as property taxes and local laws and codes?

Ugh. Low energy! (2 points)
Somewhat energetic (7 points)
Quite energetic—I love fiddling with figures (10 points)

8. Are you comfortable dealing with insurance claims and adjustors?

> No, they intimidate me (0 points)
> I suppose so, if I must (4 points)
> Yes, I am comfortable (10 points)

9. Do you see yourself as a thorough researcher who can study a neighborhood, marketplace, or a particular property?

> No, I tend to have a short attention span (0 points)
> Yes, although I hesitate to commit the time (5 points)
> Yes! I like research (10 points)

10. Can you envision yourself searching for, screening, and checking references for a management company that would run day-to-day affairs for you—and periodically reviewing its performance?

> No, that is still too much of a time commitment (0 points)
> Yes, I want a buffer between me and tenants (6 points)
> No, I prefer to be a hands-on landlord (10 points)

Final Score: _____ Points

What Your Score Means

70–100 . . . You are comfortable as an active investor and hands-on landlord.

40–69 . . . You are comfortable with active investing but you are inclined to be invisible, with day-to-day management handled by professionals.

0–39 . . . You would be most comfortable as a passive investor in such areas as a limited partnership, REIT, or tax certificate.

* * *

Do you count yourself among those who wish to be active investors—movers and shakers? Welcome to the club.

Before going further, spend a few dollars getting the standard 500 business cards printed, preferably with your photo on them. They should proclaim you "John or Jane Doe, real estate investor." Beneath that should be a phrase such as "I Buy Properties for Cash."

Once you have the cards in hand, you can get your new career under way by looking for your first purchase and by shopping for your own or someone else's money. The next chapters explain these crucial steps.

3

You're Sleeping in Your Bank

Are you one of those people who insist, "I'm so broke I can't afford to invest in anything, much less real estate"?

Yes you can. You are sleeping in your "bank."

I am not going to wave a magic wand so you can pull money out of a hat. If you live in a rental home, if you have never saved a nickel, and if you do not even have a life insurance policy of any value, you may not be a suitable candidate. If you are determined to try, you could find a deal and use OPM—other people's money. Your first deal would have to be a handyman special or fixer-upper bought for very little money, or a foreclosed property bought at 30 to 50 percent below its real worth (see chapter 9).

But I *will* wave a metaphorical wand over the house you own, live in, and sleep in, because it is a key to finding your first investing dollars.

Any wage earner who has bought a home and has equity in it, under current tax laws, can borrow against that equity. That is the definition of a *home equity loan* or second mortgage. You can then put this "found" money in your first piece of investment real estate.

Equity is defined as that amount of money that exists between what you owe on your house and what your house is worth.

Let's go back to the $100,000 house we used as an example in chapter 1. We will assume you can buy it for $10,000 down.

Meanwhile, you live in a house for which you paid $100,000 a few years ago—$10,000 down plus a $90,000 mortgage. It is now worth $200,000. You owe $80,000 on it. You have an equity of $120,000.

Various banks will offer you different arrangements, but basically you can borrow up to 80 percent of the market value in the home (80 percent of $200,000 equals $160,000) at a reasonable interest rate.

In our sample case, you can get a $10,000 home equity loan—a small portion of your maximum—at competitive rates. Better yet, equity loans are taken out tax-free.

Equity loans have proven to be a tremendous boon for consumers and lenders alike. According to the *Federal Reserve Bulletin*, 3 million home owners have equity loans, to the tune of $75 billion.

Are you willing to pull money out of this bank you are sleeping in so you can use it as down payment on your first investment house? If you follow the steps outlined in this book, the money you borrow will end up earning you more money, rather than gathering dust by figuratively sitting dormant in your own home.

True, your home is probably appreciating each year. So if you leave the $10,000 alone, and your home increases in value 10 percent a year, you are making a paper profit of $1,000 per year.

But if you decide to use the $10,000 to gain control of the $100,000 investment house or apartment, it, too, could appreciate at 10 percent a year. And that means a paper profit for you of an additional $9,000 a year, plus all the tax advantages and positive cash flow.

In other words, by using your home as your bank, you earn 100 percent, tax-free, on your money instead of 10 percent. (An appreciation of $10,000 a year on a $10,000 cash investment equals 100 percent return.)

TOO MUCH OF A GOOD THING?

It is almost *too* easy to get an equity loan these days. A lot of lenders are trying to place equity loans that really are credit cards—and then encouraging borrowers to buy sailboats and Maseratis.

What if you find a real estate deal that would require an equity loan amounting to 100 percent of the worth of the house you live in? Not a good idea. You never want to pull out more than 80 percent of the money your house is worth.

Thus, if your house is worth $1 million, don't borrow more than $800,000. If it's worth $100,000, don't borrow more than $80,000. A 20 percent cushion lets you sleep peacefully in your "bank."

Take out enough to cover the *down payment and costs only* on the real estate purchase you are working on. Do not let an overeager loan officer sucker you into borrowing more than you need to cover it.

Furthermore, keep a sharp eye on rising interest rates and on the fine print. Some equity loans can be more expensive than other loans available to you.

THE ABCS OF EQUITY LOANS, AKA SECOND MORTGAGES

A is for *Application:* Some banks charge application fees, also known as origination fees. Be sure to ask what these fees are and whether they are refundable if you do not qualify.

Another *A* about the application: Although home equity loans usually are processed faster than regular mortgage loans, find out how long it will take to get your money. One month is average; some banks take as long as three months.

B is for *Borrowing:* When you take out a home equity loan, in most cases, you are borrowing revolving credit, just as you do on your credit cards. Home equity rates are cheaper than the 18 percent and more you pay on credit cards. Nevertheless, banks allow you to obtain an 80 percent line of credit, even if you plan to use only a small amount of that. Just say no. They also allow you to write checks against your home equity line, thus adding to the amount you borrow. Don't do it.

C is for *Caps:* Some home equity loans do not have caps, or limits, on them. Thus they can keep rising as interest rates rise. Beware of no-cap or high-cap loans.

C is also for *Co-ops:* The New York City metropolitan area is unusual in that many apartment buildings are co-ops, not condos. Co-op owners pay higher rates—up to 1 percent—on an equity loan . . . and some banks ask them to pay off the loan on the co-op first. (Banks do not like second mortgages on co-ops because the "owners" do not actually own real estate; they own shares in a corporation.)

Here is additional information about home equity loans:

Most are variable rate loans: The initial interest rate is often artificially low. However, the rate suddenly jumps after six months or a year, since variable rate loans "float" or change, based on changes in the prime rate or some other index. (According to *USA Today,* three-quarters of banks tie their variable rate to the prime rate.)

Find out what index your loan is tied to, how often it can be adjusted, and whether you can convert your loan after a period of time into a fixed-rate loan. Better yet, go after the elusive fixed-rate equity loan.

Almost all have closing costs: There are almost always some closing costs on an equity loan, as there are on any mortgage. They vary from lender to lender. Some banks charge only $200 to $300, according to a *Money* magazine survey, but some places, such as Sears, charge 3 percent of your credit limit up front, whether or not you use all the money. That amounts to $1,500 on a $50,000 loan.

These costs are the fees the bank charges for doing business with you. You can finance the closing costs or pay them up front. You can also deduct closing costs from your income taxes or from the profit you pay taxes on when you sell.

Fixed rates are available: Many companies now offer a fixed rate equity loan. It is the same as a second mortgage, for the standard periods of fifteen or thirty years. Most banks won't tell you about it or do not offer it. But it is worth hunting for.

Refinancing is possible: If interest rates decline by more than 2 points, you should consider refinancing both your original home mortgage and the equity loan you have now taken out in order to make a down payment on an investment property.

YOU'D BETTER SHOP AROUND

The big mistake most people make is that they shop only one place for an equity loan. Phone or visit up to a dozen lenders who offer such loans. Make photocopies of the comparison shopping chart in this chapter, and take notes on the rate each lender offers, the length of the loan, and additional costs of each.

Notice that there is a column for checking off a bank's promise to lock in the rate quoted for a specified period of time.

Your sources of equity loans start with the bank holding your home mortgage. But that is not the only stop on your treasure hunt. Go to other banks, savings and loan companies, mortgage bankers, mortgage brokers (middlemen who have contacts with many different lenders), and credit unions.

With interest rates changing unexpectedly nowadays, it is worth the extra $200 to $350 to lock in a good rate. Otherwise, you can be in for an unpleasant shock—I call it payment shock—when, just before the closing on the loan, the bank officer informs you that his bank's rate has gone up a point in the month or two you have been waiting.

Keep in mind that an equity loan is a second mortgage. Don't borrow a cent if you are the gambling or free-spending type. You are the person who would actually go for the Maserati, even if you had every intention of using the loan for real estate investment.

The bottom line is, the home you live in is your collateral for this loan. It would be a shame if you could not repay a home equity loan, had your house taken away, and found yourself sleeping in your Maserati.

CONSUMER ALERT: EQUITY LOAN SCAMS

There have been enough complaints about home equity loan abuses to require federal investigations. Banks and other lenders are so eager to give you money that they often promise you a great deal in a newspaper ad in large type, then hedge on the goodies in the fine print of the loan papers themselves. However, some legislation has forced banks to reveal more information to consumers.

One scam that is still not covered by tougher laws allows a lender to call the loan immediately. Make sure you have a good real estate attorney read the fine print on your loan before you sign the official papers in order to avoid being burned by such a provision.

The typical loan will also be tied to a specific economic index. Some lenders, however, have been lax about revealing how much the interest rate could increase, should that index skyrocket.

Do not sign for your loan until the lender tells you *in writing* which index yours is pegged to, and how that index has performed over the past three to five years. Again, make sure your attorney reads your loan papers before it is too late.

I believe the best buy is a fixed equity loan, mentioned above. Its rate will not change, no matter what happens to the prime rate or T-bill rates. With this loan the lender gambles, not you.

OTHER SOURCES OF MONEY
FOR YOUR FIRST INVESTMENT

If you cannot get or don't want an equity loan, there are other means of raising money.

Are you a renter, with a good credit history and a good business or employment record? You can simply shop for a standard first mortgage at a fixed rate to cover the purchase price on your first rental property. You can use savings to cover the much smaller down payment.

As we mentioned before, you can shop at a variety of banks, savings and loan companies, mortgage brokers, or credit unions for a standard mortgage.

Are you holding blue-chip stocks and bonds that show a strong paper gain? You can cash them in, or your brokerage house may be delighted to offer you a credit line against your portfolio. The problem is that if you cash in your portfolio, you must pay capital gains taxes. You do not pay taxes if you borrow against your holdings.

My listeners have told me that when all else fails, they have borrowed money on their Visa or Mastercard lines of credit to get quick cash for a down payment. You pay an extremely high price for that money. So I advise credit card borrowing only as a last resort, and only if the cash flow on the property you buy is enough to cover your monthly credit card payments.

You can also seek private investors who are willing to lend you money. The loan could be in the form of a second mortgage, with your house as collateral. If your credit is bad, you might have to turn to such sources, known as *hard money*.

Why "hard"? Because it is hard to get a very good deal. Expect to pay an interest rate of ½ to 2 points more for private money than the going rate at conventional banks.

A far more preferable alternative is to seek an "angel" to become your partner. Chapter 4 tells you how to find "angels" who become your partners in a real estate investment, rather than merely your loan officer. Family members, friends, your doctor, and your dentist are also possible sources. Everyone is looking for a good place to park money these days, especially people with high income and heavy taxes.

YOUR REAL ESTATE ASSET PORTFOLIO

Now that you know how to unearth those first precious dollars for investing, you need to systematize your records and your goals.

As you build up your holdings, you should aim for a balanced real estate portfolio. To keep track of your purchases and sales, to help you better visualize your goals, and to aid you in revising your collection periodically in order to maximize your profits while minimizing your risks, your portfolio needs to be spelled out on paper.

Most people do not know what they are worth, when everything they own or have in the bank is balanced against what they owe. Yet you need a summary of your assets and liabilities to bring to lenders and potential investors to show what you have done so far.

SHOPPING FOR HOME EQUITY LOAN OR SECOND MORTGAGE

AMOUNT OF LOAN: _____

A Date Called	B Banker or Company	C Person Contacted	D Annual Percentage Rate (APR)	E Interest in $ over Term of Loan *	F Length of Loan
1					
2					
3					
4					
5					
6					
7					
8					
9					
10					
11					
12					
13					
14					
15					

*Note: The bank or lender is required by law to give you this information in writing. If you don't want to wait, simply use this example on a $100,000 house, financed at 12 percent for 30 years. You are paying $370,000 plus your initial closing costs. Your total *interest* will be $270,440 for that $100,000 house!

G Origination & Other Fees	H Closing Costs	I Total† of Addt'l Costs: F + G =	J Prepayment Penalty? Yes/No	K Lock in? Yes/No & $ Amount	L Lender's Reputation & Yrs in Biz
					1
					2
					3
					4
					5
					6
					7
					8
					9
					10
					11
					12
					13
					14
					15

†Use Column I for a quick scan comparison of closing costs.

EXAMPLE OF "BEST DEAL" ON EQUITY LOAN

Amount of loan for down payment	$ 10,000 on sample $100,000 house
Fees and costs	
Total amount of points:	$ 200 (average is 2 points)
Plus total fees:	$ 500 (application, origination, closing costs)
Equals total of:	$ 700
Divided by months of loan:	180 months (15 years = 180 months)
Gives you total of	$ 3.89 extra per month that you pay for fees over life of loan.
Plus monthly loan payment	$ 100.00 (If fixed rate at 12%)
Equals *actual* monthly cost of equity loan to you	$ 103.89

FORMULA FOR ANALYZING BEST DEAL

(Complete this chart for EACH potential lender you are comparing)

Total amount of points:	$_____
Plus total fees:	$_____ (application, origination, closing costs)
Equals total of:	$_____
Divided by months of loan:	_____ months (Example: 15 years* = 180 months)
Gives you total of	$_____ extra per month that you pay for fees over life of loan.
Plus monthly loan payment	$_____
Equals *actual* monthly cost of equity loan to you	$_____

*Use number of months you need to repay home equity loan

Especially in dealing with banks and mortgage brokers, a real estate portfolio summarizes your equity, which becomes the collateral you put up to back new loans that, in turn, help you buy still more property.

What should your portfolio include? Land and houses or apartment units, primarily.

First, 10 to 20 percent should be vacant land purchased in a growth area. This is the "land bank" part of your land/house portfolio.

The raw land is something you buy as you would numismatic coins or gold or silver. You put your deeds away, letting your land sit there for seven to ten years. You don't worry about it; it is a hedge against inflation.

Second, 80 to 90 percent of your portfolio should be residential rental property, with flat or positive cash flow.

This is the "house" part of your portfolio, and it should concentrate on affordable housing. (As I noted in chapter 1, "affordable" refers not to what you yourself can afford, but to housing within a particular community that is within reach of the majority of working people in that community.)

This section of your portfolio might contain one or more single family residences, town homes, mobile homes, apartments, co-ops, and/or condominiums.

Anyone who is serious about becoming a full-time investor should keep a running account of his or her holdings. Create a list, like the sample below, showing your assets and liabilities. This record tells you and your bank what you are worth.

As you can see, a complete accounting includes the house or apartment you live in, provided you own it. It also includes your non–real estate investments—stocks, bonds, mutual funds, CDs . . . plus your savings, your money market funds, and your cash.

I advise husbands and wives to keep their portfolios separate. However, if you hold property jointly, of course you can do a joint land/house portfolio. Furthermore, you can combine your assets when it is necessary—or prudent, in the case of a large sum—for both of you to apply for one loan.

ORGANIZING YOUR OWN PORTFOLIO

On your desk or dining room table, lay out all those pieces of paper—bank statements, deeds, etc.—and follow my "Sample Financial Portfolio" to keep track of your holdings.

You should update this chart every time you buy a property, or a minimum of once a year. Do I hear voices murmuring: "Hey, I am just entering the field. I intend to buy only one property a year!"?

That's fine . . . but remember, anything you own currently is likely to increase in value each year. So, taking into account a personal residence, a second home, and a first rental property, let us assume for a moment you are sitting on $300,000 worth of property.

In a normal market, your net worth as the result of these holdings increases at least 10 percent—$30,000—per year. Your statement should reflect this appreciation.

Why? The value of updating your portfolio comes into play when you realize you have an additional $30,000 that you can pull out of your property to invest in your next purchase. Because this represents a 10 percent down payment on a $300,000 property, your net worth on paper could double faster than you think.

Next, imagine what you would *like* your portfolio to contain in the future. Add a "wish list," showing your goals for upcoming purchases. Follow the "Sample Projected Goals Wish List" on page 32. Once you have created these two records, you know at a glance what you have, what you want, and how to go for it.

HOW TO ANALYZE A DEAL

First show the purchase price, projected closing costs, mortgage financing to be obtained and the cash investment required.

Design the yearly analysis in two columns: cash flow and taxable income.

In the cash flow column show projected annual rental income and reduce this for a reasonable vacancy percent. One-and-a-half months' rent is a conservative figure to use. This will give you net rental income.

Now show the cash expenses for management fees, maintenance, utilities, etc. These amounts are both tax and cash flow reductions. Here is where cash flow and tax show their differences: The cash flow expenses are subtracted from the net rental income to provide the investor with an amount available to service the debt on the building. Now calculate the annual mortgage payments, using the mortgage terms appropriate for the situation, and subtract to get the cash flow generated, before taxes, from the deal.

To calculate the tax liability, go back to cash available for debt service and subtract depreciation allowable, using the appropriate tax life and mortgage interest on debt payments made. You now have calculated taxable

SAMPLE FINANCIAL PORTFOLIO

Principal residence:

Net value	$150,000	
Mortgage outstanding	$ 75,000	
Equity		= $ 75,000

Lake Lot:

Purchase price	$ 4,000	
Current value	$ 6,000	
Equity		= $ 2,000

Rental House #1:

Market value	$ 90,000	
Mortgage outstanding	$ 40,000	
Equity		= $ 50,000
TOTAL Equity Worth		**$127,000**

Cash, money market funds, CDs	$ 8,000
Stocks, current value	$ 12,000
Bonds, current value	$ 5,000
Mutual funds, current value	$ 4,000
Coins & bullion, current value	$ 6,000
TOTAL Liquid Assets	**= $ 35,000**

(*Note:* do not list IRA, pensions, or term life insurance policies)

NET INVESTMENT WORTH

$127,000 Equity worth (which under normal conditions will increase 10% annually)

+ $ 35,000 Liquid Assets (add yields or deduct losses, then adjust numbers below)

= $162,000 Total Investment Capital, liquid & equity combined

If your liquid assets stay the same and you make *no* further investments, your Net Equity Worth will increase as follows:
in Year 1: $127,000 + $12,700 = $139,700
in Year 2: $139,700 + $13,900 = $153,600

income. Multiply this times the investor's tax rate, usually 28 percent, to get the tax liability.

Subtract the tax liability from pre-tax cash flow and you've calculated after-tax cash flow. The return on investment percent can now be provided by dividing the after-tax cash flow by the initial cash investment.

In the example, notice how each subtotal flows from the total calculated previously. The amounts and percents used can be changed based on each investor's individual circumstances. The key is to follow the format from top to bottom and to be sure the assumptions for pertinent data are available.

In order to fully analyze a deal be sure you have the following information available: purchase price, closing costs, mortgage financing available, mortgage terms, projected rental income, management fees, projected operating expenses, and investor tax rate.

If all these numbers are in hand, any deal can be analyzed in a matter of minutes to detail what an investor can expect to earn on an investment. The key is the cash for cash return on investment.

SAMPLE PROJECTED GOALS WISH LIST

Today's date: January 31, 1990

A. By Jan. 31, 1991 (1 year from now), I intend to buy 1 residential rental property in the $50,000 price range.

B. By Jan. 31, 1991, I intend to buy 1 residential rental property in the $100,000 price range.

C. By Jan. 31, 1991, I intend to buy 1 parcel of vacant land in the $20,000 price range.

Projected Profits: If I buy 2 houses a year at these prices, with minimum appreciation rate of 5%:

. . . By January 31, 1992, my houses will be worth:	$ 157,500
minus what I owe (price less 10% down):	135,000
Thus my worth (equity) on paper is:	22,500

Sample Projected Goals Wish List *(cont.)*

. . . By January 31, 1993, my houses will be worth: 165,375
minus what I owe (mortgage payments noted):   130,000
Thus my worth on paper is: 35,375

. . . After 10 years, using same formula,
my worth on paper is: $ 500,000

EXAMPLE OF PROPERTY ANALYSIS

Assumptions

		Cash Flow	Taxable Income
Purchase Price	65,000		
Closing Costs	3,250		
Mortgage Obtained	52,000		
Cash Investment (20%)	16,250		
Projected Rental		14,000	
Less Vacancy (1.5 Months)		(1,750)	
Net Rental Income		12,250	
Expenses			
Management Fee (10%)		1,225	
Maintenance & Utilities		2,547	
Miscellaneous		500	
Total Expenses		4,272	
Cash Available for Debt Service		7,978	7,978
Mortgage Payment (30 year fixed 10%)		5,476	
Pre-Tax Positive (Negative) Cash Flow		2,502	
Depreciation			1,655
Mortgage Interest Expense			4,928
Taxable Profit (loss)			1,395
Tax @ 28%		(391)	
After-Tax Positive (Negative) Cash Flow		2,111	
After-Tax Return on Investment Percent		13.00%	

4

Getting Started—
Your Own Money
or Someone Else's?

At this juncture, you have established your investing comfort zone, laid out your current holdings, and learned how to obtain money. Your final step before springing into action is to decide whether or not you should go it alone, or work with partners.

It must be obvious by now that if you have both time and access to money, you can reap bigger gains alone, flying solo, than if you share a property deal with a partner. You are also in complete control—you don't have to get a partner's approval. However, you are limited ultimately in the number of properties you can control.

Thus, it can be extremely profitable to use what I call OPT—other people's time—in your real estate investing . . . and/or OPM—other people's money.

Once you latch onto a good partner, your real estate career can grow dramatically. Rather than owning 100 percent of a small pie, you can own 50 percent of a much larger pie. It depends upon how you feel about sharing.

There are hundreds, even thousands, of highly motivated people in every section of the country who have not been able to put together the dollars for a real estate deal. But some of them have the brains, the free time, and the knowledge to do your legwork. All they need is the opportunity.

I have met these potential partners at seminars and spoken to them on the air. At meetings and seminars, I have helped introduce them to investors with money by asking: "How many of you have money and are looking for deals?" Then I ask, "How many have deals and are looking for money?"

Time after time, the ones with money outnumber the ones with the deals 10 to 1! Once the two groups interact, anything is possible. People constantly come back to me with fabulous success stories about fruitful deals.

A surefire way of locating partners is to attend meetings of real estate investor clubs. Such clubs operate all across the nation, and they are wonderful places to find people with both ideas and money.

Many of the long-established ones are members of the National Association of Real Estate Clubs, located in New York City. Phone: (212) 548-8934 or (212) 548-8961. Some regional branches of the association have been active for more than twenty-five years. Contact the national headquarters to learn about clubs in your area.

IF YOU HAVE THE TIME . . .

What if you are the one with the time, but no money? After you have "gone to school" learning the principles in this book, you are a candidate to receive OPM—other people's money. Remember, there are more of them than there are of you.

Make yourself known to investors with money, starting with friends, relatives, and business or professional associates. There is nothing wrong with going into business with relatives, so long as your lawyers draw up agreements that spell out everyone's contribution, their responsibilities, the terms under which you divide the profits, and the procedure for dissolving the partnership.

You can contact strangers either via ads or in person at clubs. Some fabulous properties are waiting for all of you, if you take the time to inspect and analyze them.

Another excellent venue for meeting potential partners is the real estate auction. Chat with other people at auctions and you will undoubtedly come across investors who are eager to discuss joint ventures.

"I have the money and some time, but I'm a Nervous Nellie when it comes to finance," a voice in your head is whispering.

Guess what? *Everyone* is a Nervous Nellie about money. The perfect real estate candidate is someone willing to spend his or her time and trouble to investigate potential partners first.

Once you are satisfied you have the right person, have your lawyer draw up an ironclad partnership agreement, giving each of you the right to buy each other out under a predetermined formula, so that neither one gets hurt if you go separate ways.

In a partnership, the two or three people involved sometimes have roughly an equal say in negotiating the terms of a deal. However, that is not always the case.

Let us say you have 50 percent of the down payment needed to finance a purchase. A partner offers the other 50 percent. At this point you must figure out how to structure your partnership.

Does your partner want to be an active participant? Does this person want to help make the decisions and manage the property? Your legal document becomes sort of a prenuptial agreement. It must spell out what each person's obligations and duties are, and how much power each has in making decisions.

On the other hand, perhaps your teammate prefers to be an investor/ partner. You will be the main decision maker and manager. Your teammate makes no decisions but receives a designated share of the financial gains.

Your investing partner is using OPT—other people's time—while you are using OPM—other people's money. You need a strong legal document identifying yourself as the general partner and your fellow investor as the limited partner.

Even if the two of you contribute the same amount of money—50 percent—at the outset, the percentage of the profit that each gets is negotiable. You, as the workhorse, might negotiate a larger percentage of the benefits—as much as 70 percent—while the nonactive investor/partner ends up with proportionally less.

As is the case with any deal, each person in a partnership should have his or her own attorney. A smart buyer never uses a seller's attorney . . . and smart partners never share the same attorney.

THE SYNDICATION ALTERNATIVE

Another route you can take is to form a syndicate and act as its general partner. *Syndication* is a fancy word for a relatively uncomplicated arrangement, in which a group of people pool finances to do a real estate deal. Syndicates are handy when you need a large amount of money to buy or develop a property.

A syndicate, or syndication, can take different legal forms. Ordinarily, a syndicate is very much like a limited partnership.

The difference is that syndicates include more people who each put up a smaller amount of money, while the plain-vanilla kind of limited partnership described above involves fewer people who each contribute more money. It is a bit like comparing a doubles team in tennis with an offensive unit of a football team. (The rule of thumb is that when six or more people are involved, it is a syndication . . . or a very undermanned football team!)

Usually, syndication works this way:

The person who does the bulk of the legwork is the *general partner* or *managing partner*. In active investing, you are that person. (We will talk about how you can buy into syndicates as a passive investor later in the book.)

You, as general partner, are the team's quarterback. The rest of the investors are your linemen, receivers, and running backs. None of the other investors have a voice in calling the plays.

As general or managing partner, you look for motivated sellers, find deals that will bring immediate equity and positive cash flow, and search for property that is below market value.

The general partner also takes the lead in negotiating. You make price offers and counteroffers when a suitable property is identified. As a negotiator, you have to be creative. For instance, you might take the property off the market with an option or binder. You also must put everything down on paper properly, working in conjunction with professionals such as CPAs and lawyers.

Finally, you present the deal, along with appraisals, to prospective partners. Because the deal requires a major infusion of capital, you need to approach a number of people, offering each a small share.

In forming your syndicate, you then proceed using exactly the same documents that you would need for a smaller limited partnership. Whether you call it a partnership or a syndicate, you must still persuade people to join you by convincing them that your deal will ultimately make a decent profit, as well as bring good tax benefits.

Since you, as the general partner, handle so much of the work, you negotiate your share of the deal with the other participants. Your contract, drawn up by your lawyer, shows that you will actually *own* a percentage of the property being bought, while your syndicate partners have a negotiated share. If you put no money into the deal, you get a smaller share than if you both invest in and manage the syndicate.

I am avoiding the mention of specific percentages, since everything is negotiable. Each deal and each syndication is different. They cover the entire spectrum in terms of the size of members' shares.

Each partner's liability is limited to the total amount of money he or she invests. Let us say that in a private, nonregistered syndication, an investor puts in $5,000, which represents 10 percent of the deal. That investor is responsible for only 10 percent of the debts, 10 percent of the mortgages, and 10 percent of any liabilities.

ADVERTISING FOR PARTNERS

How do you find partners outside clubs or personal contacts? A well-written classified advertisement usually does the trick:

Example 1: "IF YOU'VE GOT THE TIME, I'VE GOT THE MONEY. INVESTOR with money wants opportunities to invest in real estate. Seeks knowledgeable real estate investor who needs money but has time. Call me at XXX-0000."

Example 2: "PRIVATE INVESTOR SEEKS REAL ESTATE DEALS with fair return and strong, secure position. Call me with your deals at XXX-0000."

Example 3: "IS YOUR MONEY WORKING HARD ENOUGH FOR YOU? I have lots of time and many profitable, underpriced real estate deals. I'm looking for lazy investor who wants me to work. Call XXX-0000."

Example 4: "WANT TO INVEST IN LUCRATIVE REAL ESTATE MARKET, but don't have time to find the deals? Let me find deals for you. I have lots of deals, lots of time, but need money. Call XXX-0000."

Place your ad in the Saturday and Sunday edition of your local papers under the "Business Opportunity" or "Money Wanted" column. Try your ad for one weekend. No answers? Write a new one and put more oomph in it. Instead of the above variety, add some spice with a headline like: "High Profits" or "No Risk—High Return."

HEY, LOOK ME OVER!

Your ad does the job—you have received three legitimate-sounding replies. How do you separate a good prospect from a curiosity seeker?

Before I do business with someone, I talk to his or her family, friends, and business associates. If my choice has never had a partner before, I will check with the person's employer.

While waiting two or three weeks before getting involved in an actual deal, I run a credit check on my potential partner. The cost is minimal, and the few minutes spent writing a credit-check letter can save you thousands by alerting you to a partner with financial problems.

Some of the major credit services that issue public reports and have branches in major cities include Dun and Bradstreet, TRW Information Services Division, Allstate Credit Bureau, CBI, and Retail Credit Corporation.

Look in the Yellow Pages for other credit bureaus. Call first to find out how to proceed and how long your request will take. Some big firms have toll-free 800 numbers.

The cost, which varies according to your location, runs anywhere from $25 to $75. Do you have a friend with a retail business or professional practice, such as a doctor or dentist, who is a member of a credit bureau? You can save 40 to 50 percent on the cost by having your friend pull the credit report for you.

You can also subscribe to a computerized service called "Solutions!" which is accessed via modem on your home computer. For information on "Solutions!" software call (800) 255-6643.

New investors occasionally feel uncomfortable about credit checks. "This guy is going to put up real dough, and my contribution is just my time. Is it kosher for me to run a credit check on him?" they ask.

"Absolutely essential," is my reply. People might tell you they have money when in reality they do not. They might be getting the money from another source. If they are, you want to know more about the source.

You need to be very, very sure of a partner's financial depth. Imagine spending hours, days, weeks of your time, then arriving at a closing to hear your partner blow the deal by admitting he or she does not have the cash!

To conduct a thorough investigation, you need the person's name, address, social security number, and financial statement. It is totally acceptable in the business world to ask someone with whom you plan to invest money for an up-to-date financial statement. Why? This document will be used down the road to get mortgage money, among other things.

Be firm but pleasant about the subject. You might say, "Just as I plan to investigate carefully the properties I purchase for us, I investigate the people with whom I make those purchases. I believe in 'due diligence.' "

If potential partners balk when it comes to their financial position, you do not want to do business with them.

YOU SHOW ME YOURS, I'LL SHOW YOU MINE

The other side of the coin is that you have an obligation to let an investor know about your finances. Especially if you are the one with time but no money, you need to reassure your investing partner.

I have known numerous talented real estate people with good business heads who have temporary financial woes. They still have the expertise and the time to put good deals together. Am I describing you? You must tell your partner in advance so there won't be any surprises later on.

If there are judgments against you, or if you are having money problems, you can still become a partner who uses OPM. In such a case, your attorney needs to structure a deal that protects the deal against *your* creditors.

Suppose neither you nor your partner has ever prepared a formal financial statement. Use a document like the "Personal Financial Statement" below as a guide to gathering the necessary information. You or your partner will get a pretty good idea of the other's financial health from the facts entered here. You will have all the ammunition you need to do a more detailed credit check. Naturally, you or your CPA should verify information such as employment, salary, and current property owned.

A credit check is a valuable but impersonal document. I also like to meet two or three times with potential partners, to get to know them better on a one-to-one basis, prior to structuring any partnerships or doing any deals.

At that point, if I am pleased with someone, I have my lawyer prepare a partnership agreement. The team is ready to take the field.

PERSONAL FINANCIAL STATEMENT

PERSONAL:

Name _____ Date of Birth _____

Address _____ City, State, Zip _____

Name of Spouse _____

Telephone (residence) _____ (business) _____

Own/Rent? If Rent, how long at present address? _____

Landlord _____ Phone _____

Married? ____ years Single? ____ Divorced? ____ year Veteran? ____

Dependents, relationship, age: _____

_____

_____

EMPLOYMENT:

Occupation _____

Employed or Self-employed? _____

Name of Employer or Business _____

Your Business Address _____

Your Type of Business _____

Position _____

Name & Title of Superior _____

How long employed with this company or in this business? _____

If less than 2 years, prior occupation & other information below: _____

_____

_____

INCOME:

Base Pay or Income $ _____ per mo. $ _____ per year

Overtime $ _____ per mo. average

Bonus? _____ Commissions? _____ Amount $ _____ per mo/yr

Dividends? _____ Interest? _____ Amount $ _____ per mo/yr

Net Income other Real Estate $ _____ per mo/yr

Child Support? ____ Alimony? ____ Amount totals $ ____ per mo/yr

41

Spouse Occupation _____ Income $_____ per mo/yr
Other Income? _____ Specify: _____

REAL ESTATE OWNED:

	1.	2.	3.
Type of property	_____	_____	_____
Address	_____	_____	_____
Current Market Value	_____	_____	_____
Total Indebtedness	_____	_____	_____
Equity	_____	_____	_____
Annual Gross Income	_____	_____	_____
Annual Exps + Loan Pymts	$ _____	$ _____	$ _____
Annual Net Income	$ _____	$ _____	$ _____
Monthly Loan Pymts	$ _____	$ _____	$ _____
Total Net Value of these properties			$ _____

BANKING & OTHER DATA:

	Bank	Branch	Chkg/Svs	Other	Amount
1.	_____		__ __	___	$ _____
2.	_____		__ __	___	$ _____
3.	_____		__ __	___	$ _____
4.	_____		__ __	___	$ _____
5.	_____		__ __	___	$ _____

	Securities	Amount
1.	_____	$ _____
2.	_____	$ _____

Personal Financial Statement *(cont.)*

3. _____ $ _____

4. _____ $ _____

5. _____ $ _____

Autos:
Yr __ Make __ Lender __ Pymt/mo $ __ Orig Amt $ __ Bal due $ __
Yr __ Make __ Lender __ Pymt/mo $ __ Orig Amt $ __ Bal due $ __
Furntr & Applncs: Total Value $ ___ Pymts/mo $ ___ Bal due $ __
Net Cash Value of Life Insurance $ _____
Other Assets _____
Other Obligations/Loans/Liabilities _____

CREDIT REFERENCES:

Creditor Name	Address/ Phone	Hghst Amt owed	Reason for crdt	Date Closed
1.				
2.				
3.				

Ever Bankrupt? _____
Ever had any judgments, liens, repossessions or foreclosures? Yes/No
  If Yes, explain _____
Delinquent on Any Payments Now? Yes/No
  If Yes, explain _____

I declare this information is true and correct, and authorize its verification and the obtaining of consumer credit report.

_____   _____
signature   date

5

Your First Rental Property

Having read this much, you are probably champing at the bit. "When can I start to buy? What do I buy?" My answer: You are almost ready . . . and you should buy a residential rental property.

Why residential? Everyone knows something about a house, apartment, or town home. We all live in one and need one. Chances are you already own one. Being the landlord of a residence is only a small step away from being an owner.

Sounds like a fairly simple move, doesn't it? Now the all-important details:

Your basic credo as a novice investor is to develop as many positive cash-flow investments as possible. In my view, the best strategy is to spread your investments among small pieces of property, rather than putting all your money and effort into one huge one.

Thus, if you have a vacancy in Property A, Properties B and C will not be adversely affected.

Positive cash flow means that more money is coming in than is being paid out. You receive enough in rental income to pay the principal on your loan, your interest, taxes, and insurance, as well as repair costs, management fees, and any other expenses. As this happens, your mortgage payments plus any appreciation in the value of your property make your net worth—your equity position—grow.

Our $100,000 property example is worth repeating once more here. You buy a property this year valued at $100,000, with 20 percent down.

It increases in value (according to the national average) to $160,000 within five years.

Meanwhile, by making your monthly payments, you decrease the amount of the mortgage from $80,000 to $60,000. Result: Your original $20,000 down payment has brought you a cash-on-cash positive cash flow after five years, plus a nontaxable paper profit of $60,000.

Not bad for a $20,000 investment over five years! You will pay taxes on the $60,000 profit (the difference between the purchase price and the sale price) *only* if you sell the property for cash.

Let's go back a moment to the term *cash on cash;* it is an important term for investors. It means the amount of money you receive in exchange for the actual amount of money you have put into a deal. In this example, if your yearly income from the property is $4,000 after expenses, that is your cash-on-cash return. By pocketing $4,000 per year, you make a 20 percent cash-on-cash return on your initial $20,000 down payment. (To figure out the cash-on-cash return of any investment, see the worksheet on page 49.)

As you will see, I will be encouraging you to hold onto properties and pull equity out of them as a tax-free loan, or do a 1031 tax-free exchange.

It is now time for you to become a player.

You have scouted the real estate ads in your local paper, noticing many available single family houses, town homes, co-ops, condominiums, and small multifamily dwellings. You have perused national listings in places like the *Wall Street Journal* and *USA Today*. Perhaps you have hooked up with a partner. Where do you start?

SHOPPING YOUR LOCAL MARKET

Start with location. The most important consideration is that the property be physically close to you—within a two-hour drive of your primary residence and workplace. Even though there are properties that look great in Florida, it does not pay to put your money there unless you intend to be in Florida part of the time.

There are exceptions. By all means shop in an area that you visit regularly for business or vacation. You might look there first, if the community where you maintain your current primary residence is in the upper income sphere, or is part of a hot market where home prices have shot above the affordability level. It may be a waste of your time shopping for rental property in an inflated neighborhood, since rental income will not cover your costs.

Is your own neighborhood affordable? If so, it is the perfect starting point. You undoubtedly have walked the streets nearby a thousand times. You know which are the best blocks, where the trouble spots are, where to find the nearest or best shopping center, schools, houses of worship, and recreational facilities. You have experience with the local public transportation and commuter systems. You probably even know secret parking spots. Surely you understand how the crime rate and police protection compare with other communities.

If you are a home owner, you might even have a pretty good sense of market values. For all these reasons, you are ahead of the game.

I firmly advise you to start with a single family home, if possible. It could be the classic American dream: a detached stand-alone house on its own plot of ground with a picket fence around it. It could be a town home or condo.

How do you find it? There are myriad ways.

THE CLASSIFIED ADS BAZAAR

The obvious place to start is with the classified ads. Study them on a regular basis for the next two weeks, while you are waiting for your new business cards to be printed. Circle those that fit the description of affordable housing—a house or apartment whose rent is within reach of the majority of working people within the community.

For instance, in the Greater New York metropolitan area, a majority of families are looking for places to rent in the $400 to $700 per month range. In the Orlando metropolitan area of Florida, most people look for housing in the $275 to $400 range.

The point is, you start on the right foot by searching out housing that is most in demand in that region.

The longer a property has been on the market, the better chance you have of striking a good deal, so it pays to keep an eye on the papers for several weeks. A good system is to clip ads that interest you and paste them in a loose-leaf notebook. Even if they look like duplicates, you can note at a glance which ones sell, which ones don't, and which ones are reduced in price as the weeks go by.

From time to time, it is also worthwhile to place your own ad in the newspaper, under "real estate wanted." The ad should say you are a private investor looking for properties.

Distribute your cards to doormen and concierges at apartment houses or condominium developments in your target area. Hand them out to moving companies, local postmen, overnight delivery company drivers, and others who travel regularly among properties in a neighborhood, and who might hear that a place is available before it appears in the newspaper. Post your card on the bulletin board at supermarkets and laundromats.

Your days of being shy are over!

Join real estate clubs. The National Association of Real Estate Clubs, (212) 548-8961, can give you information on ones in your region. I mentioned them earlier as great sources for partners, but they are equally valuable for leads to properties themselves. For the same reason, attend monthly real estate seminars featuring expert speakers.

Don't hesitate to jot down phone numbers on "For Sale" signs posted in front of properties, particularly those where the grass has grown around the sign, or the windows are boarded up, or there are other signs of neglect. These clues suggest the property has been available for some time, and the seller might be extremely eager to make a deal.

Other abandoned houses in disarray might have no sign, but you can locate the owner by checking the office of the tax assessor or collector.

By checking notices filed in your local probate court, you can learn about properties to be liquidated by estates. Finally, contact the FDIC, FSLIC, and the Internal Revenue Service to get regularly printed lists of distressed properties. (Agencies and addresses are found in chapter 9.)

Once you have spread the word around that you are in the market, you will be delighted at how quickly people with deals begin coming to you.

After a few weeks, when you feel you are familiar with your chosen market, schedule drive-by tours for yourself of the houses you think have the best potential. I like to hire a car and driver so that I can concentrate on sight-seeing rather than driving. My coauthor Grace does her drive-bys on her bicycle. In urban areas, walking might be the most efficient mode of transportation.

However you do it, go out and eyeball those houses and apartments, even if you are still not confident enough to make appointments for full-scale inspections. This is a job you cannot do by phone. You might find yourself exhausted after a few days of touring, but that's part of the business.

Sooner or later, you will start answering ads, visiting real estate brokers and ringing doorbells. Time consuming? You'd better believe it. Most pros try not to squeeze too many visits into a single day, because they lose perspective after a few tours and have trouble differentiating one house from another. Don't overload yourself. You will need your stamina when it comes to the actual negotiations!

The loose-leaf notebook in which you have pasted ads now doubles as an evaluation folder. At each property, jot down details on a separate page, using the evaluation worksheets (one is for houses, another for co-ops and condos) in this chapter as a guide.

SEEKING THE MOTIVATED SELLER

Some of the smartest deals made by investors are on properties listed for sale by the owner, rather than through a broker. These properties are typically offered by that elusive prey, the "motivated" seller.

By motivated, I mean someone who is eager to sell quickly. The seller may be offering the property without a broker because he or she wants to save the 3 to 7 percent of the purchase price that is usually the broker's commission. Or, the motivated seller is building another home, is moving, needs money, or is in the throes of a family problem such as divorce. Motivated sellers also include the Federal Government, local governments, banks, and estates of deceased owners.

A real estate broker can show you a wide range of properties, but that broker rarely leads you to extremely motivated sellers.

In my thirty years of experience, I have found perhaps four brokers who truly worked their "buns" off to find me the proverbial "steal." Brokers normally do not exhaust themselves on behalf of a small investor because once they find a steal, they would rather buy it themselves. Smart brokers who are low on money will become your partners and put their commission in the deal.

I can guarantee you that with or without a broker's help, before too long, you are going to find motivated sellers and undervalued property for possible deals. Now the fun really begins.

It does not cost anything to place a bid on a property. Therefore, if you make aggressive but low bids, follow them up, and encourage sellers to make counteroffers, you will find success.

A great pianist does not play a concert every day, but does stay in concert-ready form by practicing daily. A smart real estate investor makes as many bids as possible every single day. You stay in practice that way, and by making so many offers you maximize your chances of getting acceptances, no matter how ridiculously low your bids may seem to you.

Keep in mind that you are not bound legally by an offer, so long as it contains my jump-out clauses (p. 97). You do not have to consummate a deal if you have second thoughts, or if you get more acceptances than you can handle.

Although concluding a real estate deal takes enough time for you to consider the pros and cons before signing a purchase agreement, keep in mind that there is an honorable way to back out, without explanation.

Many states have a "buyers remorse" law that allows you to withdraw from a deal within a certain number of days, whether or not you have signed a contract, if you have second thoughts. This is an especially helpful law for impulse buys at auction, and I will refer to it again in Chapter 10, which is all about real estate auctions.

DOING THE POSITIVE CASH-FLOW CHART

Before you put down major money on a property, you must do your arithmetic. I probably sound like a broken record on this subject, but unless you put pencil to paper, you cannot pass the real estate investment success

---

CASH-ON-CASH RETURN WORKSHEET

Purchase Price $_____

Outlay

$_____ down payment

$_____ appraisal

$_____ inspection

$_____ repair costs

$_____ legal fees

=$_____ Total Cash Outlay

Income

$_____ monthly rents

× 11 (1-month cushion in case of vacancy)

$_____ − management fee (optional)

=$_____ Annual Income

−$_____ Yearly mortgage payments

Cash-on-Cash Return: + or − $_____

Divide by Cash Outlay ÷ $_____

To Get Percentage of Return on Cash Investment: _____ %

course. You need to know—based on the best, hard information available—that the bottom line will be a plus, not a minus.

Here is a simple case in point:

A man telephoned me on the air one night with questions about a $100,000 1-family house in northern New Jersey. The place brought in rent of $1,200 per month. The buyer was about to put $20,000 down on it.

His monthly nut (principal and interest on his $80,000 loan, plus taxes and insurance) was $800. The place already had tenants and did not need major renovations. So, deducting his $800 payment from his $1,200 per month rental income, his monthly cash-on-cash return was $400 per month. Multiply that by 12, and he would get $4,800 a year, or 24 percent on his $20,000 cash investment, a positive return that outperforms any money market account or CD. It was a good deal.

ACTUAL EXAMPLE OF CASH-ON-CASH RETURN

Purchase price: $100,000

Outlay		Income
$20,000	down payment	$1,200 monthly rents
$ 300	appraisal	× 11
$ 250	inspection	= $13,200
$ 0	repair costs	(No management fee)
$ 700	legal fees	
= $21,250	Total Cash Outlay	= $13,200 Annual Income
		− $ 9,600 Yearly mortgage payments + taxes & insurance @ $800 per month

Cash-on-Cash Yearly Return: + $3,600
or, Percentage of Return   ÷ $21,250
on Cash Investment: 17%

For each property you think may be a good deal, do the same simple arithmetic. Your total initial cash outlay is your down payment plus other costs—inspection, title search, legal fees, and out-of-pocket repair expenses. Your gross cash income is the monthly rent times 12.

Subtract the monthly cash outlay from the monthly rental. If the cash-on-cash return on your money after expenses, on a yearly basis, before tax benefits or appreciation, amounts to 6 percent or more, you have a solid investment.

FINANCING YOUR FIRST PROPERTY

Part of your calculations will involve the size of your down payment. A general rule is, put down as little as necessary to create a positive cash flow.

In the right circumstances, you might even close a deal with *no* money down. For instance, in the case of the $100,000 property just analyzed, the owner might be willing to take a note, to be paid off at $200 a month with 12 percent interest, in lieu of the $10,000 down payment.

You would then pay off that note from your $1,000 rental receipts each month. It hikes your monthly expenses to $850 per month, but you still end up with positive cash flow.

You should point out to the seller that this is an excellent deal for him or her, too, in case the seller does not already realize it. The 12 percent return that the seller gets on the note is a higher rate than a bank pays on money market funds or CDs.

THE LIVE-IN INVESTMENT

Numerous small investors have gotten their feet wet in the rental property business by purchasing a two-family home. They live in one unit, while renting the other. The rent covers most or all of their bills, including the mortgage payment.

One great benefit of this arrangement is that at the same time your feet get wet, your eye is on your property, 365 days a year. A drawback to this arrangement is that an "antsy" or demanding tenant finds it easy to bend your ear about leaks, repairs, heat, and so on.

It is up to you to decide where your patience and privacy comfort zone lies. There is no such thing as a hands-off landlord in a two-family house in which the landlord resides.

COMMERCIAL PROPERTY
AS A FIRST INVESTMENT

I don't recommend straight commercial properties, such as a small shopping center, for the novice investor. However, there is one exception—mixed-use properties. These are buildings with a store or office on the ground floor, topped by apartments.

So long as the numbers on a mixed-use building produce a cash-on-cash return plus appreciation, it is an acceptable starting point for your investment. Problems crop up when the business occupying the commercial space fails. You end up with an empty property. Furthermore, commercial property tends to be harder to rent than residential property.

Play it safe with this formula: If the residential units in a mixed-use property do not carry the mortgage payment alone, then do not buy it.

As a novice, try to stick to either a single-family residence (including a condo, co-op, or town home) or a mixed-use building for property number one, rather than an apartment house. Owning the latter is fine as you get a bit more experienced.

If the price is right, your next property could even be a multi-family dwelling with a maximum of 4 units. One of my sons is now moving into the small apartment house arena, but he cut his teeth on single family homes.

How do you know you have reached the optimal time for making your first real estate deal, particularly on a residential rental property?

First, you analyze the marketplace, according to your research over a number of months. Second, you evaluate the property, following the worksheets below. Third, you analyze the finances of the deal, according to the "Quick Cash-Flow Analysis" on page 55, which can be applied to either a house or an apartment unit.

Your next step would be to find a tenant, unless there is already one living in the residence, or unless you are a "flipper" and plan to sell the property immediately.

The next chapter deals with becoming a landlord—finding tenants, managing them and managing the property itself. Right now, all you need concern yourself with are the numbers.

Is the monthly rent you plan to charge in line with rent for similar properties in the same neighborhood? Is it enough to give you a flat or positive cash flow? Do this homework, plus the remaining chores—getting a professional inspection of the property, title search, and so on.

Once all these elements come together, the time is right to make your deal.

HOUSE EVALUATION WORKSHEET

Address _____

Owner/Seller _____ Phone _____

View Date _____ On Market Since _____

Brief description _____

Rooms/Baths _____ Sq feet _____ Garage? _____

Asking Price $ _____ My Offering Price $ _____

Down payment (%) $ _____

Mortgage needed $ _____

EXPENSES:

Monthly payments @ _____% = $ _____

+ Property Taxes/yr ÷ 12 = $ _____

+ Insurance per yr ÷ 12 = $ _____

+ Heating costs per month = $ _____

+ Other Utilities per month = $ _____

+ Misc. Expenses per month = $ _____

= TOTAL monthly expenses = $ _____

Compare: rent per month for similar houses $ _____

ANSWER FOLLOWING ON 1–10 BASIS, 1 WORST:

Neighborhood _____ Street _____ Neighbor houses _____

Yard & lawn _____ Overall house appearance _____

Roof _____ Siding _____ Gutters/Drain spouts _____ Chimney _____

Porch/Deck _____ Foundation _____ Pitch/slope of ground _____

Garage _____ Other structures? _____

Evidence of termites? _____ Basement moisture? _____

Plumbing _____ Heating _____ Elect svs/wiring _____

Condition beams & supports _____ Traffic flow inside _____

Condition floors &/or carpeting _____ Walls _____ Ceiling moisture? _____

Insulation _____ Windows _____ Electric outlets & wiring _____

Age of house _____ A/C Yes/No _____ Water supply _____

Waste disposal _____

Other pluses _____

Other minuses _____

CONDO OR CO-OP EVALUATION WORKSHEET

Address _____ Unit # _____

Owner/Sponsor _____ Phone _____

Rooms/Baths _____ Co-op/Condo? _____ Sq Ft _____

View Date _____ On Market Since _____

Asking Price $ _____ My Offering Price $ _____

Down Payment $ _____ Mortgage needed $ _____

EXPENSES:

Mortgage payments @ ____% = $ _____ per month

+ Maintenance or Carrying Charges $ _____ per month

+ Condo Taxes per yr ÷ 12 = $ _____

+ Insurance per yr ÷ 12 = $ _____

+ Misc. expenses per month = $ _____

= TOTAL Expenses per month $ _____

Compare: Rent per mo. in Similar Units? $ _____

Seller financing? _____ If Co-op, % tax deductible _____

Age of Building _____ Renovated? _____

Move-in condition? _____ If not, est. fix-up costs $ _____

Apt vacant/occupied? _____ Walkup/Elevator? _____

Conversion date _____ % of apts sold? _____

Doorman? _____ Other security? _____

Reason for sale? _____

ANSWER FOLLOWING ON 1–10 BASIS, 1 IS WORST:

Neighborhood? _____ Location of property? _____

Street _____ Exterior of bldg _____ Hallways _____

Kitchen _____ Baths _____ Bedrooms _____ Living Room _____

A/C? Y/N Electric outlets & wiring _____ Windows _____

Insulation ____ Condition walls ____ Condition floors &/or carpeting ____

Other pluses _____

Other minuses _____

Agent/Owner & phone contact _____

QUICK CASH-FLOW ANALYSIS

Address _____ Date _____

A. Asking Price $_____

B. Down Payment $_____   (__%)

C. Mortgage Needed $_____

D. Monthly Mortgage $_____   (1st yr fixed. If using
    Payments   ARM, project all yrs
                                                          up to lifetime cap)

E. # of Units for Rent   _____

F. Monthly Rent Roll $_____

G. Yearly Income $_____   (F × 11)

H. Less Annual
    Expenses $_____   (Total expenses as
                                              shown on Evaluation
                                              Worksheet × 12)

I. Equals Net gain $_____

J. I divided by B $_____
    gives you $_____   % of return on cash
                                              invested (excluding
                                              closing costs)

EXAMPLE OF CASH-FLOW ANALYSIS

Address: <u>25 Warrington St., Englewood, NJ</u>   Date <u>6/3/89</u>

A. Asking Price   <u>$100,000</u>

B. Down Payment   <u>$ 20,000</u> (<u>20</u>%)

C. Mortgage Needed   <u>$ 80,000</u>

D. Monthly Mortgage Payments   <u>$ 800</u>

E. # of Units for Rent   <u>   1</u>

F. Monthly Rent Roll   <u>$ 1,200</u>

G. Yearly Income   <u>$ 13,200</u> (F $\times$ 11)

H. Less Annual Expenses   <u>$ 9,600</u> (Total expenses $\times$ 12)

I. Equals Net gain   <u>$ 3,600</u>

J. I divided by B   = <u>about 18%</u> on cash invested
(excluding
closing costs)

6

The Art
of Landlording

Congratulations. You have become a rental property investor. However, unless you already have a tenant for your new investment, or plan to sell the property immediately, or expect to turn the place over to a management company, you need to develop landlording skills. The bane of real estate everywhere is what I call "TNT"—Toilets and Tenants. It pays to learn how to handle them correctly.

To begin, let us say you have bought a vacant residential property, and your broker, or seller, assures you that it will be easy to find a tenant. Good deal or marginal one?

Never accept someone's promise that you will have no trouble getting a tenant. My watchword is always, "Get it in writing." Will the seller put that promise in writing? Even if the answer is yes, what happens when you are faced with an empty building? Forget about trying to sue for broken promises that are not in writing. You are asking for trouble, not avoiding it.

If the property you choose already has tenants, fine. Be sure to have your attorney examine the existing leases. If there are no leases, your attorney needs to check local laws to find out if there are controls or limits on the amount you can charge for rent. Not all controls are bad, but they need to allow you to charge enough to cover costs. Your attorney also needs to check and explain the local eviction laws to you.

If a property is vacant, you need to go further. Scan the classified ads for rentals. Then, switch hats. Become a prospective tenant, and do some detective work.

Go into the marketplace and actually shop as if you wanted to *rent* a similar property. How many are out there? How long has each been on the market? Is there a very large inventory of rental properties? In what price range?

Most importantly, ask yourself, with your detective hat on: Is the monthly rental fee what you would charge in order to get a fair, positive cash-on-cash return?

If you have projected getting $300 a month for your prospective property, while other units like it are going for $200 a month, you are kidding yourself about your cash flow.

SHOPPING FOR TENANTS

Now that you have determined that your prospective property is indeed rentable, you must put your landlord hat back on in order to find a decent tenant.

As mentioned earlier, one option for those who don't want to be a hands-on landlord is to turn the place over to a management company that would be responsible for finding tenants and dealing with them. Good management firms often have a pool of tenants from which they can entice someone to occupy your place.

A second option, for quick occupancy in an affordable low-rent neighborhood, is to go to the local office of the Housing and Urban Development. Get a list of Section 8 tenants, who are government-supported families. The government will pay the rent for such families directly to you.

The usual method is to advertise in your local newspaper's classified section. At the same time, it always helps to put a "For Rent" sign in the window, or the front of the apartment building, where zoning permits this.

Visit the best tenants nearby, or in the same building, asking if they have friends who might need housing. This technique is excellent because most people will only pass along the news of a good rental unit to people they want to have as neighbors.

If yours is an extremely competitive market, think about offering neighboring tenants, concierges, and superintendents a referral fee. Everyone likes to get an extra few dollars for a favor. This technique is perfectly acceptable in most communities. In tight rental markets such as New York City, the referral game has been honed to a profitable science.

How about a bit of mail order advertising? Send postcards to people in the area asking for tenant referrals. (Your local library should have the "reverse" telephone directory, which lists phone customers by street address, rather than alphabetically by name.)

One last alternative: Make up a neat "For Rent" flyer with pertinent information on it, have 50 photocopies made on bright yellow paper, and stuff mailboxes with it. Keep in mind that your best bet is always the classifieds, because most readers of them are in need of housing, not idle curiosity seekers.

Here is a sample of an honest, salesworthy ad:

> "FOR RENT — 3-BR 2-Bath brick home, Maplewood area. Clean, ready to move in. $400 month. References, 1st and last month's rent plus security required. Call owner at 000-0000."

HASSLE-FREE LANDLORDING

This subhead is a come-on. There is no such thing as completely hassle-free landlording. But I will show you ways to avoid some payment hassles with tenants right at the outset of your relationship by taking certain precautions.

As my friend Nick Koon, who manages more than 400 properties, says, choose tenants with your head, not your heart. Right off the bat, Nick tells callers inquiring about rentals that he charges a nonrefundable screening fee, usually about $25. This is one means of eliminating curiosity seekers or bad credit risks.

When you meet a potential tenant, first check credit references carefully. Use the same credit agencies mentioned in connection with partners on page 39. In addition, require prospective tenants to fill out the rental application form in this chapter.

Ask for the person's drivers license to make sure it shows the same face, as well as the same social security number, entered on the application form.

Call current employers and previous ones for references. Get two previous rental references. Do *not* check with the landlord the tenant is leaving—he may desperately want to get rid of this particular tenant. Do check with the landlord prior to the latest one.

If you have any suspicions, check the county records to make sure the person given as a reference is, in fact, owner of the property. (Bad credit risks could be in cahoots with a friend whose name is listed as a reference.)

Have tenants sign a customized lease, similar to the one shown on page 64. Or, modify a standard form, which you can buy in a business stationery store, by designing a lease that lets you sleep easier at night.

For instance, you can have tenants list their repair skills. Then, if they call you up with a sink problem one day, you can refer back to the lease to see if they know a bit about plumbing. "Fix it yourself," you say, "and send me a bill." Be sure to get the price in writing before you give the go-ahead. Most likely they will bill you for materials but not labor.

No law says you, as landlord, most be responsible for everything. Don't want to be bothered with stopped-up toilets? Air conditioning unit cleaning? Wall painting? Itemize those as tenant responsibilities in the lease.

Let everyone know your office hours as a landlord. Some people specify weekday mornings only—9 A.M. to 1 P.M. Monday through Friday. List a few emergencies you will respond to outside those hours, such as flooding, lack of heat, lack of water. Make it clear other problems must wait for your office hours.

Upon signing, collect a check for the first and last month's rent, plus one month deposit to cover security and damages. (Nick Koon goes a step further and collects the deposit at the time of application.) Do not permit a tenant to move into the unit until your bank clears the tenant's initial check.

A BONUS FOR PROMPT RENT

I believe in rewarding tenants for paying rent on time. At the same time, I think they should be penalized for being late. The longer into a month they fail to pay, the more penalty I require.

Here is how I arrange the penalties so that prompt payments appear as bonuses. I set fair rentals with an additional $50 per month or so built in. When payment is made on the first of a month, the tenant gets a $50 discount. When they pay on the 2d through 4th they get a $30 discount. After that they get no discount at all.

Collect your rents via mail, in the form of checks or money orders. The only reason to make in-person collections is for a problem tenant who consistently fails to pay. You might make things easier for those occasionally short on cash by allowing them to pay with a Visa, Mastercard or American Express credit card.

Do *not* accept cash, either via mail or in person. Why ask for trouble?

Every landlord has probably miscalculated at least once. Despite your credit checks and other measures, a tenant fails to pay his or her rent and moves out in the middle of the night. Provided you have done your home-work, you don't lose a bundle because you have already collected a full month's rent upon the signing of the lease, plus a security deposit.

There is no point in chasing a bad tenant. Use the extra month's rent to tide you over and to pay for a new rental ad, while you apply the security deposit to cleaning and fixing the apartment.

In any event, if you've followed my suggestions, your rental unit is in such an affordable, in-demand neighborhood that you already have a waiting list from your first go-round, or your unit will be snapped up just days after a new ad appears.

A nasty situation arises when a tenant already occupies the unit you have bought and refuses either to pay rent or move out. Have your attorney begin procedures immediately to get that tenant evicted. Do not try to handle it yourself. Turn it over to a professional. A smart landlord minimizes the most uncomfortable aspects of the job.

Don't be a soft-hearted humanitarian except in a clear, major, verifiable circumstance, such as when a person is recovering from an accident or a sudden illness. In such cases, it might be better to hold off an eviction until the situation is rectified.

Do get promissory notes signed in lieu of rent from your tenant so that you can collect later, once the crisis has passed. Somewhere along the line, you have been a tenant rather than a landlord. Ask yourself: Would your landlord have carried you for several months? The answer is no.

I want to emphasize that this is not a philosophical, political, or sociological issue. It is an unfortunately messy business issue that you can avoid by doing your homework carefully in the first place.

SAMPLE RENTAL APPLICATION FORM

LANDLORD FILLS IN BLANKS BELOW:

Today's date _____ Date house/unit available _____

Property location _____

If Apt., Unit Type _____ Apt # _____ Vacant/Occupied? _____

(CONDITIONS OF OCCUPANCY)

Length of lease _____ Date rent begins _____

Rent $_____ per/mo. Security Deposit $_____

Prorated Rent $_____ Utilities paid by tenant _____

Unfurnished/furnished? ___ Range ___ Dishwasher ___ Refrigerator ___

Children allowed _____ Pets? No/Yes Pet fee $_____

Limitations on pets _____

APPLICANT FILLS IN BLANKS BELOW:

Applicant's Name _____

Present Address _____

Home Phone _____ Date of birth _____ Soc. Sec. # _____

Present Owner/Landlord _____

Owner's Address _____ Owner's Phone _____

Present Rent $ _____ per mo. Length of Occupancy _____

Previous Address _____

Previous Owner _____

Previous Owner's Address _____ Owner's Phone _____

Previous Rent $ _____ per mo. Length of Occupancy _____

Applicant's Present Employer _____

Employer's Address _____

Applicant's Position _____ Phone _____

Present Monthly Income (gross) $ _____

Length of Employment _____ Full/Pt Time _____

Supervisor _____ Phone _____

Previous Employer _____

Previous Position _____ _____ Phone _____

Previous Monthly Income (gross) $ _____

Length of Employment _____ Full/Pt Time _____

Supervisor _____ Phone _____

Marital Status: Married/Single/Widowed _____ Separated/Divorced _____

   From whom: _____

Number of Children _____ Boys' Ages _____ Girls' Ages _____

Pets? (specify) _____

Spouse Name _____

Spouse Soc. Sec. # _____ Date of birth _____

Maiden Name _____

Spouse's Present Employer _____

Employer's Address _____

Position _____ Phone _____

Present Monthly Income (gross) $ _____

Length of Employment _____ Full/Pt Time _____

Present Supervisor _____ Phone _____

Spouse's Previous Employer _____

Previous Monthly Income (gross) $ _____

Sample Rental Application Form *(cont.)*

Length of Employment _____ Full/Pt Time _____

Previous Supervisor _____ Phone _____

Credit Cards:

Name _____ Name _____

Name _____ Name _____

Bank References:

Bank Name _____ Ckg Acct # _____

Bank Name _____ Svgs Acct # _____

Personal References:

Name _____ Phone _____

Address _____

Name _____ Phone _____

Address _____

Trade References:

Name _____ Phone _____

Address _____

Name _____ Phone _____

Address _____

Emergency (List relative or friend, not spouse or children):

Name _____ Relationship _____

Address _____ Home & Bus. Phones _____

Name _____ Relationship _____

Address _____ Home & Bus. Phones _____

I hereby deposit with owner/agent, the sum of $_____ as partial/ full security deposit on the above premises pending execution of a lease agreement. I understand that my deposit may be applied toward any rent loss, advertising costs, rerental fees, etc., if this application is approved and I am unable to fulfill the conditions of occupancy. The deposit will be returned if this application is not approved, providing all of the above questions are answered correctly and truthfully.

I have been shown a copy of the lease agreement and agree to the conditions of occupancy that are enumerated therein and find no conflict with the State code, and will adhere to the agreements if my application is approved based on the information contained herein.

I hereby grant permission to the owner/agent to verify through the Federal Adjustment Bureau Inc. the validity of all the above statements to be true and correct. I understand that this application does not constitute any oral and/or written commitments on the part of the owner/agent.

A payment of $_____ is included. This payment is made for the purpose of verifying the information included on this application. I understand that this charge is not under any circumstances to be returned to me.

_____   _____

(signature of applicant)   (date)

FOR USE BY OWNER:

Application taken by _____ Date _____

Amount Rcd. $_____ Security Dep. $_____ Balance due $_____

Rental application Approved/Rejected _____ Date Applicant notified _____

SAMPLE RENTAL AGREEMENT

This Rental Agreement is made on (date) _____ by and between _____ the owner of the premises, described below (referred to as "Owner") through its agent

_____

(referred to as "Agent"), and _____

(referred to as "Resident").

The agreement is as follows:

That Owner, in consideration of the rent to be paid and the covenants and agreements to be performed by Resident, does hereby rent the following described premises, to wit: Situated in the City of _____ County of _____ and State of _____ known as _____

_____

TERM AND PAYMENTS

Resident agrees to occupy said premises for an Original term of _____, said term to commence on the _____ 19____, and agrees to pay without demand the rental of $_____ payable on equal monthly installments of $_____ on or before the 1st of each and every month

beginning on _____ 1st, 19_____. Any and all payments to be paid by the Resident under this agreement are to be paid to _____ at _____,
or such other place as shall be designated by _____.
All payments are to be made in cash, certified check, or money orders or other method approved by the Owner or Agent.

PREPAYMENT CREDIT

In the event Resident pays any monthly installment on or before the 1st of the month, Resident may deduct $_____ from said monthly installment and the same shall be accepted by the Owner or Agent as if Resident had paid the full amount of said monthly installment.

1. ACCELERATION. If Resident fails to pay any installment of rent when same becomes due and payable, the entire amount due under this agreement shall at once become due and payable.

2. SECURITY DEPOSIT. Resident has deposited with the Owner or Agent a Security Deposit in the amount of $_____. Said Security Deposit is to guarantee the return of the premises to the Owner in the same or better condition as when accepted by the Resident, reasonable wear excepted. The Security Deposit is to indemnify Owner against damage and/or loss of value as a result of Resident's action, mistake, or inaction during the term of occupancy. The Security Deposit may not be applied by the Resident as and for payment of any rent due the Owner prior to the vacation of the premises by the Resident. Should the Resident be responsible for damage and/or loss of value to the premises greater than the value of the Security Deposit, Resident agrees to reimburse the Owner for such loss immediately upon presentation of a bill for said damage and/or loss.

3. NOTICE TO TERMINATE AND RENEWAL. Unless another rental agreement is signed by the parties hereto or unless written notice of termination is given by one party to the other thirty (30) days before expiration of this agreement, this contract shall be automatically renewed on a month-to-month basis and may be terminated thereafter by either party upon the giving of written notice to the other party thirty (30) days prior to the next periodic rental due date. Resident shall include with said notice a forwarding address if one is available. Termination shall take place only on the last day of any given month unless otherwise agreed to in writing.

Upon vacation Resident agrees to return the premises to the Owner in the same or better condition as when received, reasonable wear excepted. Under no circumstances shall a dirty or broken condition of the premises, appliances or fixtures be considered to have resulted from reasonable wear.

4. EXAMINATION OF PREMISES. Resident has examined the premises and has accepted same as habitable and satisfactory. Resident shall have 72 hours after entering the premises in which to examine same for defects or damages and report said findings to the Owner or Owner's Agent. Resident while residing in said premises shall observe and act in accordance with all Rules and Regulations attached hereto and made a part hereof as if fully rewritten herein.

5. RESIDENT'S RESPONSIBILITY. The Resident Shall:

1) KEEP THAT PART OF THE PREMISES THAT HE OCCUPIES AND USES SAFE AND SANITARY;

2) DISPOSE OF ALL RUBBISH, GARBAGE, AND OTHER WASTE IN A CLEAN, SAFE, AND SANITARY MANNER;

3) KEEP ALL PLUMBING FIXTURES IN THE DWELLING UNIT OR USED BY RESIDENT AS CLEAN AS THEIR CONDITION PERMITS;

4) USE AND OPERATE ALL ELECTRICAL AND PLUMBING FIXTURES PROPERLY;

5) COMPLY WITH THE REQUIREMENTS IMPOSED ON RESIDENTS BY ALL APPLICABLE STATE AND LOCAL HOUSING, HEALTH AND SAFETY CODES;

6) PERSONALLY REFRAIN, AND FORBID ANY OTHER PERSON WHO IS ON THE PREMISES WITH HIS PERMISSION, FROM INTENTIONALLY OR NEGLIGENTLY DESTROYING, DEFACING, DAMAGING, OR REMOVING ANY FIXTURE, APPLIANCE OR OTHER PART OF THE PREMISES;

7) MAINTAIN IN GOOD WORKING ORDER AND CONDITION ANY RANGE, REFRIGERATOR, WASHER, DRYER, DISHWASHER, OR OTHER APPLIANCES SUPPLIED BY THE OWNER AND REQUIRED TO BE MAINTAINED BY THE RESIDENT UNDER THE TERMS AND CONDITIONS OF THIS RENTAL AGREEMENT;

8) CONDUCT HIMSELF AND REQUIRE OTHER PERSONS ON THE PREMISES WITH HIS CONSENT TO CONDUCT

THEMSELVES IN A MANNER THAT WILL NOT DISTURB HIS NEIGHBORS' PEACEFUL ENJOYMENT OF THE PREMISES.

9) THE RESIDENT SHALL NOT UNREASONABLY WITHHOLD CONSENT FOR THE OWNER TO ENTER ON THE PREMISES IN ORDER TO INSPECT SAID PREMISES, MAKE ORDINARY, NECESSARY, OR AGREED REPAIRS, DECORATIONS, ALTERATIONS, OR IMPROVEMENTS, DELIVER PARCELS WHICH ARE TOO LARGE FOR THE RESIDENT'S MAIL FACILITIES, SUPPLY NECESSARY OR AGREED SERVICES, OR EXHIBIT THE PREMISES TO PROSPECTIVE OR ACTUAL PURCHASERS, MORTGAGES, OTHER RESIDENTS, WORKMEN, OR CONTRACTORS.

6. OWNER'S RESPONSIBILITY. The Owner Shall:

1) COMPLY WITH THE REQUIREMENTS OF ALL APPLICABLE BUILDING, HOUSING, HEALTH, AND SAFETY CODES WHICH MATERIALLY AFFECT HEALTH AND SAFETY;

2) MAKE ALL REPAIRS AND DO WHATEVER IS REASONABLY NECESSARY TO PUT AND KEEP THE PREMISES IN A FIT AND HABITABLE CONDITION;

3) KEEP ALL COMMON AREAS OF THE PREMISES IN A SAFE AND SANITARY CONDITION;

4) MAINTAIN IN GOOD AND SAFE WORKING ORDER AND CONDITION ALL ELECTRICAL, PLUMBING, SANITARY, HEATING, VENTILATING EQUIPMENT;

5) WHEN HE IS A PARTY TO ANY RENTAL AGREEMENTS THAT COVER FOUR OR MORE DWELLING UNITS IN THE SAME STRUCTURE, PROVIDE AND MAINTAIN APPROPRIATE RECEPTACLES FOR THE REMOVAL OF ASHES, GARBAGE, RUBBISH, AND OTHER WASTE INCIDENTAL TO THE OCCUPANCY OF THE DWELLING UNIT, AND ARRANGE FOR THEIR REMOVAL;

6) SUPPLY RUNNING WATER, REASONABLE AMOUNTS OF HOT WATER AND REASONABLE HEAT AT ALL TIMES, EXCEPT WHERE THE BUILDING THAT INCLUDES THE PREMISES IS NOT REQUIRED BY LAW TO BE EQUIPPED FOR THAT PURPOSE, OR THE PREMISES IS SO CONSTRUCTED THAT HEAT OR HOT WATER IS GENERATED

BY AN INSTALLATION WITHIN THE EXCLUSIVE CONTROL OF THE RESIDENT AND SUPPLIED BY A DIRECT PUBLIC UTILITY CONNECTION;

7) NOT ABUSE THE RIGHT OF ACCESS CONFERRED BY DIVISION (B) OF SECTION 5321.05 OF THE REVISED CODE;

8) EXCEPT IN THE CASE OF EMERGENCY OR IF IT IS IMPRACTICABLE TO DO SO, GIVE THE RESIDENT REASONABLE NOTICE OF HIS INTENT TO ENTER AND ENTER ONLY AT REASONABLE TIMES. TWENTY-FOUR HOURS IS PRESUMED TO BE A REASONABLE NOTICE IN THE ABSENCE OF EVIDENCE TO THE CONTRARY.

7. OWNER'S LIABILITY. Owner shall not be liable for any damages or losses to person or property caused by anyone not under the direct control and specific order of the Owner, Owner shall not be liable for personal injury or damage or loss of resident's personal property from theft, vandalism, fire, water, rainstorms, smoke, explosions, sonic booms, or other causes not within the direct control of the Owner and Resident hereby releases Owner from all liability for such damage. (If protection against loss is desired it is suggested that Resident secure insurance coverage from a reliable company.) Owner shall not be responsible for any damage or injury caused by the failure to keep the premises repaired if the need for said repair was not communicated to the Owner or Owner's Agent by the Resident and was not reasonably within the knowledge of either the Owner or Agent. Owner shall not be liable for damages if Resident is unable to occupy the above premises as of the _____ day of _____ 19 _____ when Resident's inability is due to circumstances not within the control of the Owner or Agent. If the Owner or Agent is not able to deliver possession to the Resident within thirty (30) days of the date set forth above for the commencement of the term, Resident may cancel and terminate this agreement.

8. UTILITY CHARGES. Resident agrees to pay all charges and bills incurred for water, sewer, gas, electricity, and telephone, which may be assessed or charged against the Resident or Owner for the Premises during the term of this Rental Agreement or any continuation thereof except those charges and bills which the Owner has herein agreed to pay.

9. ALTERATIONS. Resident agrees not to make any alteration or paint or cover walls or surfaces of the rental premises with any material whatsoever without the prior written consent of the Owner or Agent.

10. RE-RENTAL CHARGE. If the Resident vacates the premises prior to fulfillment of this Agreement, additional charges will be assessed to cover ALL costs incurred by the Owner-Agent in the re-rental of this unit.

11. EMINENT DOMAIN. If all or any part of the premises is taken by, or sold under threat of, appropriation, this agreement will terminate as of the date of such taking or sale. The entire award or compensation paid for the property taken or acquired, and for damages to residue, if any, will belong entirely to the Owner and no amount will be payable to the Resident.

12. PETS. No pets or animals will be permitted without the prior written consent of the Owner or Agent. Any permission so granted may be revoked at any time by the Owner or Agent.

13. ASSIGNMENT. Resident may not assign this Rental Agreement or sublet the premises or any part thereof without the prior written consent of the Owner or Agent.

13. OCCUPANCY. Resident agrees that the premises will be used for residential purposes only and will be occupied only by _____

_____

and _____ family consisting of _____ persons whose names and ages are _____

_____

_____

The premises will not be used or allowed to be used for unlawful or immoral purposes, nor for any purposes deemed hazardous by Owner or Agent or Owner's insurance company because of fire or other risk.

14. PROPERTY DAMAGE. In case of partial destruction or injury to the premises by fire, the elements or other casualty not the fault of Owner or Resident, the Owner shall repair the same with reasonable dispatch after notice of such destruction or injury. In the event said premises are rendered totally uninhabitable by fire, the elements or casualty not the fault of the Owner or Resident, or in the event the building of which the above premises are a part (though the premises covered hereunder may not be affected) be so injured or destroyed that the Owner shall decide within a reasonable time not to rebuild, the term of this agreement shall cease and rent shall be due only through the date of such injury or damage.

BREACH OF CONTRACT:

In the event lessee(s) is in default of any of the terms or obligations of this Rental Agreement (which includes nonpayment of rent, or any rules or regulations herein or hereafter adopted by the lessor for its buildings, its balconies, its courts, its drives, its parking areas, or grounds) and lessor requests lessee(s) to vacate the premises as a result thereof or because of said default by lessee(s), lessor initiates a forcible entry and detainer action, by delivering a notice to vacate the premises to lessee(s) as prescribed by law, or lessor files a complaint in forcible entry and detainer with the court, or lessor is awarded a judgment order for restitution of the premises, the mere act of vacating the premises by lessee(s) as a result of any of the foregoing acts does not terminate the obligation of the lessee(s) to pay rent for the remainder of the rental period for which no rent has been paid. Lessee(s) remains liable to lessor for all rent and any other damages incurred until the end of the lease term or when the premises are rerented, whichever event occurs first.

THIS LEASE SHALL NOT BE BOUND BY ANY TERM, CONDITION, OR REPRESENTATION, ORAL OR WRITTEN, NOT SET FORTH HEREIN
     PROPERTY RENTED IN THE "AS IS" CONDITION
IN WITNESS WHEREOF, Lessor and Lessee have executed this Lease in duplicate on the day and year first written above.

LESSOR _____ LESSEE _____
BY _____ LESSEE _____
     (Agent and Person in Charge)
                    GUARANTOR _____

7

The Case
for Raw Land

Raw land is sometimes called "unimproved property." Under this headline come vacant lots, farm land, mountain land, desert land, recreation land— any property that has no improvements such as buildings on it.

Just as you need raw vegetables for a balanced diet, you need raw land for a balanced real estate portfolio. I guarantee it will be a nourishing addition to your financial health. It has been to mine.

When I first sought to invest in Osceola County, Florida, the properties I looked at were mainly cattle pastures with scattered clumps of trees here and there. The land was still used for agriculture at the time.

One particular parcel captured my attention. At the county courthouse, I had discovered that it was an abandoned subdivision dating back to 1926. The land was near a lake, which the owner, a rancher, used for watering his cattle.

I tried to figure out a way to turn this pasture into housing for the thousands of construction workers who were being flown in to build the multimillion-dollar Disney World entertainment complex. No facilities were available yet, and there was hardly any time for conventional housing to be constructed.

One answer was mobile homes. At the courthouse, I checked with zoning authorities to determine if I could install mobile homes on the pastureland. Would I need to build roads? Would I have to put in sewage and water systems? Could I simply use the existing 1926 subdivision *plat* (the map showing size and shape of lots) or would I need to hire an engineer to replat and redesign housing lots?

It turned out I could indeed use the existing 1926 platted subdivision, by putting a septic tank and a well on each site. The zoning permitted me to move mobile homes onto the land. Roads could easily be built using stabilization materials such as clay and lime.

Before long, with a relatively small amount of work and money (about $300 per lot), I developed an instant community for the construction workers. And I was an almost-overnight success.

I offer this story as an illustration, not as a blueprint. Building a mobile home park is a rather elaborate maneuver not suited to a novice, but the purchase of the land is.

Raw land is great for the unsophisticated investor because it cannot call you in the middle of the night about a plumbing leak. It requires no management. You simply file away your documents and forget about it for five, ten, or fifteen years. When you take those papers out of your safe deposit box years later, you can sell the land to make a down payment on a house, to send your kids to college, or for another worthy cause.

Many people bought those individual lots that I spent $300 on for $795 apiece back in 1963, for use as mobile home sites. Five years later, they were able to sell those lots for as much as $7,000 to $10,000. That was twenty years ago. Today, those lots are selling for $30,000—thirty thousand!—each.

I compared raw land to raw vegetables before. Well, eating vegetables may not be exciting, but it is good for you. So is raw land. My rule of thumb is that a good buy in land doubles in value every ten years. A great buy in raw land doubles every five years. The Osceola County lots were originally a great buy.

AMERICAN LAND, FOREIGN OWNERS

Raw land in the United States is still a quiet bonanza. Just ask investors from Europe, Asia, or South America who have extra money. They are buying up this country as if the land were covered with diamonds and emeralds instead of soil. They use United States land as a substitute for a safe deposit box.

The foreign investors know that for the past two hundred years, our people have treated the right to own property as a given, not a privilege. Land has never been expropriated from owners by the American government without compensation, as has been the case when some parties seized power in other parts of the globe. And American land owners know that certain land is bound to be worth more years from now.

The cheapest raw land is in rural areas. You are buying lots or acreage, in most cases, farmland in others. Expect to hang on to it for at least ten years. Acreage can cost as little as $100 to $300 per acre.

The most expensive is usually suburban land, which tends to rise in value more quickly and therefore does not have to be held for as many years as rural land. In this case, you hold it with an eye to selling to a developer, builder, or anyone who needs a home site.

City land in the metropolitan area with a strong housing market and little open space (New York, San Francisco) is quite costly.

Although odd city lots in metropolitan areas can often be sold eventually to a developer or the owner of neighboring property, I do not think they make wise purchases for a novice. There are so many zoning restrictions and so much red tape involved that city odd lots are best left to experienced investors.

The best deal on urban land can sometimes be found at auctions in smaller cities. The procedure is the same whether land or buildings are being auctioned; turn to chapter 10 for details.

Who has raw land for sale? All kinds of folks: farmers who no longer want to cultivate a portion of land or who are retiring . . . raw land investors in the business of buying wholesale and selling retail . . . state and federal government agencies . . . cities with odd lots that they want back on the tax roll . . . developers . . . recipients of inherited property, and so on.

THE ODDS ARE IN YOUR FAVOR

Naturally there is risk involved in buying raw land. An unscrupulous wheeler-dealer could sell you a bill of goods by assuring you that the next Taj Mahal is about to be built on the adjoining plot. This ploy rooks unsuspecting but greedy buyers time after time. They do not investigate the claims. They pay too much for the land. The Taj Mahal never materializes, nor does the appreciation on the greedy buyer's land.

The secret to my success in raw land—and yours—has not changed in a quarter of a century: "Be where the rest of the people are going to be before the people know they are going to be there . . . and especially before anyone else knows the people are going to be there."

This suggests that I was tipped off about the bonanza of construction workers needing housing in Osceola County. You bet I was! In the business of real estate, capitalizing on inside information is legal.

How can you employ inside information to make money on raw land? The same way I did:

• Learn about demographic changes, such as longer commutes to metropolitan areas from once-distant towns that still have affordable housing. (An example is southern New Jersey, since commuters spend two hours traveling back and forth to jobs in New York City.)

• Keep tabs on new recreation areas, such as Disney World, soon-to-be designated national monuments, and state parks.

• Make notes on communities that are becoming popular with retirees, such as the sunbelt towns of Bullhead City and Yuma, Arizona.

• Look for brand new towns or communities whose growth is outstripping currently developed boundaries and nibbling at land on the outskirts. Ask yourself, "What is the direction of the nibble?"

• Look for highways that will cut across available acreage or new roads about to be extended.

• Check highway department plans to locate interchanges.

• Watch out for news about new transportation hubs, such as a proposed new airport.

• Establish a relationship with savvy brokers who will keep you up to date on the latest plans.

The drawbacks of raw land are well known. There is no cash flow to be gained, which is why I advise you to limit your holdings to 20 percent of your real estate investment portfolio.

Keep in mind, too, that you must pay taxes each year. The average bite, nationwide, is 1 percent of the market value annually. Thus, a lot that is worth $2,000 will cost you $20 a year in taxes. A $5,000 lot runs $50 a year in taxes.

Raw land is even less liquid than other real estate. Unless your land is in the path of tremendous growth, it will take longer to sell it than a comparably priced house in a boom area.

This kind of investment also takes the biggest plunge during an economic crisis. Because the demand for raw land is tied to the economy like any other commodity, it is directly affected by supply and demand. Thus, the length of time you hold it is important; like other commodities, in time the value always returns.

FINDING CHOICE PARCELS

The standard method of finding good values is to start with newspaper ads, just as you would look there for other property. But don't ignore one of my favorite advertising mediums—the sign or billboard by the roadside.

Make your intentions known to seasoned brokers in your area who specialize in raw land. Spread your name around among real estate sales people; that's what those business cards are for.

There are multiple-listing services for land, such as the one maintained by United National Real Estate in Kansas City, Mo. Call them for a copy of their catalog at (800) 999-1020.

Another source of information is the Chicago Farmers Club, 2 N. Riverside Plaza, Chicago, IL 60606. Phone: (312) 454-0857. Or try the weekly publication *Doane's Agricultural Report*, available for $62 per year. Contact Doane's at 11701 Borrman Dr., St. Louis, MO 63146. Phone: (314) 569-2700.

In addition, the American Society of Farm Managers and Rural Appraisers lists land brokers in any area of the U.S. Contact the group at 50 S. Cherry St., Denver, CO 80222. Phone: (303) 758-3513. The current price of land for sale in various areas is maintained by the Farmers National Company, 11516 Nicholas St., Omaha, NE 68154-4427. Phone: (402) 946-3276.

Moreover, government agencies, such as the General Services Agency and the Bureau of Land Management, mentioned in Chapter 11, sell land.

Finally, national newspapers, such as the *Wall Street Journal* and *USA Today*, as well as magazines, such as *Field and Stream* and *Popular Mechanics*, have whole sections devoted to land.

Consider taking out your own classified ads. A typical one might read:

"INVESTOR SEEKS UNIMPROVED PROPERTY. Must be bought at wholesale prices with owner financing. Call: 000-0000."

Many parcels advertised are offered by developers as residential building sites. Be careful that you don't buy these sites at inflated prices. Compare prices with those of parcels nearby that are offered in real estate classified ads in the area's newspapers.

There are no specific kinds of raw land that are better or worse for novice investors. To amplify what I said earlier, just as you wouldn't be eating a balanced diet if you ate lettuce alone but not broccoli, tomatoes, and carrots, you should not concentrate exclusively on residential building sites, farm acreage, and commercial or industrial sites. Check out all varieties of raw land.

The good part about buying from a developer is that certain large ones—those offering more than 50 parcels—are required to register with the state and with the Federal Government's Office of Interstate Land Sales

Registration. This means that the company must issue a property report, which has all the answers to questions you will be asking about roads, zoning, water, and sewers.

You can phone the Interstate Land Sales Registration office in Washington, D.C. for a list of developers. Another list can be obtained from the Association of Resort and Residential Developers, also in the nation's capital. Phone: (202) 371-6700.

When you make an inquiry about a development, ask if it is registered and if so, request the property report.

Although it may be more convenient to shop for raw land in your immediate area, the two-hour driving time rule does not apply here. It is acceptable to own raw land in another part of your state or even a part of the country far from your home. (Novice investors should *not* get involved in buying foreign land, however, no matter how good it looks.)

The problem here is taking time from your job and funds from your bank account to fly or drive to a site for the crucial personal inspection. Buying distant land based solely on a seller's photos or videotapes is as silly as buying a mail order bride or groom.

SCAM ALERT! RAW LAND DIRT CHEAP!

Over the years, raw land frauds have sprung up regularly like plagues of locusts despite attempts by state and federal authorities to exterminate them. It is not hard to recognize one of these scams, but a warning is nevertheless in order.

The typical scam is overpricing land that has been cut up into small slices by the unscrupulous developer. Never buy a parcel, no matter how attractive the price, without doing thorough comparison shopping.

Be especially suspicious of the overeager sales forces that want to fly or drive you into an area to examine a parcel for a sale right on the spot. Don't let yourself be flown out without doing that comparison shopping.

If you are buying land strictly based on the attractive terms offered— 10 percent, 5 percent, or nothing down—you will pay a premium on the overall purchase price for the chance to pay so little in cash. Eventually, you might be able to sell that land for more than you paid, but you will have to wait several years longer because of the initial premium, which I consider overpricing.

Another classic scam starts out with overpricing as well:

A developer sells you a parcel for $10,000 that is actually worth $4,000 or $5,000. In a few years, the developer gets in touch, explaining he or she will allow you to trade that lot in as a down payment on an $80,000 house.

Unfortunately, the house is not worth what he says, any more than the land was; the house is more likely to be worth $50,000. So your falsely priced $10,000 lot becomes a down payment on a house, and you owe $70,000!

What do you wind up with? A house for which you have paid $20,000 more than it is worth.

Other classic scams:

- Watch out for land out west that does not have water rights or public water.
- Beware of land that does not "percolate," which means a septic tank cannot be used for sewage disposal.

FIVE STEPS TO SMART LAND DEALS

Once you locate a promising site, a few simple steps can save you from being cheated and help you make an appropriate offer.

First, get in writing the following information: size of parcel, boundary survey, landscape (mountainous or rolling, streams, creeks, or roads), nearby developments, percolation test, zoning asking price, seller financing, and title policy.

Second, independently, you or your attorney should double-check at the courthouse or planning board any plans for the property and nearby land. Eyeball the parcel in person.

Third, ask yourself the following questions:

1. Is it suitable for some kind of development?
2. What kind? (A title search will tell you whether area is zoned for housing, farming, commercial development, or industrial use.)
3. Does it have adequate drainage or are there patches of standing water?
4. Are the boundaries marked by a surveyor so you know exactly what they are?
5. Is there a signed survey (paid for by the seller) available from a

registered surveyor, who independently verifies that you are buying
what you have seen?

6. Who owns parcels that border on the one you want?
7. Do the numbers on the markers correspond with the numbers on the
   area's plat map, that standard map showing parcels of land?

Fourth, do some comparison shopping. Are there many "For Sale"
signs in the same area? Compare prices of other parcels that might be
offered by competing brokers or owners, advertised on site via signs, or
listed in classified ads.

Fifth, have the land appraised by an independent, professional appraiser—either an MAI (Member, Appraisal Institute), an ASA (an associate of the American Society of Appraisers), or a member of another
nationally recognized professional appraisers group. This is a quick, inexpensive process—usually a good appraisal costs from $150 to $200 for
the whole job. Do *not* use an appraiser affiliated with the developer or
seller.

On large pieces of land, an appraisal might cost as much as 1/10 of 1
percent of the sales price. But this is not the case with small parcels such
as a new investor might begin with. Request your appraiser to do the job
for a flat fee, in advance.

On the next page is my "Raw Land Scorecard" to simplify your shopping. Keep a notebook with entries for this scorecard as you visit each
parcel.

If you do not buy an actual appraisal before closing any deal on land,
you or your real estate broker should investigate records, usually on file in
the county courthouse, showing sales of similar land in the area.

Your attorney should also do homework to make sure there is clear
title to the land, in the form of a title commitment or an abstract. The
latter is a history of the property, showing the previous owners, the prices
they paid for the land, and any debts or easements and rights of way still
outstanding. All this information is public.

ARE THERE BARGAINS ON LAND?

You bet there are! Whether land is a bargain depends on how good a
negotiator you are. Once you have done your homework and know what

RAW LAND SCORECARD

A. Parcel Site _____

B. Description _____

_____

C. Size: approx._____ acres or square ft.

D. Offered by _____ (broker or seller)

E. Asking Price $_____

F. Roads into or adjoining property _____
County/Township? _____ Surface of roads _____
Public or Private? _____ Restrictions on ingress/egress? _____Who
pays for road maintenance? _____

G. Water sources _____
Need well?_____ How deep?_____
Estimated cost? $_____

H. Sewer facilities public or private? _____

I. Percolation test?_____ Cost? $_____
Suitable for septic tank?_____ Cost?_____

J. Zoning and/or Land Use Restrictions:
Residential/Commercial/Agricultural? _____
Single Family/Multiple/Mobile Home _____
Size restrictions _____
Recreational use (Yes/No)

K. Does seller provide survey? (Yes/No)
If no, cost to you? $_____

L. Will seller provide financing? (Yes/No) Term _____
Down payment $_____ interest rate on balance _____%

similar parcels have sold for in the previous few months, as well as what
the parcel you are bidding on has sold for in the past, you can make an
informed offer.

Some of the best bargains may be obtained in tax sales or from banks
that have foreclosed on land. In the chapters that follow, you will learn all

about these methods of buying into real estate at below-market prices. Keep in mind while reading that raw land, as well as houses or other property, is available through this route. You could wind up owning land for hardly any money. I picked up lots in Florida through tax certificates for as little as $1.50 to $3 apiece!

Estates are another good source of raw land at wholesale cost (see chapter 11 regarding estate sales), as are "don't wanters"—people who, for one reason or another, are eager to get rid of lots.

Plan on paying wholesale prices, not retail, for raw land unless you have hard information about major changes in the area. What if you knew that General Motors was about to build a major plant in Tennessee? Even if you had paid retail prices for nearby land, you would have made a profit. Just make sure that the industrial or other development that you believe makes the land valuable has not been postponed or canceled.

Even as a novice, you can be privy to valuable tips on an area that is about to boom. One dead giveaway is a lot of new building permits issued by the local building department. Again, this is public information.

As a wise investor, you read the business pages of your local paper daily, plus the *Wall Street Journal, Business Week, Barrons* and other publications, which run stories on planned development. You keep eyes and ears open for similar news on radio and television.

Supplement this reading and listening by paying a visit to the local Chamber of Commerce, or Industrial or Economic Development Commission, to find out about specific, perhaps small-scale projects on the drawing boards that would affect the price of adjacent land.

Often, the brokerage community can be helpful in providing clues. Raw land brokers, who are very commonly found in small communities, tend to be more cooperative than their colleagues in the residential field, because they cannot afford to buy all the raw land available for themselves. So if you put the word out that you are in the market for good deals, brokers will keep you apprised of activity.

Some mountain areas that have experienced patterns of recreational development over the years include the Berkshires and Green Mountains in New England, the Catskills in New York, the Poconos in Pennsylvania, and the Rockies in the West. Property near or on water in such states as Florida is also a traditional growth locale.

Don't buy raw land for immediate or near-term income. Instead, buy land you expect to hold for five years or more before you see any return from it. The exception might be property in a hot area alongside a highway where you can sell the land as the site of a gas station or other business within a shorter period of time.

In an area that is drawing increasing numbers of retired people or recreation seekers, you should make anywhere from 7 to 12 percent on your money each year, on paper, until you sell it.

MAKING YOUR MOVE

Perhaps you have found a parcel of interest and have thoroughly investigated its background and potential. It is time to make an offer. There is not too much difference here between land and housing.

Offer as little as possible on land. Never pay the asking price. Be an aggressive bargainer. I myself practice this technique all the time. Recently, driving through the Pocono Mountains in eastern Pennsylvania, I saw a "For Sale by Owner" sign on a vacant site. Naturally, I inquired.

This 1-acre parcel sat between 2 lots, each of which had a house being constructed on it. Other 1-acre lots in the area were selling in the $5,000 to $6,000 range, I discovered by checking local records. The owner happened to live in New York City, a few hours away. He had inherited the land but could see no personal use for it. His asking price was $10,000.

In our phone conversation, I offered him $4,000. I knew in my own mind that I would pay up to $5,000. The owner confessed he did not know exactly what his land was worth, but would be happy to negotiate further, in person.

When we got together, I showed the owner evidence of other sales in the area to buttress my position that my price was fair. I also noted he would save the 10 percent commission that other sellers had to pay brokers.

In return, the owner told me he did not need all the cash right away, so he would be delighted to take back a mortgage. (That way, he could earn 10 percent on his money, rather than get the 6 percent his funds would earn in a money market fund.)

In a fairly short time, I was writing, in longhand, on a sheet of yellow legal paper, a deal subject to a percolation test and my attorney's approval. The price: $5,000.

The deal was successful for both sides, but not solely because I was a good bargainer. I was able to demonstrate to the seller that I had done the necessary legwork, so my offer was based upon real-world costs in his area. That, combined with his willingness to be flexible on terms, allowed me to get the land at wholesale.

After you have negotiated a price acceptable to you and the seller, the standard procedure is to pay 5 to 10 percent cash for a down payment. It is not unusual for an owner to sell to you for nothing down.

In a typical land deal, the seller finances the remainder of the purchase price. Negotiate as low a fixed interest rate as you can. Incidentally, you should not have to pay the seller points or closing costs.

Depending on how large the parcel is and how long you intend to keep it, you might have your attorney include in your contract a *release* clause or *partial release from mortgage* clause. This allows you to pay a portion of the money you owe to release from the mortgage a portion of the property that you might want to sell to someone else. The point is, you don't want to be in the position of having to pay off the entire mortgage, should you decide to sell one portion of the land.

Some of the document names for buying land include *land contract, agreement for deed, mortgage and note,* and *purchase money mortgage.*

If the seller is not financing the deal, you must shop for a mortgage. This is not going to be easy. Banks try to avoid vacant land mortgages like the plague. When they do make such a loan, it is usually short—five years is typical. Occasionally, a bank in the same area as the land will be willing to lend you the money.

That's all there is to it. Pay your taxes on your land on time (the only other costs might be lawn-mowing charges and amenity charges if you own a site within a subdivision) and in five or ten years, you will be ready to reap the benefits of raw land appreciation. Let me reiterate the point of buying land: You don't wait to buy land; you buy land and wait.

8

Raw Land as a Money Machine

How would you like to work on weekends for a gross profit of $70,000, plus a monthly positive cash flow of $3,100?

Sounds too good to be true? Think you have to knock on doors selling cosmetics or cleaning supplies? Neither is the case. Raw land is one of the easiest weekend money-makers available to the part-time investor.

My idea requires little or no money, yet fattens your wallet. It is not a new idea, but almost no real estate seminar instructor covers it in a course, since few instructors have actually done it. In this case, I have. Over and over, for more than twenty years.

All the techniques covered in the previous chapter on market value and geographic comfort zone apply here. What you are about to do is build on the knowledge you absorbed so far.

"40 ACRES AND A MULE"

In American history classes, everyone learned how pioneers would start out with "40 acres and a mule." My lesson eliminates the mule, but otherwise, you can do your own pioneering with a 40-acre parcel. Once you understand and have practiced the 40-acre example, you can project my techniques for use on bigger parcels of raw land if and when you find suitable ones.

So, here is step one: Find a 40-acre parcel with enough public road frontage so that under current subdivision rules within the local community, you can divide the parcel into four 10-acre properties.

Search for property at wholesale prices, because you will want to sell, as always, at retail in order to make a decent profit. Be especially attentive to prices of small, 10-acre parcels compared with 40-acre parcels.

I can almost guarantee what your research will show: 10-acre parcels sell for twice as much, or more, per acre than 40-acre parcels.

For example, I recently purchased a piece of raw land within three hours drive of a major metropolitan area. The size—40 acres. The price—$250 per acre. Total purchase price—$10,000. Retail prices in the area, according to my research, amounted to $500 or more per acre for 10-acre parcels.

Thus, once the 40 acres I bought were cut up into 10-acre lots, the retail value of the entire parcel was $20,000. On paper, I doubled my money.

What I was doing was subdividing. Most novice investors think this is what the big guys do, not small fry like themselves. That's quite true. But we are not talking quantum physics here. You, too, can learn to handle subdivisions. Sure, it takes time, work, knowledge, and a calculator. You have those tools at hand, right now.

MASTER OF ALL YOU SURVEY

What sort of parcel should you seek? In addition to the road frontage, the parcel should have trees. Even better is water. If the land has a stream running through it or borders on a pond, that water increases the value of your land 100 percent.

Once you have located a suitable 40-acre parcel, hire a local surveyor. Have him do a survey of the property as four distinct 10-acre parcels, each with its own road frontage.

Be sure the surveyor implants irons or cement monuments at each corner of each parcel. There should also be a stick of at least 1 inch in diameter at each corner, plus a flag. (Sometimes vandals steal the sticks; the irons or cement monuments planted in the ground allow you to replace the flags at the precise points.)

Put up a sign advertising your land on the highest tree facing the road. Nail it high enough so kids cannot deface or steal it, but low enough so drivers can read it. Signs placed on fences or stuck in the ground disappear before you can say "down payment."

I know the simplest thing is to go to a local K Mart and buy signs, but I would rather you spend the extra few dollars to have a sign custom-made by a local sign painter. After you have your first sign done, you can have copies of it silk-screened on heavy outdoor plastic or cardboard sign paper. Treat them with polyurethane, and paper your property with these outdoor ads. You can also silk-screen a single all-purpose sign for later parcels. The silk screening cuts the cost of your signs 75 to 80 percent.

The sign should read: "For Sale By Owner. Will finance _____. Low Down Payment," or words to that effect. You might want to put the actual amount of the down payment and monthly payments on the sign, if they are temptingly low. Wouldn't you telephone the number on a sign you passed if it offered you a piece of land for $1,000 down and $100 a month?

Place ads for the land in local newspapers, big dailies that sell in the local community. (The *Boston Globe* is sold across New England, for example, and the *Denver Post* is sold throughout Colorado, northern New Mexico, and southern Wyoming.) You might consider ads, too, in regional editions of the *Wall Street Journal, USA Today,* and the *New York Times.*

The ads should again emphasize "for sale by owner," not just because the phrase sounds friendly, but also because land shoppers know better deals can often be made directly with an owner.

As you begin to receive inquiries, make dates to meet potential customers on the site on weekends. Walk the property with each individual. I like to share my pride of ownership in chatting with these people, and I know how magical such phrases as "your property, your tree, your fence, your road frontage" can sound to a potential owner. All of us—you, me, and John Q. Buyer—want to own our little chunk of America.

EARNING WHILE YOU LEARN

How much will the preliminary work cost? Start with your 40-acre parcel price, which in my actual example is $10,000. The survey should cost about $1,000. Add $500 in attorney fees, $400 for signs, $1,100 for advertising. That makes a total of $13,000.

In doing a cost analysis on raw land as a money machine, make note of the fact that you will earn interest along the way. You will be selling 10-acre parcels to buyers on an *agreement for deed* or *land contract* basis. That means your buyers will be paying you in installments, just as they pay any mortgage, with an interest rate added to the basic price.

As soon as you are ready to advertise the properties, have your attorney draw up a basic "agreement for deed" or "land contract." You want your customers to sign the contract at the same time they write you a check for the down payment on the property at the point of sale.

Charge your buyers $5,000 for each 10-acre parcel. (That's the retail price once you have subdivided your 40-acre parcel.) Eventually you collect $20,000 for the 4 parcels, so your gross profit is $7,000.

"What about my cash flow?" you should be asking at this point.

Your down payment on the property would be $1,000. When you add survey costs, attorney fees, signs, and advertising, your total cash outlay is $4,000.

Now for your income. Require a 20 percent down payment on each parcel, giving you $4,000 right off the bat to recover all of the cash you put into the deal originally.

From this point on, your monthly cash flow is as follows: The payment on the $9,000 balance you owe on your 40-acre purchase amounts to $90 per month. Meanwhile, your contracts with the buyers of your 10-acre parcels bring you $100 per parcel per month, or a total of $400 per month.

This brings your gross positive cash flow to $310 per month. Your cash-on-cash return on your investment—since you have regained your initial cash down payment immediately—is almost 100 percent a year on your original $4,000 investment.

Because the down payments on your sale returned 100 percent of your original investment, however, you actually are earning $3,720 per year with no cash tied up, plus lots of interest. Show me a money market or mutual fund that offers such a stunning return!

BUYERS WHO PAY CASH

When your attorney draws up your contract for the 40-acre purchase, be sure it contains a release clause. This lets you pay off any one of the parcels at any time in order to get a deed. You need this so that you can deed pieces of the property to any of your retail buyers who prefer a cash sale.

Let us assume that two of the four buyers pay all cash. With a release clause, you can pay off your original 40-acre contract with the $5,000 you receive from each of these buyers. You then own the remaining 2 parcels free and clear. You have no money in them. Result: 100 percent pure profit for you.

"This sounds so elementary," you say. "How come the retail buyers who buy from me don't go out and buy entire 40-acre parcels themselves at the wholesale price?"

Usually, the answer is that they do not want or need that much land. The typical buyer is happy to own a small slice of the pie with a low down payment and low monthly payment. And he or she doesn't understand how to buy raw land. These typical retail customers want the land as a place for a weekend retreat, as a retirement home site, or just as a commodity to hold and then sell years from now, like a coin or stamp.

Think ahead for a moment. Imagine that you are successful with your first 40-acre wholesale buy, subdivision, and sales. You have an immediate gross profit and a handsome positive cash flow. What if you bought another parcel—80 acres this time? Using the same figures, you would make a $14,000 gross profit plus $620 a month positive cash flow.

Now double that again. A parcel of 120 acres bought wholesale brings you $21,000 gross profit, plus $930 a month positive cash flow. Can you picture 400 acres? That would bring you $70,000 gross profit, plus $3,100 a month positive cash flow.

I mentioned earlier that raw land could be a money machine. Maybe I should say a money tractor . . . or a money backhoe. Anyway, you get the idea. The formula works whether the parcel is small or large.

Incidentally, if you get tired of collecting these monthly payments, or you need more money than your positive cash flow generates, just bring your land contracts into a local bank or advertise them for sale. You can use these contracts as collateral and borrow money against them tax-free. You also can sell them for cash at a discount. Your profit will be smaller but you can get out quickly in order to go on to your next real estate deal.

SAMPLE LAND PURCHASE AGREEMENT

Date _____

Received from _____

(referred to as "purchaser") the amount set forth below as DEPOSIT on account of the PURCHASE PRICE of $ _____ for the real property in the City/Town of _____, County of _____, State of _____ consisting of approximately _____ acres, _____ sq. ft., described as _____

upon the following TERMS AND CONDITIONS:

1. Financial terms.

1-A. $_____ DEPOSIT evidenced by (check one): Cash ____ Cashiers Check ____ Note ____ Personal Check ____ Other ____, to be deposited within one (1) business day of acceptance, and escrow opened with: _____

1-B. $_____ ADDT'L CASH DEPOSIT to be placed in escrow within _____ days of acceptance and/or _____ upon removal of all contingencies.

1-C. $_____ BALANCE OF CASH PAYMENT AT CLOSE OF ESCROW.

1-D. $_____ BOND OR ASSESSMENTS of record if assumed by Purchaser.

1-E. $_____ ADDITIONAL FINANCING: (explanation) ____
_____
_____
_____

1-F. $_____ TOTAL PURCHASE PRICE (including closing costs). Any net differences between the approximate balances of encumbrances shown above, which are to be assumed or taken subject to, and the actual balances of said encumbrances at close of escrow shall be adjusted in _____ cash,_____ other: _____

2. Other Terms and Conditions:
_____
_____
_____
_____

3. Addendum. (Form covering subordination, partial reconveyances.) The Addendum to Land Purchase Agreement is/is not attached hereto and made a part of this agreement.

4. Closing. On or before _____ or within _____ calendar days of acceptance, whichever is later, both parties shall deposit with an authorized Escrow Holder to be selected by _____ Purchaser _____ Seller, all funds and instruments necessary to complete the sale in accordance with the terms hereof. Until then, Purchaser, Seller, and Broker agree not to disclose the terms of sale. The representations and warranties shall not

be terminated by conveyance of the property. Escrow fee to be paid by
_____ . Documentary transfer tax, if any, to be paid by _____.

5. Evidence of Title in the form of _____ a policy of Title Insurance
or _____ Other _____, paid by _____.

6. Broker Representing Both Parties. By placing their initials here,
Purchaser { } and Seller { } acknowledge that _____,
the broker in this transaction, represents both parties and Purchaser and
Seller consent thereto.

7. Additional Provisions. The provisions checked below are included
in the agreement on a separate page. [NOTE TO READERS: THAT
PAGE, WITH LENGTHY DESCRIPTIONS, NOT INCLUDED HERE.]
_____ Soil Tests, within _____ days of acceptance.
_____ Survey, paid by _____, based upon $_____ per
_____ acre or _____ sq. ft.

EXPIRATION

This offer shall expire unless a copy hereof with Seller's written acceptance
is delivered to the Purchaser or to his agent on or before _____ A.M./P.M.
on _____ 19 _____.

The undersigned purchaser has read this agreement, including items
on separate page [NOT INCLUDED IN THIS SAMPLE] and acknowledges receipt of a copy hereof. Purchaser acknowledges further that he/she
has not received or relied upon any statements or representation by the
undersigned Agent which are not herein expressed.

_____ Purchaser's Broker (if any) Date: _____
Signed by:

_____ Agent (if any)
_____ Purchaser
Broker's initials _____ Date _____

Acceptance. Seller accepts the foregoing offer and agrees to sell the
herein described property for the price and on the terms and conditions
herein specified.

Commission (if applicable). Seller hereby agrees to pay to _____,
the Broker in this transaction, in Cash from proceeds at close of escrow,

for services rendered: _____. In the event that Purchaser defaults and fails to complete the sale, the Broker shall be entitled to receive one-half of Purchaser's deposit, but not more than the commission earned, without prejudice to Broker's rights to recover the balance of the commission from Purchaser. The mutual recision of this agreement by Purchaser and Seller shall not relieve said parties of their obligations to Broker hereunder. This agreement shall not limit the rights of Broker provided for in any listing or other agreement which may be in effect between Seller and Broker, except that the amount of the commission shall be as specified herein.

The undersigned seller hereby acknowledges receipt of a copy hereof and authorizes Broker to deliver a signed copy to Purchaser.

_____ Seller's Broker (if any) Date:_____

Signed by: _____ Agent (if any)

_____ Seller

Broker's initials: _____ Dated _____

The undersigned Purchaser hereby acknowledges receipt of a copy of the accepted agreement.

Date: _____

Purchaser's signature: _____

9

Becoming Knowledgeable About Tax Sales and Foreclosure Sales

Even novice investors can profit from tax and foreclosure sales, great buys in either a soft or hot real estate market. It is here that an investor without a great deal of money can root out terrific values.

There are two kinds of tax sales. One involves a piece of paper called a *tax certificate*. The other involves actual real estate, which a city or state forecloses on for nonpayment of back taxes. Foreclosures occur all over the country, not merely in distressed areas. We will discuss tax certificates as an investment a bit later on, in chapter 15.

Foreclosure sales can be undertaken by banks, in cases where owners fail to make mortgage payments. The Federal Deposit Insurance Corporation (FDIC), Federal Savings and Loan Insurance Corporation (FSLIC), Department of Housing and Urban Development (HUD), Internal Revenue Service, finance companies, home improvement companies with unpaid bills, and even condominium or co-op associations with liens against an owner can bring about foreclosure sales.

Finally, the local sheriff and the Federal Government's Treasury Department sell property that has been seized from owners because of illegal activities, such as drug smuggling.

THE FORECLOSURE PROCESS

A word about correct terms: When the procedure for taking property away from its owner and offering it to the public has not yet been completed,

91

that property is said to be *in foreclosure* (sometimes known as *pre-foreclosure*).

When a property is already *foreclosed,* the paperwork has been done, and the judge has signed an order. Then, a bank or agency has title to the property, allowing a bidder to take clear title to it. Your aim usually is to find foreclosed properties. However, later in this chapter we will discuss obtaining properties during *pre-foreclosure,* which involves a different technique.

One concern that holds many people back when they hear the word *foreclosure* is the social consequences. They worry about grabbing a home out from under an unfortunate person. Some visualize tearful children with smudged faces clinging to their mother's skirt as the family home goes on the block.

Like any decent American, I care about people losing their homes. However, buying real estate that has already been foreclosed is far less emotional than those sad images evoke. The former owners of a foreclosed house are long gone. Or they are not individuals but corporations that have decided to walk away from the responsibility for a property. The homeless and those on welfare are very rarely the original owners, never having owned a home in the first place.

If a property has reached the point at which foreclosure is in progress, you, the potential buyer, are not connected at all with taking it away. The bank or government agency that does the foreclosing is the "villain." You and other bidders have no contact with the people who are losing the property.

What's more, if nobody is there to bid on a foreclosed property, it still does not revert to the unfortunate owner. The bank or other institution takes it back for a lot less than it is worth. That institution turns around and sells it for a profit.

ON THE TRAIL OF TAX SALES

You can find out about tax sales from the tax collector's assessor's or treasurer's office in the area in which you are interested. It's a good idea to call the county courthouse first and ask which specific office handles these sales.

To find out about tax and foreclosure sales, look in the records section of the courthouse under "foreclosure sales" and "final foreclosure judgments." These lists are public. The section clerk is required to tell you the date on which the government will be advertising such a sale and in which newspapers the notice will be published. The clerk should also tell you where in the courthouse the lists are posted. Bear in mind that government clerks are deluged with requests every day. Use basic courtesy and good public relations in dealing with them.

On your first such visit, simply explain that you are a private investor who is researching files for possible real estate purchases. Make it clear you are seeking information that is public. *Public* is the word that keeps you from being pushed around by impatient or unpleasant courthouse employees. As you continue to check records on a regular basis, you can develop a good working relationship with these valuable contacts.

In some states, the local government agency will be happy to put your name on a list to receive, by mail, the announcements of tax and foreclosure sales. (In some counties or other areas, tax sales might take place only once or twice a year, but foreclosure sales take place regularly.)

You may have to pay a dollar or two, and to submit your request in writing with a self-addressed stamped envelope. Your letter should read:

> Dear County Treasurer (or whichever office is involved):
> I would like to be placed on a list to receive information on the forthcoming tax/foreclosure sales [send a separate request for each] that are public information. I would also like to be notified about which newspaper this information will appear in and the date of publication, and on which bulletin board it will be posted in the courthouse.
> Sincerely,
> John or Jane Investor

Many investors, however, don't have the time to search these records. Thus, every state has services, usually advertised in the business or real estate section of the newspaper, that sell tax foreclosure lists on a weekly or monthly basis. The price of these services runs anywhere from $50 to $200 per month, depending on the number of foreclosures.

UNCOVERING FORECLOSED HOUSES

Banks are classic "don't wanters." They do not want to be in the home-owning business. Yet just because banks hold properties does not mean their lists are easily accessible. It takes a fair amount of what newspaper reporters call "legwork" to pry information loose from banks.

Go in person to the bank and ask for the officer in charge of *nonperforming assets*. These are REOs *(Real Estate Owned)* properties that the bank can now sell because it has foreclosed and repossessed them. A bank can offer them to you free and clear of liens and encumbrances. It will also finance the deal right on the spot. The government's message to banks is loud and clear: "Get rid of those REOs!"

Perhaps you have tried this before. In response to your request for nonperforming assets, the bank officer gave you a blank stare, or mumbled, "No one handles them." This is not unusual, and it sure can be annoying. The truth is, either the person is ill-informed, or the officer is withholding information from you.

One stumbling block is that banks are *not* required to give you lists of nonperforming assets, even when it is in their best interest to do so. That happens to be the way a lot of banks operate.

I get around a bank's uncooperative attitude by purchasing one share of a bank's stock. As a stockholder, I have a right to look at its books. I return to the bank with the stock certificate in my hand, demanding a look at the institution's financial statements covering nonperforming assets. I explain that I am interested in making offers on those properties.

In unearthing REOs, your targets are commercial banks (loans insured by FDIC) and savings and loans (insured by FSLIC).

Real estate brokers do list troubled properties. But keep in mind that, as mentioned earlier, properties "in foreclosure" are not yet owned by the bank. Sometimes brokers list houses for which foreclosure proceedings have begun. The idea is to bail out the owners by selling the houses before they are repossessed.

The seller of such a house is in a precarious position, however, so be a tough negotiator. Offer less for the house as the final foreclosure date nears. After all, if you don't get the property for a reasonable amount of money, the bank will get it for only the amount that is owed it on the mortgage.

There are no national sources for lists of REOs held by banks. Federal agencies publish lists of foreclosed properties once the banks give up on them, however. When banks can no longer carry foreclosed houses on their books, those properties are taken over by the various agencies that insure banks, such as FDIC, FSLIC, the Veterans Administration, and FADA (Federal Asset Deposit Association). Write to these agencies at the addresses on pages 104–106 for more information.

In thousands of cases, HUD, the Federal Department of Housing and Urban Development, gets houses after they go through the foreclosure procedure. These are houses whose mortgages were insured by the Federal Housing Administration (FHA). HUD is the agency designated to sell FHA-insured houses.

Lists of HUD/FHA foreclosed properties are available from the regional offices of those agencies, especially in economically troubled regions. Chapter 12 on government loans spells out the procedure for buying HUD houses, as well as those offered by the Veterans Administration.

Federal agencies are eager to unload foreclosed houses. They place advertisements about properties in the Friday editions of the *Wall Street Journal* ("Real Estate Corner") and *USA Today,* and in the weekend real estate sections of all major newspapers.

Other sources of lists for available below-market-price houses are Fannie Mae, the Federal National Mortgage Association, and Freddie Mac (Federal Home Loan Mortgage Corporation). The Federal Government pages of the phone book, especially in major metropolitan areas, provide phone numbers for most agencies in your region.

PURSUING FORECLOSED HOUSES

You now have a list of available foreclosed houses in hand. First, narrow your search to a specific geographic area. If there are many properties in your region, concentrate on one neighborhood—no one has the time to look at everything.

Second, make contact with a broker who specializes in properties offered by banks or governmental agencies such as FSLIC. The agencies can provide names of such brokers. Although you have to make a deal work for you, a broker will lead you through the red tape involved in actually acquiring a property. Novice investors, in particular, need help from experienced brokers to fill out confusing paperwork that is part of the bidding process.

Take a weekend, or several weeknights, to visit in person the places on your short list. Evaluate each according to the factors included in the house, condo, and co-op evaluation worksheets, which are back in chapter 5, pages 53 and 54.

Soon, you will have a collection of index cards for a variety of houses, each showing the physical condition of a house, size, asking price, number of rental units in neighborhood, current rentals in neighborhood for similar units, and so on.

Sift through the cards to discard houses that might be too big or too small, in need of too much work or too much up-front cash. Do the cash-on-cash return worksheet, page 49, to come up with a price you can offer that would make a good deal for you.

Once your maximum bid price is established, never allow yourself to go above it. Instead, have the broker you select approach the bank or federal agency involved and make an offer *below* your maximum bid.

Before you make an actual deal on a property, you will need a professional inspection of it. I urge you to refer to our book *Inside Real Estate*, in which there is an entire chapter on how to choose an inspector or engineer and how to interpret an inspector's findings.

Narrow your choices to one, two, or three properties at a time and make formal bids on them after they have been inspected. A company will give you a discount (it is negotiable—25 percent off, for example) on multiple inspections.

Many foreclosed properties will be "fixer-uppers" or "handyman specials," the kind of building that needs either cosmetic touches, such as a paint job, or more substantial repairs to make it habitable for a tenant.

Go ahead and pursue fixer-uppers, but make sure that you take into account how much additional cash you will have to lay out. That extra money must be subtracted from the annual cash-on-cash return you hope to get from the house.

I believe you should build a 25 percent cushion into the eventual market value of a fixer-upper. Thus, if a foreclosed fixer-upper is available for $50,000, and you need to put $25,000 worth of repairs into it, its cost becomes $75,000. To be a good buy, the market value should be $100,000 after fixing up. If that $25,000 cushion is not there, the house is not a good investment.

The novice investor is much better off buying a property that needs strictly cosmetic repairs, rather than costly renovations. Your goal, after all, is to start the cash flowing, not to suffer month after month of delays while repairs are completed.

Under the heading "cosmetic changes" comes a new paint job inside and/or out, new carpeting, and minor landscaping. Major renovations involve plumbing, wiring, heating, and roofing. When you spend more than $3,000 or so fixing up a house, you are cutting severely into your cash flow and losing precious time.

SETTING YOUR MAXIMUM BID PRICE

When it comes to tax-sale or foreclosed properties, I like to settle on a price that is a minimum of 20 percent below market value. Your initial bid will be even more—say 25 or 30 percent below. Expect the bank or agency to reject it. Ask them to come back with a counteroffer.

The real estate broker you have selected helps you determine what fair market value is in the neighborhood. Brokers have computerized multilist printouts of sale prices for houses sold within 90 days in an area, which you can compare with the houses you have targeted.

It is a good idea to go to a second broker as well, so you can compare reported selling prices from two sources. After all, the broker who is working for you has a vested interest in getting a sale out of you. A second or third opinion from a more objective party makes sense.

I suggest that you take one additional step before committing your bid to paper. Order an appraisal by a good appraiser registered with the American Society of Appraisers, the Appraisal Institute, or any nationally recognized appraisal association. This should solidify your ideas on the value of the property. Secondarily, an appraisal helps you get financing at the best price from a bank or mortgage company.

At this point you have a firm figure in mind. Make your bid in writing. If you are dealing with a bank, you make it on a standard "offer to purchase" form, available at a stationery store. In dealing with a government agency, you make it on the offering sheet that is supplied by the government agency in question.

"JUMP-OUT" CLAUSES

There is always a blank space on the offer sheet where you can add your own conditions, or *jump-out* clauses. I recommend that you write in the following:

1. Offer is subject to buyer's attorney's approval.
2. Offer is subject to buyer's written approval of itemized list of all personal property remaining with property.
3. Offer subject to buyer's approval of engineer's report.
4. Offer subject to buyer's final inspection of property prior to closing.

Surprise! Instead of jumping for joy at the chance to lighten its load of unwanted houses, the bank rejects your opening offer. (It happens all the time.) What then?

Ask the bank (either through your broker or directly), "Would you care to make a counteroffer?" or "Could you tell me what price range would be acceptable to the bank?" Now you negotiate with the bank until you agree on a figure.

Suppose you have offered $75,000 on a foreclosed 3-bedroom house.

"Outrageous, my dear Mr. Jones!" replies a bank officer. "We will sell it to you for $125,000."

From your homework, you know that a fair market price for the place would be $125,000. But you are not willing to go that high. "Can you give me an idea of what price range you might accept an offer at?" you reply. "Would you entertain an offer in the low $100,000 range . . . maybe $98,000 or $100,000?"

The officer returns your call in a few days, saying, "The bank's minimum is $110,000." If you have set your maximum bid at $100,000, do *not* accept this answer. Stay within your own maximum.

Those who allow themselves to be bid up by a bank or anyone else are inefficient, to say the least. They are committing investorcide!

HOW TO WIN IN CLOSED BIDDING

In some municipalities and with government agencies such as HUD, offers on homes are made on a closed-bid basis, in writing. Naturally, you take a chance on whether or not your bid will be accepted. The agency is likely to have a standard format for the bid envelope, as well as for the offer inside.

I will go into detail on HUD sales in chapter 12. Here, it is important that in any closed bidding situation, you have to make up your mind about how high your maximum bid should be. Bid that amount (or lower), with the realization that you could lose the property to a higher bidder.

The other side of the coin is realizing that if you make enough reasonable bids, you are likely to win with one of them.

PAYING FOR A TAX SALE
OR FORECLOSED HOUSE

Congratulations! You have won your bid on a house being sold for back taxes or nonpayment of a mortgage. But don't start advertising for tenants just yet. You are expected to put down 10 to 25 percent of the sale price, depending on the rules of the agency or municipality. Once you make that down payment, you have from 30 to 90 days to get a mortgage and cash the seller out.

When you bid on foreclosed property offered by a bank or a federal asset-disposition group, the bank or agency doing the selling will usually finance the purchase for you on the spot. You must have decent credit, of course. If you are an acceptable buyer, you will get a lower interest rate plus lower closing costs than you would from an outside source. The bank or agency is not being overly generous. It is simply eager to reduce its inventory through sales to qualified people like yourself.

Familiarize yourself with the agency option by scanning their ads in the *Wall Street Journal* (usually Fridays), like the one on the next page. You will see a down payment listed, along with a financing schedule, closing costs, and timetable for particular properties.

In some communities an agency will offer extremely attractive terms in order to find buyers for its houses. HUD, for instance, has offered hundreds of residences in economically depressed areas such as Denver for as little as 5 percent down, specifically to lure investors into bidding.

Thus it becomes a win-win situation. You can obtain your first property for a very small sum, while the agency has one property fewer to carry on its rolls.

Let's say you have been successful in buying a tax-sale or foreclosed house for a below-market price. What next? As you would do with any income property, you should immediately seek a tenant to rent it, even before you fix it up.

If you are turning properties over for quick profits, however, your strategy should be to put your bargain property up for sale right away, with a scale of prices: the lowest for the residence "as is," then a series of incrementally higher prices for the place as you make improvements on it.

PRE-FORECLOSURE:
LEAPFROGGING THE BANKS

There *is* a way to make a deal on a property before a bank takes it away from its owner. Such a deal is called a *pre-foreclosure* proceeding. It is a delicate negotiation that can benefit both you, the buyer, and the distressed seller.

Pre-foreclosure properties usually are in danger of being repossessed for nonpayment of mortgage installments, taxes, or other debts. A foreclosed property has already been repossessed, removing the owner from the picture. Such is not the case in a pre-foreclosure situation.

It pays to be aggressive. You *can* get pre-foreclosure information before any notices are published, as required, in local newspapers or on government lists. Once you have the names of people involved in foreclosure

proceedings, you have the opportunity to approach them with a deal before an actual foreclosure sale ever happens.

Properties in some pre-foreclosure stage are found in city, county, or state records in the "lis pendence" files, which are kept in the county clerk's office for civil cases. Remember, you or any other citizen is entitled to look at these public records.

There is another source of early information. Independent, private services throughout the United States publish pre-foreclosure property lists for various regions. Pre-foreclosure subscription services advertise in the classified real estate and business sections of local and national newspapers. You can subscribe to these lists to save time in going through court papers. The companies who sell them copy court files for you, computerize them, and send you printouts.

For instance, on the next page is a sample listing from *Investor News,* a pre-foreclosure service published by CJ Enterprise in Toms River, N.J. You might subscribe to this service if you have narrowed your geographic search to specific communities within the Garden State.

Column A (address/bank) shows the address of the property and the amount of the civil suit filed by a specific lender. For example, the first listing is at 144 W. Adams Ave. The suit by Chrysler is for $56,200.

The second listing, L/24 B/224, refers to the location of the information in the records in the clerk's office. L stands for Liber, B for book.

Column B shows the owner of the property against whom the suit is filed. In the first listing it is Rebecca Brown. MO Pymt 677/14 below her name refers to the dollar amount owed and how many payments behind she is.

Column C lists the town and zip code in New Jersey where the property is located. Column D is the lis pendence file number. ATL refers to Atlantic County.

Missing from this summary is the market value of the property. You must seek this out by consulting local real estate agents and/or appraisers.

Once you get a good estimate of the market value, subtract the sum owed (the amount of the suit, in Column A). This gives you the amount of potential equity in the house.

From doing your homework, you might already know that the Adams Avenue house has a market value of about $100,000. Thus, the potential equity is $43,800.

At this point, the proverbial light bulb above your head should switch on. There is a deal brewing on this house if you can buy it for $80,000 or less—20 percent below market value.

PRE-FORECLOSURE LISTING

A. Address/Bank	B. Owner	C. Town/Zip	D. File #
144 W. Adams Ave.	Brown, Rebecca	Pleasantville NJ	4686–88 ATL
Chrysler 56.2K	Brown, Rebecca Mo Pymt 677/14	08232	
L/24B/224 Elysian Fed 1800K	Pannullo, Joseph Pannullo, Joseph	Absecon NJ 08201	4718–88 ATL
Agassis Street K Jacobi 83K	Hargrove, Ezell Hargrove, Ezell Mo Pymt 892/10	Galloway NJ 08215	4762–88 ATL
168 Odessa Ave Janet Phillips 35K	Pitucci, Gus Pitucci, Gus Mo pymt /11	Galloway NJ 08215	4769–88 ATL
L/20.1 B/224 Elysian Fed 1800K	Pannullo, Joseph Pannullo, Joseph	Absecon NJ 08201	4717–88 ATL
Island House Condo Unit D5 Island House 6.9K	Feldman, David Feldman, David	Margate City NJ 08402	4819–88 ATL

Your next step is to send quickly a personable, friendly, nonbusinesslike letter—on personal, not company, stationery—to the defendant. It would read:

Dear Ms. Brown:

I am a private investor buying property in your area. Perhaps I can help you in your situation. If you are interested in selling your property, would you be good enough to phone me at (000) 000-0000.

Sincerely,

Do not mention the foreclosure—people in these situations are frightened and worry about being harassed by creditors. Follow the same steps in writing to many defendants who hold properties that you have determined are potential bargains. You can easily use a computer to create the same letter addressed to each different person.

You will have to send out at least a hundred such letters to get three or four replies. Many of the defendants are bailing out of the homes in question and have no interest in making a deal, or have been approached by a score of investors competing with you.

When you do get a reply, be tactful and courteous. You are talking to someone in trouble. Perhaps you get two responses like this: "I'm ready to sell my property. I want $X,000." Your reply? "Let's get together and talk. Do you want to come to my place, or shall I come to yours?"

Keep in mind that you are about to present yourself as a knight in shining armor to this person. The ultimate disaster would be for the bank or loan company to take away this person's $100,000 residence because of a $30,000 debt.

Thus, whatever you offer the owner above $30,000 is a wonderful boost. The result can be a win-win deal for both of you.

Your first obligation is to enable the owner to pay off the $30,000 debt to stop the foreclosure from proceeding. This can be done according to several scenarios:

Scenario A. You negotiate an agreement to pay the owner an amount above $30,000 but less than $80,000. The owner can then walk away with a clean credit rating and a profit, while you take title to a house at 20 percent or more below market price.

Scenario B. You negotiate the same deal, but instead of walking away, the owner remains in the house as your tenant, paying you rent. This owner-turned-tenant arrangement occurs in numerous pre-foreclosure deals.

Scenario C. You arrange to pay the owner's $30,000 debt. In return, the owner agrees to make regular payments to you on a new loan for $30,000 that you get on the property. You and the owner agree to become partners in the house in exchange for this helping hand.

When the property is sold some months or years later, you get your $30,000 back, plus a share of the remainder of the sales price. (This is similar to an "equity participation" deal, for which an investor contributes part of the cost of a house in return for a share of the equity.)

This latter turn of events shows the good side of dealing in pre-foreclosures. Before you came on the scene, the owner was about to lose his home. Now, the happy owner not only clears his debts but still lives in his own house with a chance to make a profit when the time comes to sell. *You* make an immediate profit by obtaining a share in a $100,000 house for far less money.

Once again, everyone wins.

FDIC, DIVISION OF LIQUIDATION, OFFICES

(Contact "Bank Liquidation Specialist in Charge")

Atlanta Region
1325 Barksdale Blvd., Bossier City, LA 71171-5667.
(318) 742-3290
5778 S. Semoran Blvd., Orlando, FL 32812
(407) 273-2230

Chicago Region
Regency West Office Park, 4700 Westown Parkway, Bldg. 4, Suite 200, West Des Moines, IA 50265-1004
(515) 224-1567
501 East Highway 13, Burnsville, MN 55337
(612) 894-0800
900 Oakmont Lane, Westmont, IL 60559
(312) 789-0300

Dallas Region
14651 Dallas Parkway, 2nd Floor, Dallas, TX 75230
(214) 239-3317
7324 Southwest Freeway, Suite 1600, Arena Tower #2, Houston, TX 77074
(713) 270-6565
N. Petroleum Bldg., 303 Air Park Dr., Midland, TX 79705
(915) 685 6400
999 NW Grand Blvd., Oklahoma City, OK 73118
(405) 842-7441
4606 S. Garnett Rd., Tulsa, OK 74146
(918) 627-9000

Kansas City Region
Board of Trade Bldg II, 4900 Main St., Kansas City, MO 64112
(816) 531-2212
1883 W. 21st St., Wichita, KS 67204
(316) 838-7111

New York Region
800 S. Gay St., Knoxville, TN 37909
(615) 544-4500
1607 Ponce de Leon Ave., Cobian Plaza, Lobby Level, Santurce, PR
00909
(809) 724-1740

San Francisco Region
3347 Michelson Dr., 2nd Flr, Rm C2-1-104, Irvine, CA 92715
(714) 975-5400
1125 17th St., Suite 700, Denver, CO 80202
(303) 296-4703
2870 Zanker Rd. Suite 200, San Jose, CA 95134
(408) 434-0640

FSLIC OFFICES

(Contact "Office of Liquidation")

Southern Region
1349 Empire Central, Dallas, TX 75247
(214) 905-9100

Western Region
523 W. 6th St., Suite 550, Los Angeles, CA 90014
(213) 623-7055

Central Region
10 S. La Salle St., Suite 1900, Chicago, IL 60603
(312) 419-3700

Eastern Region
285 Peachtree Center Plaza, Suite 300, Atlanta, GA 30303
(404) 880-3000

Northwest Region
P.O. Box 48269, Seattle, WA 98148
(206) 241-5505

FEDERAL ASSET DISPOSITION ASSOCIATION (FADA)

Office of Liquidation, 801 17th St. NW, Washington, DC 20036
(202) 429-9477

FEDERAL NATIONAL MORTGAGE ASSOCIATION (FANNIE MAE)

3900 Wisconsin Avenue, NW, Washington, DC 20016
(202) 752-7000

FEDERAL HOME LOAN MORTGAGE CORPORATION (FREDDIE MAC)

1776 G Street NW, Washington, DC 20006
(202) 789-4700

10

Auction Action —Another Way to Buy Real Estate or Another Way to Get Burned?

"Fifty! Do I hear sixty . . . that's fifty here . . . c'mon now, let's hear sixty. . . ." The singsong spiel of the auctioneer can be as entertaining as a show at the Grand Ole Opry, as hypnotic as the swing of a pendulum, as effective as a pickpocket.

An auction is one of the quickest ways to unload property. When the supply of homes, lots, raw land, or farms outstrips demand, there is an explosion of auctions. That is why they have become so popular among developers and government agencies in overbuilt or economically depressed communities, such as the farm belt and the oil belt.

Auctions can also be a bargain hunter's heaven . . . so long as you bid with your head, not with your heart.

An auction is an emotional event. A buyer gets a rush of instant gratification by outbidding a rival. Have you ever attended an auction, gotten caught up in the hype, walked away with an antique doodad, and then stared at it the next day, wondering, "How on earth did I get stuck with this thing?"

The answer: impulse. You were entranced by the theater of the bidding war. Almost everyone has been sucked in by an auction somewhere.

As an investor, you want to collect terrific properties at auction that seem as smart a buy the day *after* the auction as they did when you were in the midst of bidding. In other words, you want to win, but you want common sense to prevail, too. Here is how you do it.

For starters, understand that inventory clearing is one reason for a real estate auction. A sheriff's sales of foreclosed properties is another. The majority of auctions of real estate are held for the benefit of developers. These highly publicized events often are nothing more than a hype by a developer to move slow-selling properties.

The least-publicized auctions, which often have the best buys, are those of foreclosed properties for sale by public agencies and banks, at which you will be bidding against seasoned, professional real estate people.

You find out about government auctions from public notices placed in the newspaper. Interested? Contact the agency listed in the ad for more information.

Although ads for such properties talk about the "courthouse steps," the actual sale takes place on those steps only in some small communities. In larger communities, the auction is held in a meeting room inside the courthouse. The auction is conducted by a sheriff or an employee of the agency.

Yet another reason for an auction is expediency: An owner who wants to sell quickly contacts an auctioneer in order to speed up the sales process without dropping the price.

Still another circumstance is the government distress sale. The Treasury Department, for instance, holds auctions of real estate seized from drug dealers or other alleged felons. By law, public agencies must sell the property.

Local, county, and state governments also hold auctions in an effort to reduce the surplus property they have collected. Chapter 11 deals specifically with buying surplus properties, but the action at auctions—no matter who conducts them or for what reason—is very similar.

QUICK! BUY YOUR BARGAIN HERE!

In each case, the auction creates a sense of immediacy. Some auctions of a private owner's or developer's property involve a real deadline. For example, a bank may be in the process of foreclosure to take over the parcels because the seller is behind on payments.

Some auctions are phony—there is no other word for them. You can spot a phony auction by casting a critical eye at the people in the room. Is the same person bidding over and over again, without ever winning his or her bid? That's a straw man, placed there by the seller. The straw man artificially jacks up prices by bidding up honest buyers.

Should you do something if you are sure you spot a straw man? Yup! Grab your coat and leave the room.

Despite the urgency of an auction, you, as a buyer, still have to do the same homework on houses or land that you would do if you were buying it in a slower, more conventional manner. Those careful enough to research auction property can come up with fabulous deals. Auctions are often last-ditch efforts to get rid of perfectly decent housing. In overbuilt communities—certain ski resorts or beach vacation areas, for example—you can capture good houses for 20 percent or more below market value.

The auctions I urge most caution about are those in economically depressed towns, such as Tulsa, Houston, Dallas, Denver, or New Orleans, which, at this writing, are caught in the mire of the oil glut. You don't want to wind up with empty homes for which there is no rental market. It does not matter how much below market value you pay if you have a stream of red ink flowing from that investment for the next five years.

ABSOLUTES VERSUS NO-SALE

When you learn of an auction that you sense is a real one, whether it is a developer or government doing the selling, telephone the auctioneer for an information brochure well in advance.

Almost every real estate auction is conducted either by a professional auction house or by a real estate broker doubling as an auctioneer. They are paid a flat fee and/or commission by the seller.

Among the first things you should know is whether the event is an absolute auction, a no-sale, or a combination of the two. At an *absolute auction,* property must be sold, no matter how little money is bid for it.

At a *no-sale auction,* there is a floor price or minimum bid underlying each property. The seller will not accept a price that is below that minimum. You can save yourself a trip if you learn beforehand that the minimum on homes you are interested in is actually the market value price.

Hybrids exist, too. Recently, for instance, Grace Lichtenstein saw an advertisement for an auction of ranch sites in the Rocky Mountains near a major resort. The brochure she received said some properties were to be sold absolute to successful bidders, while others would be subject to acceptance by the sellers. The brochure did not say which was which. A potential buyer had to request that important detail.

It turned out that only 2 of the 30 lots, each about 35 acres, were available for whatever amount topped the bidding, without a minimum. Needless to say, both were auctioned quickly, one for just $17,500. However, other similar sites, with minimums of $40,000 to $50,000, found no takers.

SUCCESS IN THE PALM OF YOUR HAND

I went to my first real estate auction with my father when I was eight years old, and they still have a magical power over me. Even with over forty years of experience, I never enter that room without my personal secret weapon to keep my emotions in check.

My secret is a 3 × 5 index card held in the palm of my hand. On that card is a number that I have written with a bright red marking pen or crayon. No, it is not my lottery pick! It is the maximum bid I will allow myself to make on a building.

My theory is that auctions play psychological tricks on even the most sober investor. In the heat of bidding, everyone can be tempted to jump one step above a competitor. After all, what's $500 when I am so close to having that lovely three-bedroom ranch? The trouble is, $500 can become $5,000 before the numbers register on my fevered brain.

That is why I force myself to glance repeatedly at the card in my hand throughout the bidding. It helps me keep in touch with reality. If I have several properties on the list, I have a separate card for each. Sounds like a remedial math exercise, you say? Perhaps . . . yet without the cards I might act as if I were playing Simple Simon.

STEP RIGHT UP, FOLKS!

"I can discipline myself, especially with card in palm," you are now thinking. You are eager to find an auction because it might be the place to find the best values in your area. Or, you simply want to attend a free show, to get a taste of auction fever. How do you locate one?

Real estate auctions are advertised in newspapers, both in classified ads and in larger ads in business sections. Professional auctioneers, who might hold a jewelry auction one day and a real estate auction the next, are listed in the Yellow Pages. There are hundreds of auctioneers around the country who might handle real estate at some point. There are also a half-dozen companies that specialize in big or high-end real estate auctions. Several are listed at the end of this chapter.

Contact these companies requesting to be put on notice about real estate auctions; I guarantee you will not lack for announcements. Many auctions will be held right on the site of the properties, while some will be in nearby school auditoriums, hotel meeting rooms, or other public rooms.

Do not pass "go," do not collect $200, and most importantly, do not attend an auction without viewing the properties available in person beforehand. Auctioneers are in the business to sell and will gladly give you guided tours or maps to the homes or lots.

On your tour, take notes by filling in the blanks of our house evaluation worksheet (page 53) or land evaluation scorecard (page 79). The same techniques I discussed earlier apply to properties sold at auction (or in any other fashion), regardless of price. The location, the cash-on-cash return, and the tax picture must make sense.

Is there a representative of the auctioneer on hand to show you a property for which the minimum has not yet been set? Casually ask if he or she has any idea what price the seller might accept. The representative is not supposed to discuss this price, but you might get helpful clues.

GOING ONCE . . .

The first phase of your homework is now done. Next, decide what your maximum bid will be on each property that interests you. Write the numbers in red on 3 × 5 cards.

It is in your own interest to have several properties in mind. Of course, one will be your favorite. But someone else with more money could have an eye on that same parcel. To avoid disappointments, have a few backup choices.

As you enter the auction headquarters on the appointed day, your evaluation sheets, notebook, and 3 × 5 index cards in your briefcase, your first stop will be at a registration desk.

It is usual for you to be asked to show or hand over a cashiers check or certified check for anywhere from $100 to $5,000. It is made out to yourself, and it enables you to get a bidder's paddle or cardboard sign with a number on it.

This refundable check is your earnest money. You will endorse it over to the escrow company, title company, or seller, should you be a winning bidder. (Should you leave without buying anything, don't forget to ask for your check. Simply redeposit it.)

In the case of the Rocky Mountain ranch sites, a $2,500 check would be all or part of 10 percent of the purchase price—a down payment, in effect. If it turned out to be less than 10 percent, all successful bidders would be expected to come up with the remainder within five days or more.

GOING TWICE . . .

You have taken a seat in the back of the auction room. (Why crane your neck to see what others are doing, when you can have all the action taking place directly in front of you?) The auctioneer is at a podium at the front of the room, with a plat map or blown-up photos behind him.

Around the room are "ring" men—aides who help the auctioneer spot where bid paddles shoot up, or chins tilt, or heads nod. The first property is announced. Watch who is making bids. If the bidding slows down, one person might begin to bid up everybody else to get the auction flowing again, but somehow that person never does make the winning bid. Keep an eye on that person. It might be a straw man.

Strike up a conversation with the people on either side of you. Let them know what properties you are bidding on. See which ones they are eyeing. You might be able to make a deal right there that you won't bid them up on their choices and vice versa.

Perhaps, during the coffee-and-crullers or scotch-and-soda period before the auction, you overhear people talking about a property that you like. Tell them you will bid on it, too. Many times you can make a deal to go into partnership on a property before the bidding begins.

As the parcels are auctioned off, put an X through them on the list of properties you are holding, along with the winning bid price. You will get a feel for the price structure. After a few auctions, you will be able to differentiate the pricey auctions from the bargain ones.

Your moment arrives. Bidding on one of your chosen properties is under way. Is the straw man bidding you up? Do not follow up after him. A good auctioneer will quickly notice that you cannot be manipulated by straw bids.

Let us assume the opening bid is for $2,000. Raise your paddle to stay in the bidding, but never begin by offering your maximum (that card in your palm) as your opening bid. Depending on circumstances, you could win the bidding without ever reaching that red number.

. . . SOLD TO THE GENTLEMAN IN THE PLAID SUIT!

The gavel comes down on your winning bid. Before you congratulate yourself or kiss your spouse, write down the amount of your final bid.

Silly? Not at all. You would be surprised at how many arguments ensue when a bidder thinks he won an auction at one price, and the auctioneer insists it ended at a higher price. Ask one of the auctioneer's assistants for a piece of paper showing the parcel number, the address, and the price. Make sure he or she initials the information.

The usual practice after you have won a property at auction is for you to endorse your cashiers check for earnest money or the down payment in exchange for a receipt, at a special table or room set aside for this purpose. (There is no standard down payment at auctions. That's why you need to check beforehand with the auctioneer on such details.) You will get instructions after your bid is accepted on when and where the closing will take place.

As soon as possible, appoint an attorney to represent you. Have your attorney get in touch with the auction house to prepare the paperwork. As with every piece of real estate, a free and clear title is crucial. A knowledgeable attorney representing you (never use the same attorney as the seller!) should be present to close the deal for you.

Occasionally, there will be an auction at which buyers are expected to close on the spot. The title policies have been prepared in advance and so have the other necessary documents for a fast turnaround.

You have two choices in this case: Either bring your attorney with you (the better choice), or sign all documents at the on-the-spot auction with a conditional clause written in by you and initialed by an auction house representative. The condition would read: "This document subject to review by my attorney." If the auctioneers balk at this clause, don't buy the property.

In some cases, you will be expected to come up with the cash for the remainder of the bid, or to find a lender who will give you a mortgage. In one out of every four cases, the auction literature will tell you ahead of time that the seller is willing to finance a portion of the price. In these cases, you are required to put from 10 to 25 percent down, with the seller financing 75 to 90 percent.

Especially in the case of raw land, seller financing is the norm. The terms are likely to be for shorter periods than a conventional mortgage—perhaps five years with a balloon (big payment) at the end, or ten years without a balloon.

Whatever the terms are, expect to go through all the usual steps you would take in buying any kind of real estate: Have the site surveyed, do an on-site inspection with your surveyor (especially on raw land to make sure the parcel is the one you thought it was), and have a title insurance policy in hand by the closing date.

Even if land or buildings are being sold *as is,* that phrase refers to the condition of the property at the time of the auction. If someone comes along and smashes all the windows of a house you have bought a week after the auction and before the closing, the seller is obliged to fix them so the property is in the same condition as on auction day.

. . . OR, SOLD INSTEAD TO THE WOMAN IN THE PAISLEY DRESS

Mistakes and changes of heart do occur after auctions. The gentleman in the plaid suit may be all set to follow through on his winning bid for a home, until his employer eliminates his job in an economy move. Suddenly he cannot close the deal.

What happens? Most auctioneers keep a list of the unsuccessful bidders on each property. If you were really keen on the property you lost to the man in the plaid suit, let the auctioneer know you are interested in the right of first refusal. Put your request in writing in a letter to the auctioneer the following day. Then, should the winning bidder run into trouble, you will be next in line to be offered the deal.

The auctioneer will be happy to accommodate you. This is a common procedure, so don't be shy about making your interest known despite losing out.

THE "BUYER'S REMORSE" CLAUSE

Uh-oh. You bought that house at auction yesterday and now you can't sleep. Despite everything, you were so caught up in the emotion of the moment that you paid a price you really cannot afford. Should you go hat in hand to Uncle Albert to see if he wants to be your partner? How do you explain the extra payments to your spouse? Or can you back out of the deal?

You could choose to bite the bullet and pay, pay, pay for your winning bid. Fortunately, consumer advocates have made sure you probably can back out, with honor.

Many states, including New York, Florida, and California have legal *recision* periods: Consumers can change their minds about a purchase at auction within 3 to 15 days, depending on the state—regardless of signed contracts.

You do not have to give an explanation. The *buyer's remorse* law is on the books, in effect, to protect buyers against themselves, as well as to offer a safe haven after having been pressured by a pushy salesperson. It allows you to renege on a deal, provided you let the seller or company know in writing by certified mail.

Make sure never to sign a document in which you waive your right of recision. Read the documents presented to you at the auction to be certain a waiver has not been buried there among the legal phrases.

Incidentally, in states with "buyer's remorse" laws, the right of recision applies to the purchase of houses, condominiums, and other major items in any fashion, not just at auction. I mention it here because impulse buying is most likely to grab you in the heat of an auction, not on an ordinary deal.

GETTING A JUMP ON AN AUCTION

A lot of properties listed for an auction are probably buyable *before* the auction ever takes place. The seller might very well be ready to sell a house or parcel of land in advance, if the price you offer is as much as it could bring at auction.

So, what harm is there in making your offer on a property that you investigate prior to auction? None, really, provided you are satisfied with your cash-flow analysis and you are madly in love with the place. It is done all the time.

The seller could reject your offer, hoping for a better price at the auction. At that point, you make plans to attend the auction anyway, with your trusty maximum price index card in hand.

AUCTIONS FROM A SELLER'S POINT OF VIEW

Your portfolio of investment real estate has grown. You feel it is time to sell off certain properties, either because they are not performing as well as you expected, or because you think they have appreciated to a point where it is time to reap the profits. What about an auction as an alternative to conventional selling methods?

Not a bad idea . . . especially in a slow or soft real estate market, or if you are in dire need of immediate cash, or if you want to create a sense of excitement and urgency about your property. However, there are several major points to bear in mind:

Point 1: You will pay an auction house a commission, just as you would a broker. The auctioneer also gets a typical settlement fee of 1 or 2 percent if no one reaches your minimum bid.

Point 2: The auctioneer will ask you to pay an additional fee for advertising and promoting the auction. You can try to negotiate this out of the contract. Otherwise, have specific dollar amounts, publications, and an accounting (including receipts) listed in the contract.

Point 3: If you sell with no minimum bid and absolute auction, your properties will be gone by the end of the auction day. But you may not collect as much as you would, had you taken the local, rather than express, sales route.

NATIONAL AUCTION HOUSES FOR REAL ESTATE

Good & Company, (312) 346-1500.
Hudson & Marshall, (800) 841-9400
R. Thomas Ashley, (813) 885-8800
JBS, (312) 527-0777.
The National Auctioneers Association, 8800 Ballantine, Overland Park, KS 66214, (913) 541-8084, has names of auctioneers across the country. The Daily Auction Hotline, (900) 246-4000, also has information.

YOUR ANTI-IMPULSE AUCTION CHECKLIST

It is time to take a break from an auction . . .
—when you begin to feel light-headed.
—when you need to go to the rest room but are afraid you will miss something.
—when you realize you are staring at the auctioneer and nothing else.
—when you forget to look at the index card in your hand.

11

Surplus Property— How to Buy Government Castoffs

All over the United States, there are old post offices, school houses, seized property, and other buildings that the Federal Government wants to get rid of . . . a *trillion dollars* worth of property. For years, prime government surplus property has been bought at preferred prices by politically connected friends. Nevertheless, a persistent small investor can carve a niche in this profitable corner of real estate.

Here is what often happens. A congressman or an aide lets Uncle Joe or Aunt Mabel in Kenosha know, via the good old boy network, that the discarded post office in downtown Smallville, several miles away, is going to be up for sale.

Sealed bids are made, the property changes hands, and guess who has a prime piece of downtown Smallville real estate at a bargain price? Uncle Joe or Aunt Mabel.

That is probably the easiest way to get into the government surplus business. Actually, by law, the government must give anyone who asks for it a list of properties in its surplus coffer. However, right now, it is difficult—but possible—to get information because government officials are so bogged down inventorying their acres of parcels and thousands of buildings.

With luck, there are other avenues along which you, the small investor, without a nephew or niece in politics, can travel. This trip is primarily for those who are both tenacious and patient. Do these adjectives describe you? Good; read on.

Sometimes you must be aggressive in pursuing first the lists, then the properties included in them. States, counties, townships, and cities, too, must occasionally sell real estate that they cannot use. Keep dialing and asking questions until you find the agency and the officials in your state or town who are in charge of informing the public about sales of surplus, seized, and unneeded real estate. Your local, state, or federal government officials would be delighted to sell a parcel to you, once you get past bureaucratic red tape.

The majority of government surplus property is commercial, industrial, and forest land. But some sites can be developed for residential use. (My friend Norm bought a World War II prison internment camp, of all things, in the Phoenix area, which he has turned into a first-class retirement village!) Your first step is to learn what is out there.

Contact first the GSA, the nearest real estate sales office of the United States General Services Administration. (See directory, page 123.) Ask to be sent a copy of the Federal Property Resources Service quarterly publication called *U.S. Real Property Sales List*. This booklet gives you an idea of what is readily available in your region.

One hitch: GSA does not maintain an ongoing mailing list for this helpful publication. Attached to it is an application form through which you can receive the next edition, but you will have to fill out this card every quarter. You can also mail a card to get regular notices of individual sales in a specific area, within a specific price range, or both.

Since surplus-property sales are often attended by professionals, it is an excellent idea to attend a few of them purely as an interested spectator before you actually plan to start bidding. Get a ''feel'' for the way these auctions proceed. I think you will find them interesting and entertaining.

WANT TO BUY A
MILITARY BASE OR DAM SITE?

What treasures lurk in these pages? Everything from unimproved land in Riverdale, Illinois, to an old Coast Guard LORAN station on an exclusive beachfront in Kauai, to a former Air Force firing range in Oregon, to a warehouse in Brandford, Pennsylvania, to a 2-bedroom residence in Miami Beach. Military bases, abandoned border stations, hospital sites, quarries, forests, grazing land—the variety is amazing.

Common sense dictates that you confine yourself to nearby locations or to parcels in areas that you visit frequently. And although you might be curious about a firing range or a warehouse, such places are probably not the kinds of sites that are appropriate for your portfolio. Narrow your search to the most likely items.

The most obvious sites are the small ones listed as residential or as unimproved land. But do not neglect the unusual small parcels. What can you do with an abandoned right-of-way? Rent it out to a sign company for a billboard. With a bit of imagination, you can think of uses for many affordable sites.

In each case, you must inspect the property as you would any other. What does it look like? If it is a piece of land, is there water running through it? If it is a house, is it in decent condition or can it be repaired?

Let us say that you live in the Northwest and you are interested in the Linn County, Oregon, parcel of 3.2 acres, a recently listed residential property including 2 buildings. The brief booklet description tells you it will be sold via sealed bids and that you must call the sales office for the date.

Upon calling, you may find out the deadline for bidding . . . or, in this case, you may learn that the sale was canceled. (I must repeat here that you have to make lots and lots of inquiries. Some will turn up good leads, others will lead to a dead end. You must be persistent.)

If you are in the upper Midwest, perhaps you are interested in the 3.73 acres of the Headwaters Headquarters site near Remer, Minnesota. On this tract are 2 single family houses with attached garages and a separate one-car garage. The GSA describes it as "small town residential." The deadline for sealed bids is a month away. The government sends you the sealed bid form.

Sounds promising, right? So you go to Remer to inspect the buildings visually, taking the same kind of notes you would take for any residential property or piece of land. Before submitting a bid, you have the property appraised by a professional appraiser, and inspected by a professional home inspector, so you have two opinions in hand.

Then, you make your bid, based on the physical condition of the property and its market value. You can do an analysis using the formula worksheet on page 53, because this is really no different from buying a set of homes from a broker or at a private auction. Of course you would check the rental market in Remer to determine what the chances are for getting tenants at a profitable rent to create positive cash flow.

If you feel you absolutely must have this property, you must maximize your chance of winning the sealed bidding process by increasing your bid above your minimum, but still keeping it low enough so you can eventually get flat or positive cash flow out of it. My attitude is, if you cannot buy a government surplus property for the price you determine is fair and profitable, don't buy it. There are plenty of other choices.

A handy publication with surplus property information is *Commerce*

Business Daily, published by the U.S. Department of Commerce. The cost is $81 per year. Every issue lists property to be auctioned by the General Services Administration across the country.

BANKRUPTCY BUYS

The United States Bankruptcy Court sees to the distribution of all kinds of real estate and personal property in the liquidation of the estate of a debtor who has filed for bankruptcy. Everyone has heard the phrase *Chapter 11.* This is one kind of bankruptcy. However, neither Chapter 11 debtors, nor those who file under Chapter 13, a second kind, are pertinent in real estate.

The key is *Chapter 7,* sometimes called *straight bankruptcy.* In this case, a trustee (often an attorney) is appointed by the court to sell the debtor's assets in order to pay off his or her creditors.

Trustees must get the bankruptcy court's permission to sell real estate. To make sure the price is reasonable, the trustee has to get an appraisal. Then the trustee or the court itself auctions the property. Sometimes trustees hire a real estate broker, who then looks for buyers in the usual ways. There is no open notice required, nor competitive bidding.

The court does insist that the public have a chance to "upset" a broker-negotiated sale, however. In this case, the real estate agent negotiates a conditional deal. The trustee okays it. Then the court holds an auction, with a minimum amount of money above the negotiated price set as the lowest price an outsider can upset the negotiated deal.

To find out more about bankruptcy sales in your area, contact the nearest branch of the U.S. Bankruptcy Court. (They are listed in the white or blue pages of the phone book under the Federal Government "Court" listings.) Some branches maintain mailing lists for auctions. Others post notices on bulletin boards of the local courthouses.

MERCEDES AND MANSIONS:
CUSTOMS AND IRS GOODIES

When federal law-enforcement authorities take custody of merchandise or property that belongs to a person convicted of either illegal activities (such as drug trafficking) or buying with illegal funds, the government needs to sell these items. Sometimes, real estate (both raw land and buildings) is confiscated or forfeited in these procedures.

Approximately 40 offices in U.S. Customs Districts across the country hold auctions of real estate in the custody of this agency. Look in the white or blue pages of the phone book for the customs office nearest you. For more information on customs sales, contact the office at P.O. Box 17423, Gateway I Building, Washington, DC 20041.

The United States Marshals Service is called upon to sell property forfeited either through the courts or through administrative action of such government agencies as the Federal Bureau of Investigation, the Drug Enforcement Administration, the Internal Revenue Service, and the U.S. Border Patrol.

What does the Marshals Service sell? Everything from houses to autos, jewelry, yachts, planes, and fine arts. Clearly, these can be the most interesting of all government surplus auctions, but the Marshals Service does not maintain a mailing list for prospective buyers.

You can, however, find out about marshals' sales through private auctioneers and real estate brokers, who are required to advertise such sales. The Marshals Service also advertises sales in classified notices in local newspapers, and posts notices on courthouse bulletin boards.

To get more information, contact the nearest National Asset Seizure and Forfeiture (NASAF) Office of the U.S. Marshals Service. See the list on page 123.

SMALL BUSINESS ADMINISTRATION SALES

On occasion, a person or firm defaults on a loan guaranteed by the Small Business Administration, the federal agency in charge of helping handicapped and low-income entrepreneurs, as well as those with fledgling companies.

When a default occurs, the SBA must sometimes ask the local U.S. attorney to foreclose on a piece of property. This property now belongs to the government and must be sold or auctioned, like other real property handled by the Marshals Service. In many cases, local private auctioneers are hired to sell the properties.

The SBA does not maintain a list of real estate that is in its hands, nor are you likely to get helpful information via one phone call to your local SBA branch. Instead, keep an eye out for auction notices, legal notices in newspapers, or notices on government bulletin boards that mention SBA-repossessed property.

ODDS 'N' ENDS OF ROADS
CAN PAY DIVIDENDS

The Federal Government is not the only authority with surpluses. Every state has land and buildings it cannot use. A great source of information is the various state transportation agencies. The reason? Whenever transportation agencies purchase rights of way for roads, they *inevitably buy more* property than they need. They end up with odd pieces of land—sometimes large ones, sometimes slivers—because they can never figure the exact amount of space a road requires.

Thus the agencies always have surpluses that they auction, either through sealed or open bid. One of my favorite ways of making money with such properties is to buy those odds and ends right near new highways in communities and states that allow big signs. I then rent or sell these parcels to sign companies or businesses for billboards.

Here is an example: Let us say that I live in California. I have asked the California Department of Transportation to put me on its mailing list for information on real estate property auctions.

One day, I get a notice saying the agency has a vacant corner in the city of Richmond that it wants to unload. The vacant lot, zoned for residential building of medium density, consists of over 14,000 square feet (I realize this means approximately 100 × 140 feet). The state is asking for a minimum bid of $72,000, with a 10 percent "option deposit" required.

The "data sheet" that comes with the notice of sale tells me in advance that the site is hilly and that utilities are available. It also tells me the city planning department has information about how many units of housing I or another developer would be allowed to build on the site. In such a case, the value of the land is ultimately determined by how it can be used. Could someone build an apartment house? If the answer is yes, the parcel could be very attractive.

I immediately do a comparative analysis of property sold in that vicinity of Richmond within the previous three months. I decide that the minimum bid price is indeed lower than market value. (Most surplus land offered by transportation agencies does tend to be priced under going-market prices.)

I go to the auction, held at the site, with a cashier's check or money order for the $7,700 option deposit, as the announcement tells me to do. If I am the winning bidder, the state accepts my deposit (as happens at any auction) and gives me a certain amount of time (in this case 90 days) to come up with the rest of the money.

The auction notice also tells me that if I have questions, I should contact the "R/W agent." *R/W*, in this field, means right-of-way. Once you learn who the agent is in your area, you can keep in touch with the person's office for notice of other sales.

GENERAL SERVICES ADMINISTRATION— REGIONAL SALES OFFICES

Boston: (617) 565-5700
   Covers New England, New York, New Jersey, Ohio, Indiana, Illinois, Michigan, Wisconsin, Minnesota, Puerto Rico, and the Virgin Islands
Atlanta: (404) 331-5133
   Covers Pennsylvania and entire Southeast
Fort Worth: (817) 334-2331
   Covers Iowa, Missouri, Arkansas, Louisiana, Texas, North and South Dakota, Nebraska, Kansas, Oklahoma, Montana, Wyoming, Colorado, New Mexico, and Utah
San Francisco: (415) 974-9086
   Covers California, Washington, Oregon, Idaho, Nevada, Arizona, Alaska and Hawaii

NASAF OFFICES—U.S. MARSHALS SERVICE

Federal Building Annex, 77 Forsyth St. SW, 1st Mezzanine, Atlanta, GA 30303
606 U.S. Courthouse, 101 W. Lombard St., Baltimore, MD 21201
1416 J. W. McCormick, P.O. & Courthouse Building, P.O. Box 1146, Room 407, 230 S. Dearborn, Chicago, IL 60604
Room 465 Federal Building, 1961 Stout St., Denver, CO 80294 (or P.O. Box 13619, Denver, CO 80201-3619)
231 W. Lafayette St., 645 Federal Building/Courthouse, P.O. Box 2869, Detroit, MI 48231
2104 U.S. Courthouse, 515 Rusk Ave., Houston, TX 77002 (or P.O. Box 61165, Houston, TX 77208
1258 Federal Building, 300 N. Los Angeles St., Los Angeles, CA 90012 (or P.O. Box 671, Los Angeles, CA 90053)
244 U.S. Courthouse, 300 Northeast 1st Ave., Miami, FL 33132 (or P.O. Box 015979, Miami, FL 33101)
880 Front St., 1-S-1 Federal Building, San Diego, CA 92188
Room 1171, 210 Building, 210 N. Tucker, St. Louis, MO 63101

Room 1045, 450 Golden Gate Ave., P.O. Box 36036, San Francisco, CA
    94102
2842 Federal Building, P.O. Box 302, 915 Second Ave., Seattle, WA 98174.

BANKRUPTCY SALES—
UNITED STATES TRUSTEES

United States Trustee
Old Custom House
1 Bowling Green
Room 534
New York, NY 10004
(212) 668-7663

Unites States Trustee
Boston Federal Office Building
10 Causeway St.
Boston, MA 02222
(617) 565-6360

United States Trustee
60 Park Place
Suite 210
Newark, NJ 07102
(201) 645-3014

United States Trustee
Strom Thurmond Federal Building
1835 Assembly St.
Room 1108
Columbia, SC 29201

United States Trustee
421 King St.
Room 410
Alexandria, VA 22314
(703) 557-0746
(Note: this is a suboffice of the
S.C. regional office)

United States Trustee
1418 Richard Russell Bldg.
75 Spring St. S.W.
Atlanta, GA 30303
(404) 331-4437

United States Trustee
113 Saint Claire Ave. N.E.
Suite 200
Cleveland, OH 44114

United States Trustee
U.S. Courthouse
46 E. Ohio St.
Room 258
Indianapolis, IN 46204

United States Trustee
U.S. Courthouse
Room 505
110 S. Fourth St.
Minneapolis, MN 55401
(612) 348-1900
(Note: this is a suboffice of the Ce-
dar Rapids, Iowa, regional office)

United States Trustee
Columbine Building
Room 300
1845 Sherman St.
Denver, CO 80203
(303) 844-5188

United States Trustee
Custom House
701 Broadway
Room 313
Nashville, TN 37203

United States Trustee
175 W. Jackson Blvd.
Room A-1335
Chicago, IL 60604
(312) 886-5785

United States Trustee
Federal Office Building
911 Walnut St.
Room 800
Kansas City, MO 64106

United States Trustee
Transportation Center
425 Second St. S.E.
Room 6750
Cedar Rapids, IA 52401

United States Trustee
Texaco Center B
400 Poydraf St.
Suite 1820
New Orleans, LA 70130

United States Trustee
700 Louisiana
Suite 2610
Houston, TX 77002
(Note: this is also a regional office)

United States Trustee
U.S. Courthouse Room 9C60
1100 Commerce St.
Dallas, TX 75242
(214) 767-8967

United States Trustee
320 N. Central Ave.
Suite 1000
Phoenix, AZ 85004

United States Trustee
10 U.N. Plaza
McAllister St.
Suite 300
San Francisco, CA 94102

United States Trustee
Federal Building
Room 3101
300 N. Los Angeles St.
Los Angeles, CA 90012-4790
(312) 894-6387

United States Trustee
Wells Fargo Bank B
101 W. Broadway
Suite 440
San Diego, CA 92101

United States Trustee
Park Place Building
1200 Sixth St.
8th Floor
Seattle, WA 98201

SUBSCRIPTION SERVICE FOR U.S. CUSTOMS SERVICE PUBLIC AUCTIONS

Information on U.S. Customs Service sales of seized and forfeited property and general order (G.O.) merchandise is available now by subscription. Subscribers will receive sale flyers approximately two weeks before a confirmed sale date, listing the sale location, date, viewing, inspection, and registration periods, and a general description of the type of property/merchandise offered for sale. To subscribe to this service, fill out the subscription application below and enclose a U.S. Postal Money Order. (NO CHECKS PLEASE). Delivery to a foreign address requires an additional $10.00 annual charge be added to each option. All funds are directed to the U.S. Treasury. One subscription includes information on both forfeited seized property and G.O. merchandise.

Subscription options are described below:

Option 1: Nationwide
One-year nonrefundable subscription covering information for sales of seized and forfeited property and G.O. merchandise in the continental United States and Puerto Rico. COST: U.S. Delivery—$50.00, Foreign Delivery—$60.00.

Option 2: Regional—East
One-year nonrefundable subscription covering information for sales of seized and forfeited property and G.O. merchandise all states and Customs districts located east of the Mississippi River (includes Puerto Rico). COST: U.S. Delivery—$25.00, Foreign Delivery—$35.00.

Option 3: Regional—West
One-year nonrefundable subscription covering information for sales of seized and forfeited property and G.O. merchandise all states and Customs districts located west of the Mississippi River. COST: U.S. Delivery—$25.00, Foreign Delivery—$35.00.

Sorry—Self-addressed stamped envelopes not accepted.
U.S. POSTAL MONEY ORDERS ONLY!
We appreciate your interest and look forward to serving you.

Subscription Application

YES, I want to subscribe to:

	U.S.	Foreign
☐OPTION 1-Nationwide	$50.00	$60.00
☐OPTION 2-East Region	$25.00	$35.00
☐OPTION 3-West Region	$25.00	$35.00

NOTE: These prices good only through September 30, 1989.

Enclosed is a nonrefundable U.S. Postal Money Order (No checks please) payable to Northrop Worldwide Aircraft Services, Inc., for $ _____

Mail my subscription to (Please Print):

Name _____

Address _____ Apt # ____

City _____ State ___ Zip _____

Telephone (   ) _____

Signature _____

Return Application to:

Northrop Worldwide Aircraft Services, Inc.

U.S. Customs Service Support Division

P.O. Box 2065

Lawton, OK 73502-2065

I am particularly interested in purchasing or obtaining information about: (Please Specify Size/Type)

☐Cars _____

☐Boats _____

☐Airplanes _____

Merchandise

☐Clothing

☐Commodities

☐Other _____

Subscribers will receive flyers on sales in the selected region containing all types of merchandise/property and not only on sales containing their particular area of interest.

NORTHROP USE ONLY

Regional Code ☐N ☐E ☐W	Amount Received	Money Order No.	Date Received
Address Verified (Initials)	Date Posted to Mailing List	Renewal (Mo, Yr)	Posted by (Initials)

12

Government Loans
—A Triple Play

You can be flat broke and still get started in real estate investing, thanks to the Federal Government.

Three government programs—low-interest loans, low-cost housing, and VA repossessions—are incentives for you. Of course, as with any government operation, you must cut through red tape before any federal program works for you.

Let me use a young blue-collar couple from Cincinnati, the Smiths, as an example. They work for Procter and Gamble, rent their home, are raising a family, and do not have very much money saved yet for a down payment on an investment property.

By driving across the bridge to Newport and Covington, Kentucky, this couple discovers inexpensive rental property for sale in those towns, especially from the Federal Department of Housing and Urban Development. These "HUD homes" are properties that were taken over by the government after someone defaulted on a federally insured mortgage. Fixer-uppers are priced from $35,000 to $40,000, plus the cost of repairs. The houses could bring in an income of $500 to $600 in rent.

The Smiths are willing to put in time renovating such properties, but first they need an infusion of money for the down payment. They turn to HUD and the local development agencies for help.

HUD HOMES

From HUD, the Smiths get a fact-filled free booklet called "Programs of HUD," which describes the many loan programs available. Anyone can get a copy by writing or calling the Office of the Assistant Secretary of

Public Affairs, HUD, 451 Seventh St. SW, Washington, DC 20410. Phone: (202) 755-5277. (It might be easier to call your local HUD office, listed under "Federal Agencies" in the phone book.)

The booklet contains addresses and phone numbers of HUD field offices in such places as Cincinnati, where HUD works with local banks to assist eager home buyers like the Smiths in getting special, federally insured, low-interest financing.

The Smiths soon realize that savvy real estate brokers in areas such as Newport and Covington are just as eager to sell them a HUD home as they are to buy one. The brokers are authorized to give buyers a tour of any HUD home that interests them.

Where can they find a guide to these bargains? In very slow housing markets, such as Denver, HUD publishes a lift-out publication each week in the classified section of weekend newspapers that advertises many inexpensive HUD houses. They could be bought by investors for 5 percent down.

HUD houses can be bought in two ways. Sealed bids are requested weekly on new listings. Then, there is daily or open bidding on properties that do not sell via the sealed bid. It is typical for about half the houses to be offered through the weekly sealed-bidding process.

Through a broker, the Smiths make a sealed bid on the HUD home they think will work best for their investment goals. Usually, there is a 10-day bidding period. When the 10 days are up, HUD opens the bids. There can be quite a fierce competition on some houses. It is not uncommon to see five to ten bids on a single property.

If potential owner-occupants are bidding, the winning bid usually is higher than the government's asking price. Since the Smiths are investors, however, there is no reason for them to overbid. Their aim is to get a house at below-market value. Once the 10-day period is over, HUD lets the Smiths know if their offer has been accepted.

Perhaps the Smiths have chosen a house that is on the "extended" list. This is where they might find a good investment house that was not snapped up on the initial offering. Since there is no competition remaining for these properties, they can make an offer that is below the original asking price.

Extended-listing bids are submitted by brokers in writing in the late afternoon. An hour later, they are opened.

Bingo! The Smiths get the go-ahead on a $40,000 Covington fixer-upper. They make the $2,000 down payment. Their realtor, in conjunction with a local bank, arranges an FHA loan, under the Section 203(b) program, which is guaranteed by the Federal Government. The Smiths don't even have to pay the broker's fee or all the closing costs; HUD is so happy to have professionals pushing their property that the government pays some closing costs plus the broker's commission.

HUD houses come with two kinds of loans: those with insured government financing and those without insured financing. The typical insured property has been bought with an FHA loan. As an investor, you can take over this loan. The rate is lower than standard financing, and you can usually close within two months.

If there is no insurance, a property can be bought for all cash. These are among the best deals because HUD will accept low prices. The reason? It wants to remove from its inventory as many properties as it can, as quickly as it can.

Once you buy a property for cash, you get an appraisal on it. You then take the appraisal—which should come in much higher than the cash price you paid—to a bank. Your lender should be happy to provide financing at that point, thus replenishing your cash reserves. Many lenders will give you advanced approval for a loan after you tell them what HUD properties you are bidding on.

LOCAL HELP: DEVELOPMENT COMMISSIONS

Since the house needs work, the Smiths visit the Covington development commission for help with repair costs. They start by making sure that their property is in an area designated for special assistance. The commission representatives explain that if the Smiths complete the needed repairs, they will be exempt from sales taxes on the materials used.

The visit to the development commission turns up new, valuable information. Here, too, very low interest loans are available to hardworking but low income people like the Smiths from banks working with the development commission for the purchase of additional, non-HUD houses.

What's more, the commission has grant money: This Covington agency, like many agencies around the country, will actually hand over greenbacks to investors, without any interest, provided it is used to fix up houses in specific neighborhoods.

Development commissions go by different names in different cities. Try the phone book first for listings under city, municipal, or county government. Or, call the mayor's office and ask who handles urban development grants, housing grants, and sales-tax incentive plans. By now, you already know it is going to be a pain in the neck to wring information out of some harried telephone clerks. Be patient. Don't lose your cool. And keep dialing.

NEW HOMES, LOW LOANS

What if the Smiths set their sights on a new home? One popular HUD program is known as Section 235. Officially, it is the "Homeownership Assistance for Low- and Moderate-Income Families" program. Section 235 allows those people who meet certain local income limits to buy inexpensive new homes with cheap, federally insured mortgages. The point is to encourage owner occupancy. But you can buy a 235 house, live in it, and then, if legitimate circumstances require you to move, you can move out and rent it ethically.

The great part about 235 purchases is that federal insurance enables the lender to give the buyer a mortgage at 2 to 3 points below market-rate interest. There are restrictions, of course. The house must cost $40,000 or less. The buyer must put a 3 percent down payment on the house, and set aside at least 20 percent of the family's adjusted gross income each month for mortgage payments.

Let us assume the Smiths find a new $40,000 house. Together they make $21,000 a year, so they are eligible under a formula that limits the program to people with incomes of 95 percent of the median income in the Covington area for a family of four. The Smiths then make a $1,200 down payment. (With the amount of the down payment that low, the Smiths could probably borrow it from their office credit union or even get a cash advance on a credit card!) Each month, they make mortgage payments of $306.10—20 percent of their adjusted gross income. Meanwhile, they rent out the house for $550 a month. Thanks to HUD, the Smiths, despite very modest salaries and savings, have become real estate investors.

There are other HUD programs for different kinds of investments. For instance, Section 221(d)2 provides mortgage insurance on 2- to 4-family homes for eligible low- and moderate-income families. Section 231 is specifically designed to help investors get money for housing that will be occupied by the elderly. Call HUD's question line, (202) 755-6685, for details on specific programs. Pages 132–133 show a sample HUD sales contract.

INVESTING IN VA REPOSSESSED HOUSES

Another popular way of getting into investing, for those with not much money but plenty of time, is through housing repossessed by the Veterans Administration. The VA has thousands of houses. You don't have to be a veteran to qualify for a VA home in the repo stage. In fact, you don't have to be a citizen, nor do you need good credit.

Sales Contract

U.S. Department of Housing and Urban Development
Office of Housing
Federal Housing Commisioner
Property Disposition Program

OMB Approval No. 2502-0306 (exp. 9-30-89)

HUD Case No.

1. I (We), _____
(Purchaser(s)) agree to purchase on the terms set forth herein, the following described property
in _____ County, State of _____
The legal description of the property is:

The address is: _____
(Street Number, Street Name, Unit Number, if applicable, and City)

2. The Secretary of Housing and Urban Development (Seller) agrees to sell the property described above at the price and terms set forth
herein, and to prepare a deed containing a covenant which warrants against the acts of the Seller and all claiming by, through or under
him. Title will be taken in the following name(s) and style: _____

3. The agreed purchase price of the property is . . . . ▶   3. $ _____
Purchaser has paid $ _____ as earnest money to be applied on the purchase price, and agrees to
pay the balance of the purchase price, plus or minus prorations, at the time of closing, in cash to Seller.
The earnest money deposit shall be held by _____
_____ .

4. ( ) Purchaser is applying for HUD/FHA insured financing with a down payment of $ _____
in cash due at closing and the balance secured by a mortgage in the amount of $ _____
for _____ months (does not include HUD/FHA Mortgage Insurance Premium).
( ) Said mortgage involves a repair escrow amounting to . . . . ▶   4. $ _____
( ) Purchaser is applying for conventional or other financing not involving HUD/FHA insured financing.

5. Seller will pay reasonable and customary, but not more than actual, costs of obtaining financing and/or
closing (not including broker's commission) in an amount not to exceed . . . . ▶   5. $ _____

6. Upon sales closing, Seller agrees to pay to the broker identified below a commission of . . . . ▶   6. $ _____

7. The net amount due Seller is . . . . ▶   7. $ _____
(Purchase price, Item 3, less Item 4 escrow, if any, less Items 5 and 6)

8. Purchaser ( ) will ( ) will not occupy this property as the primary residence.

9. The sale shall close not later than _____
Closing shall be held at _____ .

10. If Seller does not accept this offer, Seller ( ) may ( ) may not hold such offer as a back-up to accepted offer.

11. ( ) An addendum is attached hereto and made part of this contract.

12. This contract is subject to the Conditions of Sale on the reverse hereof, which is incorporated herein and made part of this contract.

Certification of Purchaser - The undersigned certifies that in affixing his/her/its signature to this contract he/she/it understands all the contents
thereof (including the Conditions of Sale) and is in agreement therewith without protest.

Purchaser(s): (type or print names, social security nos., and sign)	Purchaser(s) Address
	Phone No. Date Contract Signed by Purchaser(s)
Seller: Secretary of Housing and Urban Development By: (type name and title, and sign)	Date Contract Accepted by HUD

Certification of Broker - The undersigned certifies that: (1) neither he nor anyone authorized to act for him has declined to sell the
property described herein to or to make it available for inspection or consideration by a prospective purchaser because of his race,
color, religion, sex, or national origin; (2) he has executed and filed with HUD, form HUD-9556, Joint HUD-VA Nondiscrimination
Certification (Sales Broker); and (3) he is in compliance with HUD's earnest money policy as set forth in Agreement to Abide

executed on _____ , 19 _____ .

Name and Address of Broker (include Zip Code)	Social Security No. or Employer ID No. of Broker (include hyphens)	Area Code & Phone No. of Broker
	Signature of Broker	

This section for HUD use only. Broker notified of:	By	Date
☐ Acceptance ☐ Back-Up No. _____ ☐ Rejection ☐ Return Earnest Money Deposit		

Previous Editions are Obsolete   Original   form HUD-9548 (8/88)
ref. handbook 4310.5

Conditions of Sale

A. All assessments, including improvement assessments which are available for payment without interest or penalty for advance payment, taxes, rent, and ground rent, if any, shall be prorated as of the closing date.

B. Purchaser will accept the property in the condition existing on the date of this contract. Seller does not warrant the condition of the property, including but not limited to mechanical systems and dry basement, or compliance with code requirements and will make no repairs to the property after execution of this contract.

C. Should Purchaser refuse or otherwise fail to perform in accordance with this contract, including the time limitation, Seller may, at Seller's sole option, retain all or a portion of the deposit as liquidated damages. The Seller reserves the right to apply the earnest money, or any portion thereof, to any sums which may be owed by the Purchaser to the Seller for rent.

Purchaser(s) Initials:_____

Seller's Initials:_____

D. Seller may rescind this contract and return Purchaser's earnest money deposit under the following conditions:
  1. Seller has not acquired the property.
  2. Seller is unable or unwilling to remove valid objections to the title prior to closing.
  3. Seller determines that purchaser is not an acceptable borrower.
Tender of the deposit shall release the Seller from any and all claims arising from this transaction.

E. Risk of loss or damage is assumed by Seller until sale is closed, unless Purchaser takes possession of the property prior thereto, in which case state law shall apply. If the property is damaged prior to the date of closing, Seller reserves the right to terminate this contract. Tender of the earnest money deposit shall release the Seller from any claims arising from this transaction.

F. If this property is being offered with HUD/FHA insured mortgage financing available, Seller's acceptance of this contract constitutes a commitment to insure, conditioned upon Purchaser being determined by Seller or Direct Endorsement Underwriter to be an acceptable borrower, and further conditioned upon Seller's authority to insure the mortgage at the time the sale is closed.

G. Purchaser understands that Seller's listing price is Seller's estimate of current fair market value.

H. No member of or Delegate to Congress or Resident Commissioner shall be admitted to any share or part of this contract or to any benefit that may arise therefrom, but this provision shall not be construed to extend to this contract if made with a corporation for its general benefit.

I. Purchaser warrants that no person or agency has been employed or retained to solicit or secure this contract upon an agreement or understanding for a commission, percentage, brokerage, or contingent fee, excepting bona fide employees or bona fide established commercial agencies maintained by the Purchaser except as provided herein. For breach or violation of this warranty, Seller shall have the right to annul this contract without liability or in its discretion to require Purchaser to pay, in addition to the contract price or consideration, the full amount of such commission, percentage, brokerage, or contingent fee.

J. Purchaser and Seller agree that this contract shall be binding upon their respective heirs, executors, administrators, successors or assigns but is assignable only by written consent of the Seller.

K. If this property was constructed prior to 1978, Seller has inspected for defective paint surfaces. Seller's inspection found no defective paint surfaces, or if defective paint surfaces were found, Seller has removed or will remove such defective surfaces in a manner prescribed by HUD prior to closing. **Purchaser understands and agrees that the Seller's inspection and/or removal is not intended to, nor does it guarantee or warrant that all lead-based paint and all potential lead-based paint hazards have been eliminated from this property.** Purchaser acknowledges that he has received a copy of a brochure which discusses the lead-based paint hazard.

L. The effective date of this contract is the date it is signed by the Seller.

M. If the amount stated in Item 5 (obverse) exceeds actual allowable financing and/or closing costs, according to the list of such allowable expenses provided to the Broker by Seller, such excess shall not be paid by Seller and may not be used by Purchaser to reduce amount(s) owing to Seller.

N. Seller's policies and requirements with regard to earnest money (including forfeiture thereof), extensions of time in which to close the sale, back-up offers, and allowable financing and/or closing costs are detailed in instructions issued to selling brokers.

O. This contract contains the final and entire agreement between Purchaser and Seller and they shall not be bound by any terms, conditions, statements, or representations, oral or written, not contained in this contract.

The program exists because the VA has guaranteed loans that banks have made to eligible vets. When the vet defaults on such a loan, the bank forecloses on the house and then gets its money back from the VA. The VA thus ends up with a tremendous inventory of houses.

There are two ways to get one of the VA's properties, which are handled in a manner not unlike the bureaucratic procedures governing HUD homes: You obtain a list of the houses, with minimum acceptable bid prices, from the VA property management offices. (Call the Veterans Administration in your area for the address of the nearest property management office.) Or you can work with a broker who specializes in VA houses.

These brokers, who are registered with the agency, will be happy to help you purchase a VA house. (In some cases, the brokers also handle HUD homes.) They are familiar with the paperwork involved. They have keys to VA houses, so you always have the opportunity to look at the inside of a VA-repossessed house. (Some government agencies do sell surplus houses "as is," and you cannot inspect them before they are auctioned off.)

I strongly recommend working hand in hand with a broker experienced in VA houses. He or she will be able to tell you if the price you have in mind for a given house is in the ballpark. Furthermore, since the VA pays the broker's commission, it is in the broker's best interest to have you buy a house at the price you want.

Normally, the down payment on a VA house is in the $500 range. Using a specific form, you place a bid through the broker on the house you have chosen and give the broker your $500 deposit. Within 14 days, the VA either accepts or rejects your bid. What if your bid is rejected? If the house remains on the market, you can make a second bid.

Officers at the VA are the ones who determine whether your bid is acceptable. Experienced brokers who have a working relationship with these VA people can usually help you set the right price.

Almost without exception, VA-repossessed houses are in affordable, low-cost neighborhoods, not in the $200,000-and-up districts. The minimum bid prices are usually below market value. You can be sure that if a newly repossessed house is on the VA list for the first time at below market value, there will be other bids on the property in competition with yours.

When a house is listed for the first time, there is a 5-day wait before the VA starts accepting bids. It pays to submit a bid that is slightly *above* the minimum in order to win the competition. You need to stay in close contact with your VA broker to learn about exceptionally good buys as soon as they appear on a list, and to submit your bid before the agency closes bidding.

How can you make fairly certain you will win a bid on a house if it initially listed at 20 percent or more below market value? I suggest bidding 5 percent above the minimum. Make enough bids at 5 percent over the minimum (after doing a comparative analysis of prices in the neighborhood) and you are going to end up winning the right to buy some houses.

Financing? Practically a snap. Once you make a purchase, the VA will give you the names of banks in your area that do VA loans. The VA will guarantee your mortgage, even if you are not a veteran yourself.

There is one fly in the VA ointment. I have found that of all the government properties I have bought, VA repossessions have been in the worst condition. So before making your bid, it behooves you to investigate closely. Pay the fee for a certified home inspector to analyze these battered houses, in order to figure in the cost of repairs. Especially in cold climates, VA managers don't always keep an eye on such problems as freezing water pipes. You can't see the damage in the winter when pipes are frozen, but you can bet you will know about them when spring comes.

STATES HAVE LOW-COST BUCKS, TOO

So far I have mentioned federal and local programs. Your state undoubtedly has grant and loan money as well. The first problem is finding the agency that hands it out. The second problem is qualifying for it as an investor.

Most states have special low-cost loan programs for first-time home buyers. One innovative program now in a pilot stage in Michigan allows qualified people to buy their first homes for just one dollar. Some of the houses are in Highland Park, a Detroit suburb. The program also lends to those buyers who move in a total of $10,000 to repair plumbing, wiring, or structural deficiencies in these dilapidated houses.

Residents must live in the house and maintain it for 5 years, paying all taxes and utilities. They must show they can pay $150 a month for insurance and utility bills.

After 5 years, the loan is forgiven, so it becomes a grant. Residents then own the home. This allows the state to expand its tax base, since the owners of the $1 home are now paying taxes on it.

In your case, however, you might already be a home owner. Is there a way to pry some bucks out of the agency for an investment house?

Maybe. Almost every state has "target" areas, often run-down, inner-city neighborhoods, in which the state welcomes developers. Your state might be willing to waive the "first time home buyer" requirement on a

low-cost loan if the investment house you want is in that target area. It is
worth a few phone calls to find out.

Whom do you call? Ah, there's the rub. The agencies vary from state
to state. The best source of agency names that I know of is Wayne Phillips's
book, *Government Loans: The Road to Real Estate Wealth*, published by
Simon and Schuster. It contains a list of every state housing finance agency
in the U.S.

The crucial elements in getting government loans and grants with a minimum of red tape are twofold:

One, you must play by the rules, which means you need to be within
the income eligibility range and to find out which blocks or communities
are covered by the various programs.

Two, you still need to analyze the numbers to make sure the deal works
for you. You can't buy a place just because it is cheap. Before you spend
time nailing down an individual property, find out how much repairs will
cost, and whether you plan to do them yourself or hire a contractor. Get
an appraisal of the house in its present condition. Then, have the appraiser
add an addendum onto that appraisal noting what the market value will be
once the property is fixed up according to the detailed plans you have drawn
up. This second appraisal value (of the property restored to perfect shape)
is known in the industry as *turnkey* condition.

When you have your appraisal information, show it to the local authority and the lender. After the bank and the local authorities have approved your project, you can expect to get checks from them without too
long a wait. Usually, the checks start coming right after the closing.

I won't insult your intelligence by telling you that taking advantage of
government loans and grants is easy. Yes, there is paperwork to be done.
Yes, the process of finding property and then money to fix up that property
can be long and tedious. The effort involved in investing in property in
emerging urban communities such as Covington, or Camden, New Jersey,
or East Los Angeles may not appeal to you.

But the financial and psychological rewards can be marvelous for those
of you who are attracted to this kind of investment. You can be helping to
build—or rebuild—your town while you are building your bank account.
And you can be providing a decent place to live for your fellow citizens at
a fair rent. You could call this the reverse of baseball's triple play . . . it's
a win-win-win arrangement where everyone scores.

13

No More Paperwork: Using a Property Management Company

Once you start seeking your first property, whether through conventional means, via a tax sale or an auction, or any other method, you need to surround yourself with a solid team of professionals—real estate broker, lawyer, house inspector, and certified public accountant. But the work does not end there. Once you have closed on a house or apartment, you must find a tenant, collect rents, pay bills, and keep the house or apartment in good repair.

At the outset, I explained why you reap the biggest profits by doing these landlording chores yourself. But many successful real estate investors either do not have the time (or a partner's time) or the energy to handle this side of the business. If this is your situation, you need to hire a professional: a competent property management company to free you of the housework and paperwork.

A manager or management company does more than relieve you of duties you cannot take care of yourself. It also affords you privacy. Your tenants do not have to know your name or your telephone number. When a leak occurs or there is not enough heat, tenants lay these typical hassles at the feet of the management company.

I emphasize the word *professional*. Uncle Joe or Aunt Sally may be terrific relatives who live in the neighborhood of your new investment, but they are not necessarily qualified to run a business for you. Owning property is your new business. Managing it is yet another business best assigned to a leader in that field.

The Yellow Pages is the standard starting point in your search for a property manager. Perhaps the broker who handled your deal can recommend a manager as well. In addition, go to buildings or rental houses that convey an image of good management, talk to tenants about whether the place is well managed, and find out who is in charge.

Contact The Institute for Real Estate Management at 430 N. Michigan Ave., Chicago, IL 60611. Phone: (312) 661-1930. This national organization will give you the address and telephone number of the chapter in your area. Members of the local chapter should be quite happy to hear from you. However you get the names, do not make the amateur's mistake of hiring the first person with whom you chat.

Discuss your needs with at least two likely managers or companies. Then, examine their qualifications. The most important element in the manager's resume is his or her track record.

Is your potential manager a member of the national institute mentioned above? Is he or she licensed by either the state or the local real estate board? Does your candidate have the designation CPM (Certified Property Manager)?

If you plan to have the manager do repairs, is the person bonded or insured against damages or injuries that cost the owner money? Can the management company give you references, preferably from invisible landlords of properties in the same locality as you?

Be firm and persistent in getting complete answers to questions like these. After all, these people will not only represent you, but also collect precious rental money for you. I ask to see a client list. Then, I ask if I can follow up by interviewing at least two owners—I pick them at random from the list—for whom they are managing property.

Finally, to be certain there are no bad marks against the company or person, I phone the local Chamber of Commerce, Realty Board, and Better Business Bureau.

BECOMING AN INVISIBLE LANDLORD

A management company will handle whatever services you want. There are at least three levels of service that allow you to be a slightly visible landlord, an almost transparent landlord, or a totally invisible landlord.

At the first level, you turn over only a few specific duties to a management company. For instance, some owners hire management companies strictly to look after maintenance. The company's job is to make necessary repairs, mow lawns, shovel snow from sidewalks, and so on.

Perhaps you feel confident about day-to-day management of your rental property but you would rather leave the delicate business of finding a tenant, doing a credit check, and negotiating a lease to a pro. A management company often will perform these services for a flat fee.

At the next level, you have managers handle both maintenance and rent collection. But you are often in contact with them and request that they get clearance from you to do additional jobs such as contracting for major repairs.

At the most expensive level of service, you figuratively wave a magic wand and render yourself totally invisible by assigning all the work to a full-service "turnkey" management group. (As you might guess, the phrase connotes turning a key to the property over to the management company and letting it do the rest.)

For this kind of service, I prefer a person to be a CPM—certified property manager. This designation is issued by the National Association of Realtors, IREM division, to people who have taken extensive seminars and courses.

You sign a comprehensive agreement under which a CPM advertises a vacant apartment or house, qualifies tenants, negotiates leases, terminates leases of bad tenants, hires contractors for major repairs, hires lawyers for eviction proceedings—indeed, does everything except (or sometimes including!) windows. The manager keeps the books, opens a special bank account for the owner, writes himself a check each month or quarter for a portion of the rental income, and mails a check for the balance to you, the owner.

CHARGES AND OVERCHARGES

Based on which services you choose for a company to do, you negotiate what percentage of the rentals the management company will be paid. You can expect to pay anywhere from 7 to 20 percent, with percentages varying in different parts of the country. Management agreements usually last 1 year and are renewable each year at the option of the owner.

What happens when an air conditioner dies in your rental house in mid-July? In a comprehensive management agreement there is usually a maximum amount of your money that a manager can spend on repairs or materials (usually $50 to $100) without consulting with you. Make sure that after you give your approval in a phone call, your manager follows with a written memo.

Suppose you get bills that are within your approval limit but seem high or frequent. It is hard to avoid being overcharged by an unscrupulous company unless you take certain precautions. Check with other owners to find out if charges are consistent across the client list.

It is also fair to do spot checks. Let us say a monthly statement includes $20 for four fluorescent bulbs for a tenant's kitchen. Call your tenant to find out if those bulbs were actually installed. "What fluorescent bulbs?" responds the tenant.

Your next call, obviously, is to the management company. "I noticed you bought some fluorescent bulbs for my Unit A," you say, "but my tenant Mr. Jones tells me he is in the dark about them. When do you plan to put them in?"

This lets your management company know that you intend to shine a careful spotlight on its repair and billing practices, without advance notice. Why pay a premium for service calls when you are already paying a company a share of your rental income?

Also, if bills for labor seem unfairly high, you have a right to question them in writing. In a serious enough situation—numerous, expensive plumbing bills, for instance—you yourself can quietly call in a second plumber for an evaluation of the completed work and its cost.

Another way I keep an eye on my property when it is in the hands of a manager is by requiring managers to send a Polaroid photo of my houses with my monthly statement, so I can see that the exterior is being maintained properly. Managers tend to scream and holler at this request, but you should insist on it. There is nothing more terrible than making a drive-by inspection of a property that you have not seen in six months and discovering it's covered with graffiti.

The most sensible strategy is to insist on constant two-way communication with your manager. Keep the lines open by demanding that statements be mailed to you on time, and by requesting the home telephone number of your management company representative. In return, make sure the phone on which the company calls you is answered twenty-four hours a day, either by you or a machine. Real estate needs tending all the time, not just on weekdays during business hours.

DO MANAGEMENT FEES NIBBLE AWAY AT PROFITS?

How much of your expected profit will a manager cost you? The real question to ask is how much your time is worth.

Start by using the worksheet below to estimate how much time you

must spend yearly if you do the managing yourself. Then compare the cost
with the management company's basic percentage charge:

Annual Time Cost of Managing

1. Finding and qualifying tenant   _____ hours

2. Signing of lease & collection of security   _____ hours

3. Monthly rent notice & collection ___ hours
                                    × 12 = _____ hours

4. Answering calls on maintenance & utilities   _____ hours

5. Cleaning in between tenants   _____ hours

Total hours you spent _____

Multiplied by cost of your time per hr. × $ _____

Equals cost of self-managing = $ _____

Meanwhile, annual rental income $ _____

Multiplied by mgt. co. fee (%) ×   _____

Equals annual cost of hired manager = $ _____

If you fill in the hours on the above chart honestly, you should show
at least 100 hours spent each year being a visible landlord. At the measly
rate of $10 per hour, that means your cost of self-managing will be $1,000.
(You undoubtedly think your time is worth more than that, but let me
complete my argument.)

Now let us assume you are asking $600 per month rent on a $50,000
property. Your mortgage is $30,000. Your monthly expenses, including
mortgage principal payment and interest, taxes, and insurance come to
$300 per month. Your preferred management company wants to take 10
percent, or $60 per month, the national average. If you use the manage-
ment company, instead of taking a $300 per month positive cash flow, you
get only $240. Your additional cost per year is $720.

It might be worth it to you to have the management company save you
all that time. On the other hand, numerous owners enjoy the duties of
being a landlord.

Before making a decision, you still have a crucial question to ask. Will
your own rental property still bring you flat or positive cash flow if you
hire a management company? Simply subtract the annual cost of a management company from your cash flow worksheet on page 49 to see if a

management company significantly gobbles up profit from your investment. Managing a property yourself might be the difference between positive and negative cash flow.

Many of you will wind up leaving your current full-time jobs to become full-time real estate investors and managers. That's a different story. In that case, you are probably better off spending the time learning how to manage in order to maximize the profit from your investment.

TAXING MATTERS

A final point: Management fees are among your tax deductions for operating your property as a business. So you are not really paying 10 percent, or whatever a management company will charge you. Those of you in the 20 percent tax bracket would be paying not $60 per month, but 20 percent less, or $48.

Despite hiring a property management company, you can still qualify as an "active" manager and collect all tax deductions due you under the current tax laws. In anticipation of possible IRS challenges, follow every phone call with a written memo to your manager. Keep a copy in your files and make a note of the phone call in your business diary or phone log. Also keep a file of the regular statements you receive from the management company.

Feel you need to know more? The best book I know of on this subject is *Managing Residential Real Estate* by Paul Lapides, published by Warren Gorham & Lamont.

TEN QUESTIONS TO ASK
PROSPECTIVE PROPERTY MANAGERS

1. How long have you managed property in this county/ town/ neighborhood?
2. What kind of management license do you have?
3. Are you a Certified Property Manager?
4. Are you bonded and/or insured?
5. Can I see some property you currently manage near here?
6. May I see your client list for reference?
7. Can you give me the phone numbers of a few owners I choose at random from this list to discuss your performance?

8. What percentage of the rental income do you receive for the services I have outlined?
9. May I see samples of your management contracts?
10. How often are management agreements renewable?

SAMPLE AGREEMENT WITH PROPERTY MANAGEMENT COMPANY

In consideration of the covenants contained here, _____ (Owner), agrees to employ _____ (Agent), to rent, lease, operate and manage the real property situated in the City of _____, County of _____, State of _____, known as _____ _____ (name and address of building), for a period beginning this date and terminating at midnight of _____, and continuing on a month-to-month basis afterward, subject to _____ days written notice of intent to terminate by either party, upon the following Terms and Conditions:

AGENT'S AUTHORITIES AND OBLIGATIONS

Owner hereby confers on Agent the following authorities and obligations, where initialed by Owner:

_____ To advertise the availability for rent or lease of premises and to display For Rent or For Lease signs. To screen and use diligence in selection of prospective tenants and to abide by all fair housing laws.

_____ To negotiate leases as may be approved by Owner. Lease terms not to exceed _____.

_____ To execute leases and rental agreements on behalf of Owner.

_____ To collect rents, security deposits, and all other receipts, and to deposit such monies in a trust account with a qualified banking institution.

_____ To serve notice of termination of tenancies, notices to quit or pay rent, and such other notices as Agent may deem appropriate.

_____ To employ attorneys approved by Owner for the purpose of enforcing Owner's rights under leases and rental agreements and instituting legal action on behalf of Owner.

_____ To provide all services reasonably necessary for the proper management of the property including periodic inspections, supervision of maintenance, and arranging for such improvements, alterations, and repairs as may be required of Owner.

_____ To hire, supervise, and discharge all employees and independent contractors required in the operation and maintenance of the property. Compensation shall be in such amounts as approved by Owner and the employment of any employee shall be terminable at will. It is agreed that all such employees are employees of the Owner and not of the Agent. To prepare payroll tax returns for Owner, where applicable, and to make payments of such taxes to the appropriate agencies from gross revenues.

_____ To contract for repairs or alterations at a cost to Owner not to exceed $ _____.

_____ To contract for emergency repairs at a cost to Owner not to exceed $ _____ per repair.

_____ In the event Owner is not available for consultation, to contract for such repairs and expenditures as are necessary for the protection of the property from damage, or to perform services to the tenants provided for in their leases.

_____ To execute service contracts for utilities and services for the operation, maintenance, and safety of the property as Agent deems necessary or advisable. Provided that the terms of any such contract shall not exceed _____ months and the amount payable each month shall not exceed $ _____ without written approval of Owner.

To pay from gross receipts all operating expenses and such other expenses as may be authorized by Owner, including:

_____ Mortgage Payments
_____ Property Taxes
_____ Payroll Taxes
_____ Insurance Premiums
_____ Other: _____

_____ To maintain accurate records of all monies received and disbursed in connection with management of the property. Said records shall be open for inspection by Owner during regular business hours and upon reasonable notice.

_____ To submit monthly statements of all receipts and disbursements not later than the _____ day of following month.

OWNER'S OBLIGATIONS

Owner agrees to pay to Agent fees for services rendered at the rate set forth below. Such compensation is due and payable on demand and may be deducted by the Agent from receipts.

COMPENSATION FOR MANAGEMENT SERVICES (initial where applicable):

_____ $_____ per month for each single family residence.

_____ _____ % of gross monthly collections, provided that the minimum compensation is at least $_____ per month

_____ $_____ flat fee per unit per month.

COMPENSATION FOR LEASING:

_____ New Leases: $_____ or _____ %.

_____ Renegotiated leases: $_____ or _____ %.

COMPENSATION FOR MODERNIZATION OR CAPITAL IMPROVEMENTS: $_____

_____

COMPENSATION FOR REFINANCING: _____

COMPENSATION FOR OTHER SERVICES: _____

Owner shall indemnify and save the Agent harmless from any and all costs, expenses, attorney's fees, suits, liabilities, damages from or connected with the management of the property by Agent, or the performance or exercise of any of the duties, obligations, powers, or authorities granted in this agreement to Agent.

Owner shall not hold Agent liable for any error of judgment, or for any mistake of fact or law, or for anything which Agent may do or refrain from doing hereinafter, except in cases of willful misconduct or gross negligence.

Owner agrees to carry, at Owner's expense, Workers Compensation Insurance for Owner's employees. Owner also agrees to carry, at Owner's expense, bodily injury, property damage, and personal injury public liability insurance in the amount of not less than $500,000 combined single limit for bodily injury and property damage. The policy shall be written on a comprehensive general liability form and shall name the Agent as additional insured.

Owner shall immediately furnish Agent with a certificate of insurance, showing that the above coverage is in force with a carrier acceptable to Agent. In the event Agent receives notices that said insurance coverage is to be canceled, Agent shall have the option to immediately cancel this agreement.

Owner assumes full responsibility for payment of any expenses and obligations incurred in connection with the exercise of Agent's duties set forth in this agreement.

Owner shall deposit with Agent $＿＿＿＿＿ as an initial operating reserve and will cover any excess of expenses over income within 10 days of any request by Agent. The Agent may terminate this agreement immediately if the request for additional funds is not paid. Owner understands that it is not Agent's obligation to advance its own funds for payment of Owner's operating expenses.

OTHER TERMS

All notices required to be given hereunder shall be in writing and mailed to the parties at the addresses below.

In the event of any legal action by the parties arising out of this agreement, the prevailing party shall be entitled to reasonable attorney's fees and costs, to be determined by the court in which such action is brought.

ADDITIONAL TERMS: ＿＿＿＿＿＿＿＿＿＿＿＿＿＿＿＿＿＿＿＿

＿＿＿＿＿＿＿＿＿＿＿＿＿＿＿＿＿＿＿＿＿＿＿＿＿＿＿＿＿＿

Agent accepts the employment under the terms hereof and agrees to use diligence in the exercise of the obligations, duties, authorities, and powers conferred herein upon Agent.

Date: ＿＿＿＿＿＿＿

Agent: ＿＿＿＿＿＿＿＿＿＿   Owner: ＿＿＿＿＿＿＿＿＿＿

By: ＿＿＿＿＿＿＿＿＿＿＿   Owner: ＿＿＿＿＿＿＿＿＿＿

Title ＿＿＿＿＿＿＿＿＿＿＿   Soc Sec # ＿＿＿＿＿＿＿＿

Address ＿＿＿＿＿＿＿＿＿   Address ＿＿＿＿＿＿＿＿＿

City, State, Zip ＿＿＿＿＿   City, State, Zip ＿＿＿＿＿＿

PART TWO

PASSIVE INVESTING

14

Investor Equity
Participation

Remember back in chapter 2, where I described the different kinds of investors? One category belonged to *angels*—people who backed deals with their own money but left active management to a partner. That is what investor equity participation is about.

Equity participation involves two partners plus money, which is used for the buying and selling of real estate. The investing angel, or *passive partner,* makes the down payment on a property, period. His or her investing stops at that point.

Meanwhile, the equity participant lives in the property, makes the monthly payments, and manages the property by keeping the place in good condition. The two investors split the profits when the property (often a house or condo) is sold. It can be a straight 50/50 split, but sometimes it is not; the division of the profits is fully negotiable.

There are all kinds of variations on this theme. A common one: The equity participant finds you, the investing angel, and then purchases property for the team, but does *not* actually live in that property. Instead, the active partner selects a tenant, manages the property, collects rent, and splits the profit.

Whoa! cries the potential investor who has turned to these passive investment chapters. I want a hands-off arrangement, but I also want protection. I'm a conservationist; I believe in careful preservation of capital. There are no government authorities watching over this kind of deal, no SEC to regulate them, no glossy brochures from brokerage houses, or detailed prospectuses. Isn't equity participation dangerous?

THE FEEL-GOOD INVESTMENT

True, it is not shielded under the umbrella of a government securities law. Chances are your stock broker or financial advisor will never breathe a word of it to you. It is rarely mentioned by investment books.

An equity participation deal, however, can be the most gratifying investment imaginable—from the nonmonetary point of view. Among other things, it is a way for family members to help relatives realize their dream of home ownership. In its classic and most familiar form, equity participation consists of parents making the down payment on a first home for a newly married son or daughter.

A less familiar but equally pleasing alternative allows a stranger to help a young couple or family trying for a new start to move into that first home.

Whatever the situation—parents helping children, children helping parents or aging relatives, strangers helping the less fortunate—equity participation contains an emotional intangible that few investments can match: It makes the investor feel good. At the same time, it is an opportunity to make a profit. If this sounds angelic so far, read further.

As you have gathered, the standard equity participation scenario features a primary residence. The active partner is a person or family with the ability to make the monthly payment for a property, but without the savings or credit for the initial down payment.

SPREADING THE WORD

Good news travels fast, so you might never need to take out a classified ad to find an equity participation deal. As a first step, you can spread your angel's wings by putting out the word to family members that you are ready to help. Let them know that if they find a decent property at a good price, you are willing to invest a certain amount in the down payment.

Make it clear that family members should be willing to move into, or manage, the property, and to pay off the monthly note—including principal, interest, taxes, and insurance. Set the situation up in a businesslike way—with a written agreement. No defaults or missed payments allowed. Drive home the idea that even though you are the angel, you won't allow your relatives to test your good faith by letting them fall behind on payments or do slipshod repairs.

"I'm lucky; nobody in my family needs my help," you say. Or perhaps you are ready to be an angel, but the only relatives who want your help are bums. Glance through the classifieds in your local newspaper and I bet you see at least one possible equity participant who seeks an investing angel.

Here is a typical ad:

YOUNG COUPLE LOOKING FOR INVESTOR. We found a great house and cannot afford down payment. You make down payment and we will make monthly payments and we will split profit with you. Call 111-0000.

If you want to be more aggressive, go out and find the property yourself first, then run your own ad. It might read:

INVESTOR HAS PROPERTY FOR SALE, NO MONEY DOWN. I'll make down payment, you make monthly payments and live in house. Split profit when sold.

Another way to get started is to contact attorneys, mortgage companies, bankers, and real estate professionals. These people talk to potential home buyers every day. Let them know you want to finance young or needy people who are looking for homes but lack a down payment, although they can handle monthly payments.

Have you heeded my suggestion about joining a local real estate club? Next time you go to a meeting, let the club know you are interested in equity participation deals. Your prospective partners will flock to you.

Finally, you can spend a few dollars on a classified ad, stating your willingness to play the angel for someone. Imagine the response you can get to an ad that reads like this:

50 PERCENT OF SOMETHING is better than 100 percent of nothing. Have money, will make down payment on your house if you make monthly payments and are willing to split profit on sale of house after your move. Call 111-0000.

I guarantee you will get replies. In fact, be prepared for calls the very morning the paper hits the newsstands.

HOW TO STRUCTURE AN
EQUITY PARTICIPATION DEAL

Your lawyer or CPA can write out a contract for you and your partner to sign. Have this professional structure the deal so that after you have tied up your money, you get an excellent return over a period of time. As is the case with most smart deals, this means finding a place at below its market value.

Here is a fictional example: You buy a 4-bedroom house with a government employee, his wife and his two children in New Jersey. The house has a value of $100,000, but you are able to get it for 20 percent below market value, or $80,000. It requires a down payment of $10,000. (Thus, as soon as you make the down payment, you have already earned $10,000 on your investment.) The New Jersey family makes the monthly payments of approximately $700 per month. The house is to be sold at the end of five years.

Since you won't be earning income on your dollars until the property is sold, you should have a deadline for the sale. The date should be agreeable to both participants.

Let us assume that after five years, the New Jersey house is worth approximately $150,000. If you and the government employee go ahead then and sell it, you split a handsome profit. First, you get back the original $10,000. The numbers work as follows:

Original price: $80,000.
Selling price: $150,000.
Profit: $70,000.

At closing, the investing angel gets $10,000 for the original investment, plus half of $70,000, or $35,000. Your return on your $10,000 investment in 5 years becomes $45,000. Net profit: $35,000.

That's a good deed, a great deal, and a healthy return on your money.

WHEN YOUR PARTNER
WANTS TO KEEP THE HOUSE

In structuring such an arrangement, be sure to give your partner an option to "take you out" at a particular time. That way, if they want to stay where they are and keep the house beyond the deadline for sale, they can return a fair profit to you while buying the house for the family.

Going back to our New Jersey family as an example, a well-structured contract would provide that after 5 years, should the government employee want to stay put, an appraiser would be brought in. The appraiser, in this case, puts a market value of $150,000 on the house. Now it is up to your partner to pay you $10,000 (your initial investment) plus $35,000 (your share of the appreciation), for a total of $45,000.

How can the family in New Jersey keep the house? Simply by refinancing. At this point, if they get a 90 percent loan on the $150,00 house, they collect enough money to pay you in full and remain in the house.

Equity participation has become especially popular in regions where the price of single family homes has soared beyond the means of the average working American. For home buyers, the escalating cost of residences in some areas is unfortunate, but it creates an opportunity for you, the small investor.

HOW SAFE IS THIS UNREGULATED INVESTMENT?

Equity participation offers distinct advantages over some of the other passive investments you will learn about in later chapters. To begin with, it is safe, perhaps safer in terms of preservation of your initial investment than any kind of security.

Why? Because no one wants to lose his or her home. And if your partner does default, your contract permits you to step in and take over the house. Once you do this, your $10,000 investment, using the example above, is secured not by 50 percent of the equity in the house but 100 percent. Thus, after five years, that $10,000 can be converted to $150,000, factoring in normal appreciation.

Since you already know how to avoid pitfalls that trap novice investors, the only cautionary note I would add is to refuse any equity participation deal in which the house is purchased for full market value. If a family has money problems, or a divorce occurs, you get caught in a default that requires you to repossess the house. Reselling it without losing money can become a long, tedious process.

In private real estate deals like this, there are several crucial points to keep in mind:

• Always play out the worst-possible-case scenario in your mind, even if you don't expect it to occur. How easy would it be to sell the house if there is a default?

• Always get a "deed in lieu of foreclosure," a document that makes it simple to repossess the property without a long and expensive court proceeding.

• Always follow the standard rules in evaluating location, condition, price, and market in the choice of a house. That means you must make sure to enter into a deal at 10 percent or more below market value.

• Follow the suggestions on choosing partners (see chapter 4) before putting your money on the line. If you fail to do a thorough personal investigation and credit check on your partner, you put your money at risk. That means running a credit check on your son, daughter, Aunt Millie, or Uncle Sol, as well as a stranger.

• Keep your valued team members in place for this deal as you would for any other. Use an attorney who has done previous equity participation deals. Don't be put in the position of teaching your attorney what he or she should already know.

• Set a timetable for ending your involvement in the deal and stick to it. Your role as an investing angel must be limited in order to make a profit. Never allow your participation to go beyond ten years.

OOPS! GOTTA GET CASH QUICK!

Equity participation is not a one-way street. There could come a time before your contract runs out when you, rather than your partner, need the money you have put into the deal. How do you withdraw that money?

Every contract should have a *buyout clause,* often referred to as a *buy/ sell agreement.* Should you need money before the original time period runs out, this type of clause provides a way for your equity participant to buy you out.

The first way this can be done is for you to refinance the house or to have your equity participant get an equity loan. The second way is for you to use a note with a second mortgage, which would include time payments plus interest.

For an example, let's go back to the deal in New Jersey. Say you want to cash out after the first year. Using a normal appreciation of 10 percent, the $100,000 house would be worth $110,000. You and your partner paid $80,000, which gives you a gross equity after 1 year of $30,000. Your 50 percent interest in that equity is $15,000. If you add the $10,000 that you originally put in, and are entitled to, you are owed $25,000.

Your equity participant can sign a note and second mortgage in the amount of $25,000, to be paid over 30 years at 12 percent interest (or whatever the prevailing rate is). You could sell this note very fast at a 50 percent discount and collect $12,500 on the spot. That still gives you a $2,500 profit. Since your initial investment was $10,000, you have received a 25 percent return.

You might decide instead to keep the note for a longer period, collecting the income, or you might hold it a while longer in order to sell it at a smaller discount.

Most equity participation deals are wrapped up and completed before the deadline set in the initial contract. Some might end with the sale of a house after just one year; others might last as long as a decade.

Incidentally, if, as an investor, you feel not completely satisfied merely putting your $10,000 into the New Jersey property and then waiting five years to make the return on your investment, you can get more deeply involved by having your name on the mortgage and the deed. You then lease the house back to your equity participant under a lease-with-option-to-purchase arrangement. You can still incorporate the split profit that I talked about earlier.

This variation gives you the benefit of ownership of a rental property. You would be able to deduct interest and depreciation from your taxes. Usually, equity participants do not need the tax benefits anyway. Ask your CPA if your financial situation warrants this kind of deal. You must be careful that the amount of rent you charge (covering the principal, interest, taxes, and insurance) is equal or close to the market value of rentals in that neighborhood. Otherwise, the IRS could disallow the deductions.

The first equity participation arrangement I did concerned a $30,000 house in Weirsdale, Florida. I made the 10 percent down payment—$3,000—for a young couple. They paid the principal, interest, taxes, and insurance. Before too long, the young man was transferred to another city. So, just four years later, the house sold for $50,000.

It was a terrific lesson for me in good deals and good deeds. I got my $3,000 back, plus $10,000 (half the $20,000 on the profit from the sale). The young couple ended up moving to Atlanta, where they bought a $75,000 house. Their share of the profit on the sale in Weirsdale allowed them to make the down payment and pay most of the closing costs.

What a wonderful way to get a young couple started on their life together!

The following is a sample equity participation agreement, followed by a "Short Form Memorandum." The first document is the actual agreement that spells out details binding the two parties. The second document is a notice specifically designed for recording the agreement in the public record.

SAMPLE EQUITY PARTICIPATION AGREEMENT

THIS AGREEMENT entered into this 3d day of March, 1988 by and between I.M. Angel, hereafter referred to as INVESTOR, and A. Participant, hereafter referred to as CO-INVESTOR, WHEREAS, INVESTOR is purchasing the property located at 173 CLUB PLACE, ABSECON, NEW JERSEY 08215 and wishes to sell an undivided 50 percent interest in such property to CO-INVESTOR as TENANTS IN COMMON, and WHEREAS, the parties desire to provide for financing, management, and disposition of such property. IT IS, THEREFORE, agreed as follows:

1. TERMS OF AGREEMENT
The term of this agreement shall be for a period of 60 months, unless otherwise agreed upon in writing.

2. VALUE OF PROPERTY
The value of said property is agreed to be ($80,000) EIGHTY THOUSAND AND 00/100 DOLLARS

3. INVESTOR'S CONTRIBUTION
The INVESTOR'S contribution, including all closing costs, on such property shall be contributed by INVESTOR and title to such property shall be taken in the names of both parties, subject to required financing and security documents INVESTOR SHALL CONVEY TO CO-INVESTOR an undivided 50% interest in such property, conditioned upon full compliance by CO-INVESTOR with all terms of this Agreement. INVESTOR'S contribution is ($10,000) ten thousand and 00/100 dollars.

4. CONSIDERATIONS FOR THE CONDITIONS OF CO-INVESTOR'S PURCHASE OF AN UNDIVIDED INTEREST.

(a) INVESTOR will execute a Bargain and Sale Deed with Covenants, to CO-INVESTOR for an undivided 50% interest in said property upon the acceptance and agreement by the CO-INVESTOR to the following terms and conditions of this Agreement and the integrated lease agreement.
CO-INVESTOR will execute A Deed In Lieu of Foreclosure in favor of the INVESTOR, which will be held unrecorded by John Doe, Esq. as Trustee. In the event that CO-INVESTOR is in arrears ten (10) days or longer on any payments, as set forth in subparagraph (b) of this paragraph 4, and provided that INVESTOR or INVESTOR'S designee has filed A NOTICE OF DEFAULT upon the CO-INVESTOR in writing, and provided that Trustee has received a written notification of CO-INVESTOR'S

default, Trustee is instructed to record the Deed In Lieu of Foreclosure from CO-INVESTOR, and CO-INVESTOR, at option of the INVESTOR, shall be deemed a month-to-month tenant under all the terms of the lease provisions of this Agreement and is liable for all payments due to INVESTOR OR INVESTOR'S designee until the lease term is expired.

(b) CO-INVESTOR agrees to sign a lease agreement for INVESTOR'S 50% for 5 years or until the property is sold, unless terminated earlier with the consent of the INVESTOR or by the purchase by CO-INVESTOR of INVESTOR'S interest in the property. Said lease is attached hereto as EXHIBIT A and is fully incorporated herein.

(c) CO-INVESTOR agrees to pay to the INVESTOR or his designee, for the term of this Agreement, monthly payments of ($_____)_____ AND 00/100 DOLLARS with a down payment of ($____)_____ NO DOLLARS in advance when accepting and signing this Agreement. The monthly payments shall be in advance including ___X___ Principal, ___X___ Interest, ___X___ Taxes, ___X___ Insurance, and ___X___ Maintenance Fees, which shall be based on the actual amount of payments due on all notes encumbering the property. Any positive cash flow, in excess of Mortgage Payments, received from CO-INVESTOR will reduce the amount owed to INVESTOR and will be credited to CO-INVESTOR on buy-out or sale of property. Said payments may increase or decrease in amount, depending on the type of existing financing or any variance in taxes or insurance. Payments are due on the first day of the month and shall be delinquent if not received by the INVESTOR or his designee by the fifth day of every month. INVESTOR'S designee is _____ of _____ Phone _____. Said monthly payment shall be credited as follows: ___50___ % of the payment shall be deemed to be a purchase payment to INVESTOR for CO-INVESTOR'S ___50___ % interest in the property. The remaining payment share shall be a lease payment to the INVESTOR for the ___50___ % interest retained by him in the property. Any partial or late payments shall be applied first to late charges, secondly to rent and any remainder to monthly purchase payments. The INVESTOR, or his designee, shall make all monthly payments to beneficiaries and to taxes and insurance upon receipt of the monthly payment received from the CO-INVESTOR.

(d) CO-INVESTOR agrees to execute a   Mortgage in favor of the INVESTOR for the purpose of securing:

(1) Payment to INVESTOR for INVESTOR'S CONTRIBUTION as set forth in paragraph 3 above.

(2) The performance of each agreement of CO-INVESTOR incorporated by reference or contained herein.

Mortgage is to name_____

_____as

Mortgagees.

(e) CO-INVESTOR acknowledges that his ____50____ % interest in the property is subject to Notes and Mortgages securing said property in the amount of ($_____) THOUSAND AND 00/100 DOLLARS plus any and all contributions made by the INVESTOR hereafter.

(f) CO-INVESTOR agrees to maintain said property as his sole expense and be responsible for any and all repairs or improvements up to one percent (1%) of property value at that time. CO-INVESTOR shall not make or allow to be made, any major repairs or improvements to the property without having first obtained the written consent of the INVESTOR, which consent may be given or withheld at INVESTOR'S sole discretion.

Major repairs and improvements shall mean any job, the cost of which exceeds one percent (1%) of the property value. Any repair expense in excess of 1% shall be paid according to each party's ownership interest. Prior to commencement of such repairs or improvements, CO-INVESTOR shall cause to be recorded and posted in a conspicuous place on the property, a legally recorded NOTICE OF NONRESPONSIBILITY. A copy of the recorded NOTICE OF NONRESPONSIBILITY shall be sent to INVESTOR before any work starts. CO-INVESTOR and INVESTOR shall agree in writing, the maximum allowable cost before work is started. When the property is sold at the end of this Co-Tenancy Agreement, CO-INVESTOR shall be entitled to recover the actual amount expended beyond one percent (1%), by CO-INVESTOR on the property. This amount is not to exceed the amount agreed upon before work started.

(g) CO-INVESTOR shall not dispose of any real or personal property connected with the home without written consent of the INVESTOR.

(h) At the signing of this Agreement, CO-INVESTOR shall pay for a Homeowners Insurance Policy naming INVESTOR as a Co-Insured. Fire insurance coverage shall be a Replacement Value Policy with the amount never less than ($ 80,000.00) EIGHTY THOUSAND DOLLARS. In the event of total loss, CO-INVESTOR shall assign his interest of monies paid by the Insurance Company to the INVESTOR to cover his investment, including closing costs as set forth in paragraph 3. Any excess monies will be divided equally based on each partys' ownership interest. In the event of a loss of CO-INVESTOR'S personal property, investor agrees to assign his interest of any monies paid by the Insurance Company for CO-INVESTOR'S personal property, to the CO-INVESTOR.

(i) Mortgage life insurance paid by CO-INVESTOR is not included in this agreement.

5. ENCUMBRANCES AND ASSIGNMENTS
CO-INVESTOR shall not sell, assign, transfer, or encumber his interest in the property, this Agreement, or his lease of the property without the prior written consent of the INVESTOR.

6. DEFAULT BY THE CO-INVESTOR
The occurrence of any of the following shall constitute a default by the CO-INVESTOR.

(a) Failure to make any payment under paragraph 4 when due and if failure continues for ten (10) days after notice has been given to the CO-INVESTOR, CO-INVESTOR is in default.

(b) Abandonment and vacation of the premises (failure to occupy the premises for ten [10] consecutive days shall be deemed abandonment and vacation, unless notice to INVESTOR is given in advance.)

(c) Failure to perform any other provision of this Agreement and Exhibit A, and if failure to perform is not cured within ten (10) days after notice has been given by the INVESTOR, CO-INVESTOR is in default. Notices given under this paragraph shall specify the alleged default and the applicable agreement provisions, and shall demand that CO-INVESTOR perform the provisions of this Agreement or make the lease or purchase payments that are in arrears, as the case may be, within the applicable period of time, or quit the premises. No such notice shall be deemed a forfeiture or termination of this Agreement unless INVESTOR so elects in the notice.

7. INVESTOR'S REMEDIES IN CASE OF DEFAULT
INVESTOR shall have the following remedies if CO-INVESTOR commits default. These remedies are not exclusive; they are cumulative in addition to any remedies now or later allowed by law.

(a) If CO-INVESTOR commits any default under Paragraph 6 herein, INVESTOR may terminate the lease provisions of the Agreement and regain possession of the premises in the manner provided by the laws of unlawful detainer in the State of NEW JERSEY in effect at the date of such default, notwithstanding his ownership interest in ___50___ % of the premises. At INVESTOR'S option, he may continue the lease provisions of this Agreement in effect for so long as INVESTOR does not terminate CO-INVESTOR'S right to possession by notice in writing, and INVESTOR may enforce all of his rights and remedies under this Agreement, including his right to recover the rent as it becomes due. INVESTOR'S rights hereunder shall be in addition to those provided in the default section of Exhibit A attached hereto.

(b) If CO-INVESTOR fails to make any payment within ten (10) days after notice of default as set forth in Paragraph 6a above or defaults on any of his obligations under Paragraph 6b or 6c above, the entire amount of past due payments and charges, plus the entire amount of monthly payments due for the term of the lease under Paragraph 4b, plus the entire value of INVESTOR'S CONTRIBUTION as set forth in Paragraph 3, shall become immediately due and payable to INVESTOR and INVESTOR may foreclose on the Mortgage as set forth in Paragraph 4d above. Upon the sale or repurchase by INVESTOR of CO-INVESTOR'S ___50___ % interest in the premises, CO-INVESTOR shall be deemed a month-to-month tenant as to the *entire* premises and shall be obliged to pay to investor as *rent* an amount equal to all principal, interest, insurance, tax, and assessment payments due on such property, until his leasehold interest in the premises is terminated as set forth in Paragraph 4b and/or Exhibit A.

(c) CO-INVESTOR acknowledges that if any monthly payment due from CO-INVESTOR is not received by INVESTOR when due, INVESTOR will incur costs the exact amount of which is extremely difficult and impractical to fix. Therefore, CO-INVESTOR shall pay to INVESTOR an additional sum of six (6) percent of the overdue rent and purchase payment as a late charge. The parties agree that this late charge represents a fair and reasonable estimate of the costs that INVESTOR will incur by reason of late payment by CO-INVESTOR.
Acceptance of any late charge shall not constitute a waiver of CO-INVESTOR'S default with respect to the overdue amount, or prevent INVESTOR from exercising any of the other rights and remedies available to him.

8. DEFAULT BY THE INVESTOR
(This clause is used only if INVESTOR collects the payments). Upon the signing of this Agreement, a Request for Notice of Default shall be given to all lenders on behalf of the CO-INVESTOR. If the INVESTOR fails to make any payments as received from CO-INVESTOR on the property when due, he shall be in default. If INVESTOR fails to make said payment within ten (10) days after Notice has been given by the CO-INVESTOR,

CO-INVESTOR can cure the default at INVESTOR'S cost. Any sums paid by the CO-INVESTOR shall be due immediately from the INVESTOR, and if not paid shall bear interest at the rate of twelve percent (12%) per annum until paid. If INVESTOR does not cure his default within ten (10) days after Notice has been given by CO-INVESTOR, CO-INVESTOR may thereafter, at his option, make all purchase payments directly to the holder(s) of the note(s) and policies of insurance covering the premises and to the appropriate governmental authority for tax assessment payments due on such property.

9. OPTIONS TO PURCHASE OR SELL
Each party shall have the right to purchase the interest of the other party in such premises under the following terms and conditions: Option purchase price is based on Fair Market Value of the property at the time the option is exercised. INVESTOR'S CONTRIBUTION, Paragraph 3; CO-INVESTOR'S Down Payment 4C.

(a) At any time during the first _____ months after purchase of the premises, CO-INVESTOR may purchase INVESTOR'S interest in the premises or this Agreement for one-half (½) of the difference between the Fair Market Value of the premises and the balance on the existing First Mortgage, together with the sum of _____ which represents the Investor's Contribution.

(b) If CO-INVESTOR should elect not to purchase INVESTOR'S ___50___ % interest as set forth in paragraph 9a, INVESTOR shall then have the option to purchase CO-INVESTOR'S ___50___ % interest for the same amount as stated in paragraph 9a minus the INVESTOR'S contribution, and plus CO-INVESTOR'S Down Payment. In order for the CO-INVESTOR to receive a reimbursement for repairs or improvements, a written agreement must be provided in advance, and reimbursement shall be limited to that amount agreed to in writing before repairs or improvements are made, or the actual dollar amount expended on the property, whichever is less.

(c) By mutual agreement, INVESTOR and CO-INVESTOR may extend this Agreement for an additional period of time.

(d) If neither INVESTOR nor CO-INVESTOR elect to purchase the other's interest, or to extend this Agreement, the INVESTOR and CO-INVESTOR hereby agree to offer the property for sale at appraised value, and at the time specified herein to accept a valid cash offer in the amount of the appraisal. If an offer has not been accepted within sixty (60) days after listing, the parties agree to exercise good faith and business judgment in reducing the offering price and in considering offers involving seller financing, as then may be necessary to sell the property without undue delay. If the property has not been sold within thirty (30) days after the natural expiration of the lease and Co-Tenancy Agreement, both parties agree that the INVESTOR shall have an additional return on his original contribution of ___12___ % per annum, beginning at said expiration date. The final decision for sale is reserved to INVESTOR and CO-INVESTOR will abide by INVESTOR'S decision.

10. SALE OF PROPERTY

Upon the sale of the property, the net proceeds shall be distributed as follows:

(a) INVESTOR shall first receive a sum equal to his contribution, including costs, as set forth in Paragraph 3, reimbursement for any other monies expended, or interest earned on the property by the INVESTOR.

(b) CO-INVESTOR shall receive _____ or $ _____

(c) The remainder of the sales price shall be divided between INVESTOR and CO-INVESTOR, based on their percentage of ownership, after all costs of sale have been deducted.

(d) Selling party shall furnish Buyer with a marketable Title free of Liens and Judgments evidenced by a policy of Title Insurance.

(e) All options stated in Paragraphs 9a, 9f, and 9g, shall be in writing and given to the respective party at least sixty (60) days prior to the exercise of each option.

11. NOTICES

Any and all notices and other communications required or permitted by this Agreement shall be served on or given to either party by the other party in writing and shall be deemed duly served and given when personally delivered to any of the parties to whom it is directed, or in lieu of such personal service, when deposited in the United States Mail, using a registered letter with a return receipt attached, first class postage prepaid, addressed to INVESTOR at P.O. BOX 000, CLIFTON, NEW JERSEY 07015 or CO-INVESTOR at the property address or such forwarding address that the CO-INVESTOR gives to the INVESTOR.

12. ARBITRATION

In the case of any controversy between the CO-INVESTOR and INVESTOR concerning, but not limited to, the validity, construction, or interpretation of this Agreement, or the validity of the appraisal, the parties shall refer such dispute in writing to an Arbitrator to be jointly agreed upon, or

Sample Equity Participation Agreement *(cont.)*

failing an agreement, to the American Arbitration Association for referral to a single Arbitrator. Said Arbitrator shall promptly determine such dispute and deliver a written decision to each party by personal delivery or certified mail. Both parties agree to pay the arbitration fee based on their percentage of ownership in the property. The decision of the Arbitrator shall be final and binding on both parties and shall be enforceable as any Arbitration award. The Arbitrator may hold meetings, hearings, and take testimony of witnesses and receive evidence, but shall not be empowered to compel the attendance of any person or the production of any evidence.

13. INTEGRATED AGREEMENT
INVESTOR and CO-INVESTOR agree that this instrument is and shall be incorporated into and become a part of the Co-Tenancy Agreement executed by them and further agree that this instrument and said Co-Tenancy Agreement shall be deemed to collectively set forth their rights and obligations to each other concerning the demised premises. Any agreement or representation respecting the demised premises or the duties of either INVESTOR or CO-INVESTOR in relation thereto not expressly set forth in this lease or the Co-Tenancy Agreement is null and void.

Dated MARCH , 1988 _____
INVESTOR _____
INVESTOR _____
CO-INVESTOR _____
CO-INVESTOR _____
MANAGER _____
MANAGER'S ADDRESS _____
MANAGER'S PHONE _____
STATE OF New Jersey _____
COUNTY OF _____

On, March , 1988, before me, the undersigned, a Notary Public in and for said County and State, personally appeared: _____
_____
known to me to be the person(s) whose names(s) is (are) subscribed to the within instrument and acknowledged that __they__ executed the same.

_____   _____
Notary Signature line   My commission expires:

SHORT FORM MEMORANDUM OF AGREEMENT FOR SHARING EQUITY AND LEASE

THIS AGREEMENT FOR SHARING EQUITY AND LEASE, is made this _____ day of __MARCH__, 19_88_, by and between _____

_____
Hereinafter called "INVESTOR", and _____
_____ hereinafter called "CO-INVESTOR"

1. The parties hereby agree and acknowledge that they have entered into a certain recorded Agreement for Sharing Equity and Lease of a residential property, the terms of which are hereby incorporated herein by reference. Said Agreement pertains to that certain real property situated in: the City of __Absecon__, County of __Atlantic__, State of __New Jersey__, with a legal description of __Lot 1.17.302 in Block 741 on the Tax Map of the Township of Galloway__

AKA _173 Club Place, Absecon, New Jersey_
which property shall hereinafter be referred to as the "Property".

2. The Agreement for Sharing Equity and Lease, provides that the parties will purchase the property as tenants in common and further provides for the monthly contributions by each party for the payment of all costs and expenses regarding the property, including but not limited to, all mortgage payments, insurance, taxes, maintenance, major repairs, and in the case of townhouses or condominiums, the home owner association charges, property management fees, if any, and reasonable anticipated reserves for the foregoing. The Agreement for Sharing Equity and Lease further provides that the CO-INVESTOR will pay certain rent payments to the INVESTOR for the CO-INVESTOR'S use of INVESTOR's interest in the property.

3. The Agreement for Sharing Equity and Lease contains certain options to allow a party to purchase the other party's interest in the property, pursuant to certain specific terms and conditions. The Agreement specifically prohibits the transfer and/or assignment of either party's interest in the Agreement or property.

4. The Agreement for Sharing Equity and Lease, further provides that the INVESTOR will record subordinate lien deeds of trust against the CO-INVESTOR's ownership interest in the property, and to secure the

performance of the CO-INVESTOR (Co-owner) to all the terms of the Agreement.

5. It is understood that the only purpose of this instrument is to give notice of the existence and terms of the Incorporated Agreement for Sharing Equity and Lease, and should there be any inconsistency between the terms of this instrument and the terms of said Agreement incorporated herein, the terms of the Agreement for Sharing Equity and Lease shall prevail.

IN WITNESS WHEREOF, the parties have caused this Short Form Memorandum of Agreement for Sharing Equity and Lease to be executed the day and year first above written.

THE UNDERSIGNED HEREBY ACKNOWLEDGE THEY HAVE READ AND UNDERSTAND ALL THE PROVISIONS OF THIS AGREEMENT, AND HAVE RECEIVED A COPY HEREOF.

Dated ___ MARCH ___ , 1988 ___

State of ___ New Jersey ___)
County of _____) ss.

On ___ MARCH ___ , 1988 ___
before me, the undersigned, a Notary Public in and for said State, personally appeared

_____

_____

known to me to be the persons whose name are subscribed to the within instrument and acknowledged that they executed the same. WITNESS my hand and official seal.

_____
Signature of INVESTOR

_____
Signature of INVESTOR

_____
Signature of Notary

_____
(This area for official notary seal)

Dated ___ MARCH ___ , 1988 ___

State of ___ New Jersey ___)
County of _____) ss.

_____
Signature of CO-INVESTOR

Short Form Memorandum of Agreement for Sharing Equity and Lease *(cont.)*

On _____ March _____ , 1988 _____
before me, the undersigned, a notary Public in and for said State,
personally appeared

_____

Signature of CO-INVESTOR

_____
_____
_____
_____

known to me to be the person
_____whose name is subscribed
to the within instrument and acknowledged that he executed the
same. WITNESS my hand and official seal.

_____

Signature of Notary

_____

(This area for official notary seal)

15

Tax Certificates

Tax certificates are pieces of paper that can earn you extremely high amounts of interest.

Have I captured your attention? You'll like the next part even more; as an investment, tax certificates are as safe as savings bank money market funds, government bonds, or savings and loan CDs, and a heck of a lot safer than shares of mutual funds.

Don't confuse a tax *certificate* sale with the sale or auction of a property for back taxes; the latter is the disposal of actual real estate and was dealt with back in chapter 9.

Governments rely on taxes to run their communities. When a property owner does not pay his or her taxes, the government looks for other ways to collect that needed money. So if Jane Shmoe in Teaneck forgets to send in her property tax check that is due March 31, the Bergen County tax collector's office is going to wait only so long. Then, that department will include Ms. Shmoe's property when it holds its annual sale of tax certificates. The sale represents the amount of taxes owed by all such neglectful taxpayers.

Tax certificates are issued by a state or local agency and sold to the public to bring in income. When you buy a tax certificate, the document states that you have paid the overdue taxes on someone else's property and thus you are guaranteed, in return, a certain rate of interest.

The interest rate varies from state to state, community to community. Some places pay as high as 90% interest. (In recent years, the average has been 15 to 18 percent.) In each case, it is considerably higher than current bank rates, to make the purchase of the certificates more attractive to you. By law, you must hold the certificate for a period of time, during which the property owner may redeem it.

The main reason to hold a tax certificate is to collect high interest on your money in a safe manner. In 99 and 44/100 percent of the cases, the original property owner does redeem the tax certificate that you hold. Otherwise, that person could lose his or her property to you.

Few owners are willing to let real estate slip from their grasp because of a couple of hundred or even a couple of thousand dollars. The owner typically pays, once he or she receives a notice from the tax collector that the certificate has been sold.

In numerous cases, a house is in the process of being sold, but the owner cannot close until the tax bill is satisfied. So the owner pays the tax collector the back taxes plus interest.

As the certificate holder, you then receive a check from the tax collector for the amount you paid in back taxes, plus the interest. It might take 6 to 12 months following the sale for you to get your money, but the government guarantees payment.

Here is an example: Let's assume that Bill Jones of Pitkin County, Colorado, failed to pay $1,000 in property taxes. The county notified everyone that certificates for this and other back taxes would be sold on Nov. 3, 1987, at its annual tax certificate sale. There, the certificate for Jones's taxes was bought by John Doe, at an interest rate of 9 points above the discount rate. That amounted to a 15 percent interest rate at the time.

Two months later, Bill Jones paid to redeem the certificate. The result? John Doe got his $1,000 back, plus $25, or 15 percent annualized interest for two months.

Another example: Jane Smith bought a Florida certificate for back taxes for $2,000 at 18 percent. Just one year later, the property owner redeemed it. Ms. Smith got back her $2,000 plus $360 profit in interest. The same money in a savings account would have earned $120. The tax certificate earned three times that amount safely.

By now, you undoubtedly realize that buying tax certificates is an almost surefire way to make your dollars earn good money for you. So what's the catch? Why haven't you heard about this before?

There really is no catch, friends. Tax certificates happen to be a totally public, yet still largely unnoticed, method of making money in real estate.

Most governments hold regular sales of tax certificates, announced through standard channels, such as the posting of notices in a court house, tax collector's office, or other bulletin board.

In some places, the sale is actually an auction. The bidding starts with the highest amount of interest allowed by local law. You bid against someone by offering a lower interest rate than the announced one. Thus, if Sam Blue bids on a $500 certificate at 15 percent—the going rate—you can try to obtain the certificate by bidding 14 percent.

In other places, where there are numerous bidders eager for a piece of the action, the sale is conducted on a rotating basis. As the name of each player is announced, that person announces that he or she will, or will not, buy the certificate under consideration. The sale continues with all bidders, in turn, being given a chance to grab a certificate as their names come around.

Occasionally, where there is huge demand for certificates, bidders are allowed to offer a nonrefundable premium over and above the face value of the certificates. This happens in such places as Pitkin County, which includes Aspen, the gilt-edged resort town.

In one typical case, a certificate with a face value (representing back taxes) of $1,760 at 15 percent interest was awarded to the bidder who offered a $45 premium, making his total cost $1,805. Two months after the sale, the delinquent taxpayer redeemed the certificate. The county kept the extra $45, while the successful bidder got back $1,750 plus two months' worth of interest.

Buying at a premium (over the face value of the certificate) simply means that you are hoping the owners either do not redeem, so you get the property, or take enough time for you to recoup the premium in interest payments.

In some municipalities, once a tax certificate sale is over, the agency entertains "open buying." You can buy any remaining tax certificates at the maximum interest rate.

No need to bring a wad of greenbacks to these sales. The standard procedure is to pay 10 percent of the value of your certificates with a cashier's check, then pay the balance three to ten days later.

PLAYING THE TAX CERTIFICATE GAME

Ready to jump into this lucrative real estate market? While working on this book in Aspen, Colorado, Grace Lichtenstein and I decided to see how easy—or difficult—it was to get information on tax certificate sales in that gorgeous resort. So we strolled over to the Pitkin County court house.

In the treasurer's office, a friendly clerk was extremely cooperative in providing this public information. She was happy to give us a sheet of paper explaining the sale, which occurs every November, and took time to show us actual certificates purchased the year before.

You can do the same. In a metropolis such as Manhattan, Chicago, or Los Angeles, digging out the proper information does take more than a stroll down the street, but it is still eminently doable.

Phone the main information number of your county clerk first to determine which office—tax collector, treasurer, or another—handles tax certificates. Then, make a trip in person to that office, to learn when the next tax certificate sale takes place. Ask how you find out what is available. The rules vary greatly from one community to another, so take along the checklist at the end of this chapter.

Once again, this information is public. A clerk will be able to tell you where a notice of properties involving certificates will be posted, in which newspapers that notice will also be published and on which days (a legal requirement), and how to get on a mailing list, if there is one, for more details.

According to law, you hold the certificates for a specified minimum period—usually one to three years. (The period of time given an owner to pay up differs from state to state.) In those rare cases when an owner does not redeem the certificate by the end of that period, you can file papers forcing the state to put that land up for grabs at a tax sale—an auction at which you can bid on the actual real estate. In some states you simply apply for a tax deed, while in others you go through the full foreclosure procedure. No auction or bidding is required.

Canny investors obtain the lists of properties involved in tax certificate sales in advance. Then, they visit the properties in person, searching for the elusive one in a thousand that appears to be abandoned or could be part of an estate.

There are parcels for which the certificates may never be redeemed. An investor who identifies such a property bids for the certificate either at 0 percent or at a big premium, guaranteeing that he will walk away with it.

As an alternative, the investor could contact the delinquent owner, asking, "Are you having trouble on taxes? I would like to buy your tax certificate, or perhaps you would like to talk about selling your property." At this stage, the investor could well cut a marvelous deal for the abandoned property at far below market value.

What if you root out an apparently abandoned building, buy the tax certificate on it, wait the allotted period of time, and then find there is no sign of the owner?

As the expiration date approaches, have a local attorney prepare foreclosure papers to be filed the day after expiration. Arrange to pay the attorney a certain amount simply for beginning the process (sometimes it costs $50 or $75 just to file the first notice), then additional fees as other steps are required.

The delinquent owner will probably ante up the money quickly after receiving a foreclosure warning. If not, your attorney asks for a hearing, after which a judge signs a document turning the property over to you once a waiting period (typically 30 to 90 days) is over. The delinquent taxpayer can still redeem the certificate at this late hour, but he or she must pay your legal costs as well.

There are also times when no one buys the tax certificate. In this case, the agency ends up foreclosing on the property for back taxes. This happens a lot in large metropolitan areas. Some beleaguered communities hold tax certificate sales as often as every month.

Once a property is offered at a foreclosure sale, the holder of the tax certificate is in the best position to buy it. The holder is first in line, and in some areas no one else is allowed to bid on the property.

CERTIFICATES ON RAW LAND

One means of increasing the admittedly slim odds of your claiming the property itself is to bid on certificates that cover vacant land. Often, the land is owned by absentee owners who are ready to walk away from it, rather than pay back taxes.

Remember the land near the Disney World site that I mentioned in the chapter on raw land? In the early 1960s, I picked up tax certificates on lots near Kissimee for as little as $1.25! The absentee owners never even bothered to appear for the foreclosure proceeding. I ended up owning iots of lots of Osceola County for pennies, which I eventually sold for thousands of dollars.

In conclusion, you might think of tax certificate sales as "no-sweat equity." The only "active" work involved is first eyeballing the property attached to the certificates, then attending the sale, and finally keeping track of the ones you bought.

Oh, yes, there are two other "activities": watching the calendar for the expiration date, just in case someone defaults . . . and breaking into a grin when a check for your investment, plus interest, arrives in your mailbox from the tax collector.

12 QUESTIONS TO ASK
YOUR LOCAL TAXING AUTHORITY

1. When, where, how often, and at what time does this community hold its sales of tax certificates?
2. Is there a brochure showing rules and regulations of such sales?
3. On what date, and in what newspapers, will the notice be published?
4. Where will a list of the properties involved be posted?
5. What is the method of sale—rotation, auction, other?
6. What is the length of time the certificates must be held before the property itself becomes available?
7. What is the interest rate paid?
8. What kind of deposit is required from buyers of certificates?
9. Where can a record of the most recent previous sale of tax certificates be found?
10. What is this community's procedure for handling unsold certificates?
11. What method is used to foreclose on and get deeds to unredeemed certificates?
12. If you don't sell the certificates, who gets to bid on the properties taken over by you for failure to pay property taxes?

Don't forget your key magic door-opener phrase: I'm looking for public information.

STATES, INTEREST RATES,
REDEMPTION PERIODS

In the chart on the following pages, the first two columns indicate the type of form a state uses. Some merely issue a receipt for payment of taxes instead of an actual certificate. In those states, you must apply for the deed after the redemption period on tax certificates has expired. The column for interest rate is blank for those states in which it fluctuates from year to year, from county to county, or both.

State	Deed	Certificate	Interest Rate	Redemption Period
ALABAMA		X	6%	3 yrs.
ALASKA	X			1 yr.
ARIZONA		X	10%	3 yrs. to 5 yrs.
ARKANSAS		X		2 yrs.
CALIFORNIA	X			1 yr.
COLORADO		X	Federal Reserve Rate on 9/1 + 9%	3 yrs.
CONNECTICUT	X		12%	1 yr.
DELAWARE		X	15% to 20%	1 yr.
FLORIDA		X	18%	2 yrs.
GEORGIA	X			1 yr.
HAWAII	X		12%	1 yr.
IDAHO	X			3 yrs.
ILLINOIS		X	18% to 90%	6 mo. to 2 yrs.
INDIANA		X	10% to .25%	2 yrs.
IOWA		X	$3/4$% per mo. & 5% per yr. penalty	2 yrs. 9 mo.
KANSAS	X			None
KENTUCKY		X	12%	3 yrs.
LOUISIANA		X	12%	3 yrs.
MAINE	X			18 mo.
MARYLAND		X	6% to 21%	6 mo. to 2 yrs.
MASSACHUSETTS	X		16%	6 mo.
MICHIGAN		X	$1 1/4$% per mo. & 50% penalty after 12 mo.	6 mo.

State	Deed	Certificate	Interest Rate	Redemption Period
MINNESOTA		X		3 yrs.
MISSISSIPPI	X		12%	2 yrs.
MISSOURI		X	8%	2 yrs.
MONTANA		X	8%	3 yrs.
NEBRASKA		X		3 yrs.
NEVADA	X			
NEW HAMPSHIRE		X	18%	2 yrs.
NEW JERSEY		X	18%	6 mo. to 2 yrs.
NEW MEXICO	X			
NEW YORK		X	8% to 10%	1 yr. to 3 yrs.
NORTH CAROLINA		X	9%	6 mo. to 1 yr.
NORTH DAKOTA		X	9%	3 yrs.
OHIO	X			
OKLAHOMA		X	8%	2 yrs.
OREGON	X			
PENNSYLVANIA	X			2 yrs.
RHODE ISLAND	X		10% to 16%	1 yr.
SOUTH CAROLINA		X	8% to 12%	18 mo.
SOUTH DAKOTA		X	8%	4 yrs.
TENNESSEE	X			
TEXAS	X	X	25% to 50%	2 yrs.
UTAH	X			
VERMONT		X	12%	1 yr.
VIRGINIA	X			
WASHINGTON	X			
WEST VIRGINIA	X		12%	18 mo.
WISCONSIN		X		3 yrs.
WYOMING		X	11%	4 yrs. to 6 yrs.
DIST. OF COLUMBIA		X	12% to 29%	2 yrs.
PUERTO RICO		X	10%	1 yr.

16

Buying, Selling, and Holding Second Mortgages

Say you have $16,000 in a savings account. You can put an ad in your local paper that says "Need Money? Private investor will buy your second mortgage." This is one of my favorite safe ways to make money in real estate.

When a person signs a mortgage on a house, that person also signs a personal note, guaranteeing that if something happens to the house he or she will be responsible for the money. Thus, you can recover money from someone who has other assets in addition to the house, if that person defaults on a mortgage.

Investors who are involved in second mortgages make money by lending a home owner money at an interest rate higher than the first mortgage, with the home as collateral for the loan.

Right at the beginning, let me state Sonny Bloch's Golden Rule on mortgages. My approach is conservative: If the existing first mortgage and the second mortgage that you would hold as the lender (known as the mortgagee) exceeds more than 50 percent of the market value of the property, don't do the deal. Stick to this formula and you won't get hurt, because you can always sell a property at 50 percent or more of its market value.

In other words, you can always get your money back plus interest. Keep this rule in mind as you learn more about second mortgages. Others may be comfortable buying second mortgages worth 70 percent or less of a property's market value, but I prefer to stand by the more conservative 50 percent limit.

There are several ways to get involved in the second mortgage market. You can buy existing mortgages. . . . You can create new mortgages. . . . You can accept mortgages and notes ("paper") on deals you are buying or selling. . . . Or you can deal with mortgage brokers or dealers who make a business of buying and selling mortgages and notes.

BUYING EXISTING
SECOND MORTGAGES

A simple way of buying a second mortgage is to go to the original owner of a property. Those people have sold their home to someone who could not make the full down payment. That owner agrees to *carry back paper*—to finance part of the down payment in the form of a second mortgage—in order to complete the sale.

For instance, a couple of senior citizens in New Jersey decide to retire to Florida. They sell their New Jersey home for $100,000, but the buyers can only come up with $10,000 as a down payment, and they qualify for only a $70,000 mortgage on the home. That leaves $20,000 to be covered. The retirees carry a second mortgage of $20,000.

This is where the investor steps in. You try to buy the second mortgage for as much *below* its face value as you can.

Second mortgage holders, such as the retirees in this example, have a variety of reasons for selling the note. Perhaps they need the cash to buy their Florida house, to furnish it nicely, or to buy a boat for recreation in Florida. Perhaps they simply get tired of the responsibility of collecting the payments via long distance.

For whatever reason, a partial chunk of the $20,000 today, immediately, in cash, looks better to these folks, even though it is discounted, than $20,000 over a five or ten year period.

If it is a new note, you offer to buy it at a discount of 25 to 30 percent, or for about $16,000. Once you buy it, you have already made a paper profit of $4,000. That is better than a 30 percent return on your money, right out of the starting gate.

The note and mortgages you buy should carry an interest rate of at least 1 percent above the current rates for first mortgages, as advertised by banks in the region.

For example, take the second mortgage in the example above. Let's say it has a face value of $20,000. You have bought it at a discount of 30 percent, for $16,000. The going rate on first mortgages in your region is 10 percent. Be sure this second mortgage is being paid off at 11 percent or more. Thus, you earn 11 percent interest on $20,000—the full value—not on the $16,000 you have actually paid.

Be discriminating about the length of the second mortgage. Long-drawn-out payment schedules are a red flag. Only buy second mortgages with a life of less than ten years. I prefer those in the five- to seven-year range.

How do you find existing second mortgages? At the beginning of this chapter I mentioned an ad. Never underestimate the number of people out there who want cash in hand right now. Run an ad like the one above in the appropriate classified section of your local paper, and I promise you will get plenty of calls. Negotiate each deal on an individual basis.

Depending on the cash requirements of the callers, you might be able to bargain for a bigger than 30 percent discount on someone's second mortgage.

Let us pretend a Mr. Judson is one of those who answer your ad. He and his wife are retirees who are moving from New Jersey to Florida. They have taken back a $20,000 mortgage on their New Jersey home to facilitate a quick sale. If the $20,000 owed to them, plus the existing first mortgage, total 50 percent or less than the market value of the house, you begin negotiations.

"Tell me how much you want for the second mortgage, Mr. Judson," you ask. His initial answer: "$20,000, of course."

"Since I will have to wait ten years for my money, I would like to offer you less. Would you accept $12,000 to $15,000?"

While he considers your offer, you ask Mr. Judson: "Is the interest on the note 11 percent or more? And do you have a recent appraisal of the house?"

Your goal is to buy the paper for 30 percent off face value or less. If you return enough calls that come in response to your ad, you will have all the second mortgages you ever wanted, at a good discount. Use the worksheet later in this chapter to do your arithmetic.

Once you and Mr. Judson agree on the price, have your attorney draw up assignment papers of the mortgage and note. Double-check to make sure that your attorney executes and records the documents properly. It should also be the attorney's job to arrange for the title policy to be changed to show you as the new second mortgagee, and for the first mortgagee to be advised about the change.

You must have a closing on the deal, since your attorney will have to check on possible hidden or forgotten debts against the property. You also need to do a credit check on the home owners. Then sit back and wait for the checks to arrive each month.

BUYING NEW SECOND MORTGAGES

Every major Sunday newspaper in the country carries hundreds of classified ads from people ready to lend money for second mortgages. The interest rates run anywhere from 1 to 3 percent above the going rate for first mortgages on residential properties. For commercial properties the second mortgage interest rate runs even higher.

You, too, can place such an ad as a private investor. Once again, you can virtually be assured of a bunch of calls. There are loads of people who want to pull equity out of their property, and one way of doing this is by refinancing their home with a second mortgage.

Once again, before you make such a loan, get an appraisal on the property, have your debtor's credit checked carefully, and have your attorney handle the necessary documentation at the closing. Here, too, you must have a formal closing.

BUYING SECOND MORTGAGES
FROM DEALERS

There are dozens of professionals who deal in second mortgages in every geographical area. You can spot the pros by the ads they run offering second mortgage paper for sale. The most critical thing to check, in order to avoid being bitten by a scam bug, is the legitimacy of the notes and mortgages they are selling.

There is always a risk of fraud in any financial dealing, and buying second mortgages is no exception. A lot of phony paper is being sold.

Don't set yourself up for fraud by taking shortcuts. If you go through the basic closing procedures outlined in the sections above, and notify the current owners of the property in question, and if your attorney does "due diligence" at the closing, you should have no problem buying from a dealer. Your internal warning signal should go off when a dealer says, "You don't need an attorney," or "You don't need a closing."

SECOND MORTGAGES ON YOUR OWN DEALS

The final way to generate second mortgages is by creating your own. When you are selling land or property, let the public know, either through brokers or in your own ads, that you will accept mortgages on other property as either partial or full payment.

Here is where the paper game gets really interesting! Perhaps there is someone who very much wants a property from you. Instead of all cash, the person offers, as partial payment, a mortgage with a face value of $20,000, but the discount will be considerably deeper than 30 percent.

Some of the best deals I have ever done have involved accepting *paper*—second mortgages and notes, sometimes discounted as much as 50 percent (½ of face value), as payment for the property I was selling. The reason is, the buyers want the property I have . . . more than they want the second mortgage they are holding.

PROFITING FROM PAPER

Whether you deal in existing second mortgages, new ones, or one of the other variations I have described, dealing in paper can bring you a return on your investment that is five to ten times greater than you would get by putting your money in a money market fund or a certificate of deposit.

Spread your money around to reduce the risk. You are better off with a large group of small second mortgages than with only two or three large second mortgages. I would not recommend buying second mortgages on large buildings or pieces of land, since that puts all of your monetary eggs in a single basket.

The cardinal rules stated earlier in this book apply here as well. Stay away from mortgages on properties in a region driven by a single product or industry, such as oil. Seek out areas in which houses are selling at a brisk pace and the neighborhood is either stable or up-and-coming.

HOW TO PRICE A SECOND MORTGAGE

A. Appraisal price of house (less than 6 mo. old) $ _____

B. Balance due on Second Mortgage $ _____

C. Balance due on First Mortgage $ _____

D. Total of B & C $ _____
   (D should be 50 % or less of A)

E. Rate of Interest on Second Mortgage   _____ %

F. 70% of Balance due (B minus 30%) $ _____

Note: F or less is the amount you should pay for the Second Mortgage.

Pretty soon, you could have ten second mortgages, each with a face value of $10,000 apiece, for a total of $100,000, that you have bought at an average discount of 30 percent, or $70,000. Should one of those deals go awry, you won't be hurt, because the money you lent plus the first mortgage is less than half what the house is worth. Eventually, perhaps within six months to a year and a half, you will turn that defaulted $10,000 second mortgage into a sale for double your money or more—even if you sell the property for below its market value. Here's how I figure out the profit:

$100,000	$40,000 1st mg	Both mtg= $50,000.
house	$10,000 your 2d mtg	You foreclose. Your new $100,000 house cost you $50,000. You sell for $80,000 & put $30,000 profit in pckt

If there is such a deep discount offered on a note that is irresistible, buy it, then turn around and sell it immediately to a dealer. Second mortgages are a commodity that can be traded almost as easily as stocks and bonds. You can almost always find someone who is looking to buy, if your price is low enough.

For instance, if you buy a second mortgage with a face value of $20,000 for $10,000, you can be sure of finding someone who will buy it from you for $15,000 or $16,000.

A HANDFUL OF HINTS
ON SECOND MORTGAGES

When you hold a second mortgage, you should get a certificate that is updated on a yearly basis from an insurance company covering the house, just in case the property involved is destroyed in a fire or some other disaster. The certificate will show that you are the loss payee, up to the amount of money you are owed on that property.

You should also have on file, at the insurance carrier, a letter stating that you are the second mortgage holder (mortgagee). The letter should state that you are to be notified if the insurance premiums are not being paid on time. This is more important than a mere bookkeeping chore. If a house burns down, and a check for the insurance is issued to the person living in the house, you might not get your money. The "owner" could simply cash the check and disappear without rebuilding the house. That leaves you holding a worthless second mortgage.

As far as the residence itself, don't buy a second mortgage and note unless the property is one you yourself would like to own as an investor. Make sure, too, that the owner agrees in writing to place you on the policy as a loss payee.

There are certain kinds of property whose mortgages you should not buy: churches, bars, restaurants, motels, or any facility that has a limited use. If you are thinking about mortgages on commercial property, check local zoning ordinances in advance of the deal to be certain that the shop or service facility is not in violation of local laws. If a business for which you hold a mortgage closes down, the debtor will stop making payments. If that space cannot be used for a similar purpose, you could end up with a washout.

Another *don't* on my list concerns the nature of the mortgage holder. Don't buy second mortgages if the monthly payments are paid by a trust, trustees, corporations, or partnership. You want your money to come from real people with real assets. It is very hard to get a straight answer from a trust or corporation when a monthly payment is missed.

The smartest idea—one that I try to follow—is to reserve your second mortgage portfolio exclusively for single family residences.

Ever hear of an *estoppel* certificate? Perhaps you have not, but your attorney should know about it. This document shows the interest due and principal remaining on a mortgage. Make sure your attorney gets this certificate from the person paying the mortgages—both yours and the existing first mortgage.

An estoppel certificate is important in proving quickly how much you are owed. It settles disputes over how much money might be due or discrepancies between what someone thinks he has paid and what the mortgage company says he has paid.

HAPPY SHOPPING!

Shopping for mortgages is very similar to shopping for good real estate deals of any kind. Do your homework, study the market, shop with discrimination, talk to plenty of people, and you will have no trouble finding good second mortgages for sale with deep discounts and high yields.

Once you have bought a second mortgage, don't be in a hurry to sell it. The older it gets, and the more payments that are made on it on time, the more valuable it becomes, especially in the first three years.

For this reason, start with low amounts—$5,000 to $10,000. Later you can work your way up to higher-priced mortgages. There is a tremendous profit built into second mortgages bought at a discount, so there is no point in unloading them early.

If you do need a big sum for another kind of deal, you can bundle your mortgages together into a single package and borrow against it, using the bundle as security.

REMICS: THE SECURITIZATION OF MORTGAGES

Individuals such as yourself are not the only investors who bundle mortgages. Companies that issue mortgages also bundle them together and sell them to wholesalers. The wholesalers then turn around and sell interests—shares of the bundles—to the public. This is the pooling, or packaging, part of the business.

The sale of interests in these pools, or packages, has become very popular in recent years. As the Federal Government was pulling out of the housing market during the Reagan years, it decided to encourage the private sector to invest in these pools of mortgages to generate lots of liquid funds in the mortgage market.

In an attempt to make these investments more beneficial to more investors, Congress recently created a new real estate investment vehicle known as the REMIC. This new breed is for the hands-off, ultraconservative investor.

REMIC stands for Real Estate Mortgage Investment Conduits. They are corporations, partnerships, or REITs (Real Estate Investment Trusts) that hold a portfolio of mortgages. They sell a piece of the action as mortgage-backed securities. You buy stock or a share of the mortgage pool.

In other words, they use bundles of mortgages as the security for your investment in the deal. The companies invest strictly in mortgages, buying paper on properties with a very definite percentage of return on investment. Typically, the return is 9 to 11 percent, depending solely on the general economic climate at the time of investment.

REMICs are treated as if they are partnerships for tax purposes. Thus, they have the same tax benefits that a limited partnership has. Income from a REMIC is not treated as portfolio income but as passive partnership income. That could be very important if you have passive income losses, like depreciation and negative cash flow.

The main drawback of REMICs is that buyers do not participate in the appreciation of the real estate itself. Furthermore, as an investor, you should understand that REMICs are owned by an intermediate party and controlled by someone else. You are not buying a direct mortgage, like those I detailed earlier in this chapter. You can also lose your long-term benefit on this investment if the owners of the properties on which the mortgages are held decide to refinance or prepay.

A key to the attractiveness of REMICs is that the entity holding the mortgages is not taxed at the mortgage-pool level.

By law, all mortgages held by a REMIC must be purchased within three months of the creation of the mortgage. If one of the mortgages in the pool defaults, the REMIC can obtain a replacement mortgage. A REMIC can also own an interest in another REMIC and can own property acquired as the result of a foreclosure on a mortgage it holds. However, the government has set a strict time limit on the holding of these properties. The REMIC is required to dispose of these properties within twelve months from the time of foreclosure.

There are two ways to own a REMIC: One is as a regular interest holder; the other is as a residual interest holder.

Being a regular holder is just like holding a note or any kind of debt instrument. You get an unconditional right to receive interest at a fixed rate, or a variable rate in some cases. In addition, you receive specific payments of principal.

Being a residual holder puts you in the class of a person holding an equity. This is chancy, so you get a higher interest rate. As a residual holder of a REMIC you are also subject to servicing fees of 1 to 2 percent. You are also subject to quicker cash-outs. However, you can get an equity kicker, a piece of the action that means partial ownership of the real estate deal on which the mortgages are held.

I do not recommend investing in REMICs as a residual interest holder, only as a regular interest holder. If you want to gamble on property values in equities, I would rather see you in a master limited partnership (see chapter 18), where the primary purpose is equity investing, not debt investing.

A REMIC can also liquidate its portfolio at any time without paying capital gains taxes on the sale of its assets. It simply files a plan to liquidate and must pass along to the investors their proportional shares of the profits.

Many REITs and real estate mutual funds are buying REMICs as part of their portfolios. I explain these securities in the next chapter.

REITs are part of a growing trend toward what the industry calls the securitization of real estate. This is the transformation of real estate from a wholly owned, controllable asset into a freely transferable liquid security.

17

REITs—Buying Real Estate on the Stock Exchange

Do you realize that now, any of us can become "partners" with the Rockefellers in owning Rockefeller Center? This famous collection of buildings has been opened to public ownership through the creation of a REIT—a Real Estate Investment Trust. *REITs* are public companies that buy real estate. Shares are bought and sold on public exchanges just like stocks. They give small investors a chance to become part of the larger real estate scene.

After a bumpy start back in the 1960s, these products have proven to be reliable, high-quality investments for the passive real estate investor. They are highly liquid, just as any other stock bought and sold daily. The underlying asset is real estate and/or mortgages, instead of traditional companies. Thanks to federal law, REITs do not pay corporate taxes. Furthermore, they are required by law to pass along 95 percent of their profit to investors.

REITs make money for you by returning a decent yield through appreciation and cash flow. For the past few years, REITs have returned an average yield of 8 percent or more.

REITs contain a tax break for you as well. Up to 40 percent of a dividend paid to you by a REIT may be treated as a return of your capital. This creates tax-deferred income. You can defer your taxes on that part of the dividend until you actually sell your shares.

The stability of REITs is comforting. For example, on Black Monday, October 19, 1987, REIT shares fell an average of 9.1 percent, less than half the plunge experienced by the Standard and Poor 500 stocks. My strategy as a small investor would be to hold REITs for at least five years to capture both appreciation of the property and the swing in real estate cyclical markets.

As an owner of REIT stock, you have voting rights. A group representing a majority of stockholders must approve property purchases and sales. Interestingly, stockholders must be independent from the day-to-day managers of the REIT's holdings.

The professionals who have formed REITs, master limited partnerships, and real estate mutual funds are trying to correct what is perceived to be real estate's greatest drawback—the lack of liquidity. These are also attempts to sidestep the mortgaging of property and the payment of huge amounts of interest on those mortgages. With REITs, money is raised from the general public through the purchase of shares of a REIT stock, a development that was originally attempted to keep mortgage costs down.

In my opinion, the securitization of real estate has not worked the way the originators of the idea hoped. Costs have become heavier with layer upon layer of administrative and sales costs. All the expenses involved in forming, running, and selling the product, and all the layers of administrative and marketing personnel, have cut into the basic profit that goes directly from ownership of property to the investor.

On the other hand, the creators of REITs *have* succeeded in bringing Wall Street and real estate more closely together. Wall Street—the investment community—now considers real estate one of the safest, most stable investments available in the U.S. today.

In creating REITs, the pros have indeed reduced the risk, but they have also greatly reduced the profit potential. Nevertheless, they are the perfect nonactive investment choice for certain people. Are you a conservative real estate investor who likes liquidity and low risks? Are you willing to accept low rewards in exchange? If you answered yes to both questions, read on.

A SECURITY THAT ACTS LIKE A COMPANY

REITs operate the way you would if you were a major firm with millions of dollars to invest in real estate. In general, they buy residential and commercial properties, holding them from three to five years. They then flip, or sell these properties (at prices higher than the original purchase price, in the best scenario) and buy new ones.

According to government rules, a REIT must invest solely in real estate. All income must come from real estate or real estate-related investment, such as mortgages.

REITs come in several versions, including the FREIT, or Finite Real

Estate Investment Trust. This kind is set up with the understanding that it will liquidate all holdings within a specified number of years. The danger is that if the time set for the liquidation occurs in a down real estate cycle, you could be in for a big loss. Start-up investors should stick to standard, ongoing REITs.

There are three basic varieties of REITs, in terms of their ingredients: equity, mortgage, and hybrid.

The ingredients of equity REITs are familiar to you by now—real estate properties that the trust goes out and purchases, with the intention of selling them in a few years. Because of appreciation, this variety has the most potential for profit.

Mortgage REITs are, in effect, mortgage companies that lend money on buildings and bring you a stable but conservative return. The return is based on the interest rates on the mortgages they grant, the investor's hope being that the mortgage is not paid off before its maturity.

Hybrid REITs are combination portfolios. They both lend money on buildings and buy actual buildings.

There are also some "blended" REITs. These invest heavily and participate in mortgages with a "sweetener" to the lender for a percentage of the cash flow on the property and a percentage of the appreciation on it, a so-called *blend* of debt and equity benefits. In other words, blended REITs lend money in return for a piece of the action.

The danger in investing in mortgage REITs is that if mortgage rates begin to drop, building owners refinance, and your investment suffers because you don't get as big a return.

HOW REITS RATE AS
PASSIVE INVESTMENTS

I would choose REITs over both RELPs (Regular Limited Partnerships) and MLPs (Master Limited Partnerships), which are discussed in the next chapters, because REITs have a much longer track record. But there is another important consideration. You can feel fairly safe in REITs because Congress and the Internal Revenue Service have basically left this form of investment alone.

On the other hand, the rules governing both regular and master limited partnerships are constantly changing, with the result that syndicators still continue to fiddle with the partnerships they offer.

Keep in mind that if you do sell a REIT at a loss, the amount is deductible against your portfolio income. This makes REITs different from other real estate investment losses, which are offset by passive income, because REITs are treated as if they were stocks. REITs also have an advantage over mutual funds specializing in real estate, in that independent REITs don't have heavy expenses paid to managers. (I will talk about the pluses of real estate mutual funds later in this chapter.)

INTERPRETING A REIT PROSPECTUS

Before you buy a REIT, read its prospectus, as you would with any market investment. What should you look for? Overall, the rudiments of making a profit in real estate, as explained throughout this book, must be applied in analyzing a specific REIT.

As a start, turn to the "Summary," a section usually included in most prospectuses. There, you should be able to get a quick fix on the *company itself*, the *trustees*, and *its previous REITs*, as outlined briefly.

The summary might also tell you about past experiences of the trustees in managing real estate trusts or as developers. Check both the *management team* and the *trustees*, who are the owners of properties. By law, those who manage the company and those who own it have to be two different sets of people. The prospectus should say that.

One question that should be answered in the summary is, what is the trust's *investment policy*? Ask yourself whether you think the types of purchases the company is committed to will meet today's real estate investment requirements. Does it buy in places where the people are going to be located before the people are actually there?

The following paragraph, from an actual prospectus, illustrates a different approach:

> Sierra Capital Realty Trust VIII will purchase equity ownership interested in a diversified portfolio consisting primarily of retail, light industrial, distribution facilities, and other income-producing commercial real estate located in major and emerging metropolitan areas of projected growth throughout the United States. Diversity in both geographic location and property type will be considerations for investment. . . .

In other words, this REIT is a *blind pool* or *slush fund* that will raise money first, then look for properties. Are you considering such a trust? Hunt for the track record of earlier trusts put together by the same company, or group of people, which should be in the prospectus. It should show good management and a good return. Keep in mind that it will take a "slush fund" REIT a few years (the prospectus should say how many years) to accumulate its properties. You should have some reservations about these kinds of REITs, as I'll explain a bit further on.

Here are more questions that a good prospectus answers: How are the directors and the managers compensated? Is there some incentive program that drives managers to look for investments that will make both them and their investors happy? A good board of directors will have a long and profitable real estate investing background.

The investment policy section of the prospectus tells you what kind of properties a company will seek and where. In the paragraph cited above, "equity ownership" means it will buy buildings and/or space (not mortgages) for a portfolio of commercial real estate—anything from strip shopping centers to parking lots.

A typical REIT could name more specific properties in more specific locations. The prospectus tells you whether the plan is to leverage purchases or to buy for all cash.

If its properties are not in good locations, if it has invested in overbuilt markets with lots of vacancies, or if properties are not maintained and managed properly, the REIT will fail, just as the properties would fail if they were owned by you directly.

The summary should tell you whether a REIT will be finite or ongoing. However, some include "jump out" clauses, saying, in effect, if it's not the right move to liquidate a finite arrangement, the managers won't do it.

Use common sense when reading the prospectus. For instance, look for a yield of 8 percent or more. (Some trusts guarantee a minimum return.) Has the REIT already begun to deliver a return on its shareholders' investment? If not, it will say when the yield begins. You will also discover what exchange the REIT is traded on—the New York or American Stock Exchange, as a rule.

When you come to information on price/earnings (P/E) ratios, note that this is the price of the stock in relation to what the company earns. In the case of REITs, it is *not* as important as the valuation of the underlying assets of the stock, which consist of the properties the trust owns.

You certainly want to know what your shares are worth, but more important is what the properties held are worth. A good REIT will send you a statement at least once a year estimating the value of the properties held in the REIT's portfolio.

The financial sheet within the prospectus tells you the market values placed upon the properties held. I look for REITs that have undervalued properties. Market value here is determined by qualified appraisers, the same people you would call upon to evaluate an individual building or piece of land.

Ask yourself these questions:

1. Is there a perception in the marketplace that the area in which some properties are located is either rundown or a poor risk?
2. If so, do I have information suggesting the area has either bottomed out or is about to come back?
3. Do I know that smart-money people are indeed buying into that area?

The answers determine whether this REIT could be an excellent buy, especially if the stock is selling at or below *book value*—the amount of money for which the firm purchased its properties. When this area in which the properties are located shows appreciation that is not reflected in the financial data, the stock itself is undervalued.

Now let's go a bit further into an examination of real estate held by a REIT. Perhaps some of the properties are located close to a new development, such as a city's rehabilitated downtown district. Perhaps the properties are in the path of a growing geographical area and will soon become contiguous with the growth area. Perhaps they are near a manufacturing plant about to be expanded or modernized. Any of these situations makes me a lot more interested in the REIT.

I recommend buying REITs with property holdings already in place in areas where the market is not yet overbuilt. REITs heavily invested in overbuilt places, as Houston and Dallas were in the 1980's, are not going to show a major return on investment for at least eight to ten years. What's more, look for those REITs in which the maximum mortgages on the buildings held are 65 percent.

The prospectus should give you the REIT's track record so far. How has the REIT done in good and bad times? REITs have been in business long enough to ride through both up and down economic cycles.

A good REIT generates regular dividends. The prospectus will show how regular its distributions have been. What is the source of the stock's distribution and cash dividends? The operating statement will spell out these payments. The operating statement will also tell you about the REIT's cash situation. Is it accumulating cash reserves for repairs on existing buildings and for future purchases?

WHAT ABOUT START-UPS AND MATURE REITs?

Perhaps your broker or financial manager trumpets a brand new start-up REIT, such as the one whose prospectus we quoted on page 187. How can you make a wise decision?

First, be sure to scrutinize the roll call of managers and ponder their track record, inasmuch as the REIT itself won't have its own track record. Second, find out if the new trust has identified actual properties, or kinds of properties, that it plans to invest in. Watch out for "blind pools" or "slush funds." A *blind pool* REIT promises risk takers good returns, in exchange for a belief in the savvy of its managers.

One hint for a smart buy is to look for a "closed" or "finite" REIT that is a few years away from the *end* of its designated life, because at the end, the stock will be selling at close to the value of its underlying assets, namely the properties it owns. If those properties are in a strong market, buyers who jump in a few years before liquidation reap the rewards of appreciation on those properties.

THE CAL STATE REIT TEST

Your broker should be able to provide you with investment house research on REITs. Both Standard & Poor and the Value Line Investment Survey also evaluate REITs, judging them on safety and long-term growth potential.

In addition, two professors from California State University at Sacramento, James Kuhle and Josef Moorhead, have developed a set of six tests by which you can grade a REIT, based on public information. Try out this system on your picks. Any REIT that gets at least 16 points is rated a good buy:

1. Dividend yield: Divide the per-share dividend by stock market price per share. The number must equal at least two-thirds of the average yield on triple A-rated corporate bonds. Score 4 points for dividend yields that qualify.

2. Price-earnings ratio: Is the P/E ratio of the REIT 70 percent or less of the average P/E ratio of S & P's 500 stock index? Score 4 points.

3. Price-to-Book-Value Ratio: Figure the book value by subtracting a REIT's liabilities from its total assets, as shown on its balance sheet. Is the stock's market price less than 80 percent of book value? Score 6 points. Between 80 and 100 percent? Score 3 points.

4. Debt-to-Equity Ratio: Is the REIT's debt less than its stockholders' equity? Score 4 points.

5. Earnings Growth: Has earnings growth averaged at least 9 percent over the past five years? Score 6 points.

6. Diversification: How many different types of properties (residential, commercial, industrial, etc.) does the REIT hold? Score 1 point for each, up to a maximum of 4.

At first glance this might seem complicated, but I believe the professors' system is quite useful. Using the rating system on 102 REITs traded between 1977 and 1985, the Cal State team came up with 20 that passed. These 20 averaged a whopping annual total return of 31 percent.

HOW DO REITS AFFECT YOUR TAX RETURN?

Once you have decided on a REIT, don't forget to talk to your CPA about the tax benefits. If you sell your REIT at a profit, you will pay the capital gains tax on it. As noted before, however, returns are not counted as income until you sell your REIT stock.

If you need additional passive income to offset passive losses that you are carrying, then you should buy a limited partnership (RELP) or master limited partnership (MLP) with a good track record.

But if you do not need passive income and like the idea of regularly issued dividends—portfolio income—a well-structured REIT is for you.

REAL ESTATE MUTUAL FUNDS: DIVERSITY PERSONIFIED

The 1980s have witnessed the growth of a whole slew of mutual funds that specialize in real estate. Many of the big mutual fund companies, both those that charge sales fees and the "no-load" companies (of which Fidelity is the largest), now offer real estate mutual funds. These funds typically hold stock in REITs, real estate companies, and master limited partnerships.

The first great advantage to these funds is that you get diversification—an opportunity to hold a small piece of a larger variety of stocks. The fund manager acts as the overseer, watching the stocks on a daily basis. You get the benefit of his or her personal attention and expertise.

The second great advantage is that, like REITs, these real estate mutual funds are completely liquid. You can buy shares on Monday, sell on Tuesday.

The third advantage is the small commitment involved. Real estate mutual funds require as little as $500 for the first purchase. So even if you don't have much money to start, you can dip your toe into the business. I suggest that an initial investment should be from 5 to 10 percent of your real estate portfolio. This will give you a feel for a new, safe way to invest in real estate without tying up a lot of your money.

Real estate mutual funds are investments that you should buy with an eye to holding for longtime growth and income, not a quick one-month or six-month profit. They don't go up in value fast enough to make a quick killing.

A SELECTION OF REITS RECOMMENDED BY BUSINESS PUBLICATIONS I TRUST

IRT Properties (NYSE)
Washington REIT (ASE)
United Dominion (OTC)
Federal Realty (NYSE)
First Union Real Estate Investments (NYSE)
Property Capital Trust (ASE)

Note: Initials stand for the trading vehicle: New York Stock Exchange, American Stock Exchange, or Over the Counter.

18

RELPs—Finding Honest Real Estate Limited Partnerships That Aid the Small Investor

Real estate limited partnerships come in all shapes and sizes. They can be *public* or *private*. This chapter deals with the public version, often referred to in written matter as a RELP. (The next chapter deals with private partnerships, which also come in different forms.)

A RELP is a registered security protected by various federal and state laws. Most public real estate limited partnerships are collections of numerous investors who have bought shares in a deal, much as they would buy stock.

RELPs are passive investments, long a favorite tax shelter for the wealthy. The 1986 Tax Act took away most of the tax advantages, but it also forced managers of RELPs to sweeten them with better returns on invested income. The change makes public partnerships good products for small, not-so-wealthy investors.

The biggest reason for buying RELPs is that they give you an opportunity to get involved in major real estate deals handled by professional managers who know what they are doing.

When you buy RELP shares, you participate in real estate without doing any work whatsoever. You hope to profit from long-term appreciation, but you won't know until a few years have passed.

In a way, investing in RELPs is like taking a ride in a limousine down a long but straight highway. The driver, who is the general partner, does the work of steering the limousine in the right direction, while you, as a limited partner, are an interested passenger. There is the opportunity, down the road some seven to fifteen years hence, of benefiting from the appreciation of property that the partnership has bought. And if the driver is astute, you should collect some tribute, or income, along the way.

Unlike tax certificates, with which there is always a big guaranteed payback, there are fewer guarantees with RELPS. Unlike REITs, they are *illiquid,* or not easily sold on a public market.

Sometimes, you sign up as the partnership is being formed. This can be a "blind pool"—you don't know yet what specific properties the group will actually buy. More typically, a RELP will tell you the kinds of properties it plans to concentrate on—shopping centers, apartment buildings, etc.

The major drawback of public partnership shares is that they can be hard to sell. If you are forced to unload them, you are likely to get far less than you paid. In most cases, public limited partnerships, which are registered as securities with the Securities and Exchange Commission and subject to "blue sky" laws, the common term for state securities regulations in each state, are traded on a growing, but still small, secondary market. More about this later.

For all these reasons, public limited partnerships belong in the "High Risk/High Reward" segment of your portfolio.

HERE COME THE SYNDICATORS

RELPs are usually developed by professional syndicators (the general partners), who pool money from hundreds or even thousands of investors. Many of the offerings you are likely to see are done by syndicators with years of experience in putting together these kinds of deals.

For example, JMB Realty of Chicago, which went into business in 1968 and now promotes itself as the leading sponsor of limited partnerships in this country, manages a multibillion dollar property portfolio for some 200 pension, endowment, and foundation funds, according to the *New York Times.* JMB and its affiliates have a total of 350,000 individual and institutional investors. The Balcor Company, another large syndicator, has managed as many as ten public partnerships at a time.

Once the RELP has raised the money it needs, it buys properties— perhaps a dozen, perhaps more—with the idea of selling them within seven to ten years. Until the properties are sold, investors collect income, mostly from rents, of anywhere from 2 to 15 percent a year return-on-cash investment.

Most public partnerships are *leveraged,* just as any real estate purchase is. In other words, they use the money they raise to put down payments on properties. Then they borrow anywhere from 25 percent to 80 percent of the total purchase price. According to *Money* magazine, most financial planners now prefer moderately leveraged partnerships, which borrow 30 to 60 percent.

For instance, Carlyle partnerships, which are sold by JMB, emphasize the purchase of office buildings and shopping centers. Some are bought entirely for cash; others have a 60 to 70 percent mortgage debt level. One Carlyle offering, XVII, seeks to raise $100 million by selling units of $1,000 each, with a minimum of $5,000 per investor.

Whereas many large RELPs buy every variety of property, others specialize. There are RELPs that buy only raw land, others that buy only mobile home parks. Each partnership must be evaluated on its own merits.

Finally, there are a group of RELPs that specialize in buying distressed properties at prices far below market value. These are the so-called "vulture" RELPs.

All the big syndicates have funds to buy distressed properties. They are the longest shots and the riskiest, because the properties need to be turned around. Vulture funds, therefore, should be purchased by high rollers and big-risk takers only.

WHAT ARE THE KEYS TO THE
SUCCESS OF A PARTNERSHIP?

I personally look for RELP portfolios with income-producing properties, such as apartment buildings, office buildings, and shopping centers. I also prefer *no-load* deals, meaning the stock broker, financial planner, or other sales person does not take a commission on the sale of shares to you. There are not too many of these, but its worthwhile digging them out. If the sales agent makes 10 to 20 percent up front, that takes away from the profit potential of the partnership.

Administrative costs and real estate commissions are involved when a fully subscribed partnership, having collected the money it needs, goes out to buy properties. You can expect administrative fees and real estate commissions to be in the deal.

The big question is, how much? If it becomes too costly—more than 14 to 20 percent—then you should think seriously about not getting involved.

A Limited Partnership consists of the General Partner, who is manager, decision maker, or chief executive officer, plus the Limited Partners, who make up the rest of the investors.

Limited Partners have nothing to say about how the money is invested. But standard procedure calls for a RELP to distribute any income to limited partners first, before the general partners get any of the money.

Among the questions you want answered when you are approached to invest in a RELP are: When do you start distributing profits? How is the distribution made and how often?

You make money in two ways in a RELP: first, from the cash flow—rents and leases, usually—generated by the properties bought; and secondly, from the sale, several years down the road, of those properties. If your RELP has made good choices, those properties will appreciate nicely over the years, although you never can be sure. A number of RELPs have been stuck with properties in depressed markets, such as Houston or Dallas, whose value plummeted in the 1980s.

Let us assume your General Partner makes wise decisions and the properties are worth twice as much when they are sold five years later. How much do you get? If your investment amounts to 10 percent of the partnership, you get back 10 percent of the profit from the sale.

Along the way, a decent partnership should pay you 8 percent or more a year in income, starting in the first year after the plan is fully subscribed. A well-managed RELP can make lots of money for its investors. Standard Pacific, to name one, has delivered a 12.3 percent annual yield.

ARE RELPS STILL GOOD FOR YOUR TAX RETURN?

RELPS were considered terrific investments for wealthy physicians, attorneys, and other investors before 1986, because much of their income was sheltered. If you invested $10,000, you could subtract that amount or more from your taxes, so it cost you little to nothing to get involved. Taxable income from partnerships was regarded as capital gains and thus taxed at a lower rate than regular income.

Now, of course, some of those benefits are gone. Tax reform has forced syndicators to construct new partnerships with cash flow and appreciation, not tax shelters, in mind.

Still, partnerships can be excellent passive investments, because you can put your money in the hands of professionals who already have been winners in the real estate game, and because you are not taxed on anything until you get something out of your investment. Besides, as a passive investor, you don't have to worry about day-to-day management.

HOW TO READ A RELP PROSPECTUS

When you are presented with a partnership deal, ask for the prospectus. This description of the deal gives you most of the information you need to make an informed decision. If you don't understand the prospectus, ask your Certified Public Accountant to go through it with you.

Start by investigating the background and track record of General Partners. Who are they? How long have they been in business? For instance, in the Carlyle XVII, there are three and a half pages of small print devoted to the "Prior Performance of the General Partners and Affiliates." Among other things, you learn that since 1968, affiliates of the General Partners have sponsored 37 public RELPs and 67 nonpublic ones.

In almost numbing detail, the prospectus tells how those previous partnerships raised billions of dollars, how hundreds of properties were acquired, and how many of those properties were sold.

Further along, the prospectus provides a description of the people who will manage the partnership. I like groups that have been putting limited partnerships together for ten years or more.

What are their backgrounds? Read all about them in the prospectus. In this particular case, there are a chairman, a president, four executive vice presidents and thirty-nine additional vice presidents! If you are a prudent investor with a lot of time, you can read brief biographies of each. Incidentally, *Sylvia Porter's Personal Finance* magazine advises people to seek general partners with expertise in real estate itself, not just finance, and I agree.

Are they putting any of their own money into the deal? If not, are they putting in their time in a big way? Find out.

Second, check on the objectives of the partnership. For example, in Carlyle XVII, a very general answer can be found in the section of the overall summary that is labeled "Partnership Objectives":

To obtain: (i) capital appreciation; (ii) current cash distributions (expected to commence in the calendar quarter following the calendar quarter in which the offering terminates); and (iii) tax losses during the early years of operations from deductions generated by investments (which excess tax losses may generally be used by Holders of Interests, under present Federal income tax laws, to offset passive activity income from non–publicly traded partnerships).

As in every prospectus, there is ample warning that you might not make money on this investment:

The objective of capital appreciation, in particular, may not be achieved since it is predicated on certain assumptions as to the real estate market in general and the future values of particular properties which are not now ascertainable.

Why is this warning included? Because there is risk involved. (The people who write these documents are always very careful to cover their rear ends!)

Third, look for an indication of how highly or moderately leveraged the deals will be. In other words, what percentage will the partnership put as a down payment on each property, leaving what percentage to be borrowed?

In our Carlyle XVII example, the prospectus says in the summary that maximum leverage "will not exceed the sum of (i) 80%" and that "it is expected that it will be in a range of 60 to 70%." Diligent students who continue to read learn, forty pages later, further details about the borrowing and other financing of the partnership.

Fourth, look for the distribution of the money generated by the partnership. Pay particular attention to "compensation and fees." How much of the operating cash flow will be distributed to you and other limited partners? How much will the general partners keep for themselves?

By now, you are probably trying hard to keep your eyes open. Let's face it, the writers of limited partnership prospectuses won't give Stephen King any competition. These documents are not what you'd call page turners! But you and your CPA need this information to make intelligent decisions. (Indeed, considering how much King earns writing novels, I would not be surprised if his CPA has urged him to invest in RELPs!)

In a well-run partnership, at least 90 percent of the net cash flow is passed along to limited partners. So take into account how the partnership will divide money generated by sales or refinancing. Sometimes when a property becomes very valuable, a partnership refinances it in order to pull some money out for distribution to limited and general partners.

For example, let us assume a partnership owes $50,000 on a building worth $100,000. This building brings in enough rent to make payments on a bigger $85,000 mortgage, and it might be a good idea to get that bigger mortgage. Once the partners get this refinanced mortgage for $85,000, they have $35,000 to distribute to limited partners first, then the general partner.

The prospectus should say what percentage of sale or refinancing money will go to the limited partners, what percentage to general partners.

Another question the prospectus should answer is how often the general partners report back to you. The answer should be at least quarterly. Each year you should also get a summary, telling you how much various properties increased or decreased in value.

One final point: I am a firm believer in reading the "footnotes" in a prospectus, often relegated to the back pages. That's where you will find the balance sheets, estimates of taxable income or losses, and other interesting stuff. Continuing with Carlyle, there is a section buried on page 116 of the document that is headed as follows:

PRO FORMA ESTIMATE OF TAXABLE INCOME (LOSS) AND FUNDS GENERATED FROM BLUE CROSS BUILDING BEFORE ALLOCATION OF GENERAL AND ADMINISTRATIVE EXPENSES OF THE PART- NERSHIP.

Below the heading are the words: "For a Twelve-Month Period (Unaudited)." What follows is an impressive set of numbers suggesting an income of over $1 million from this building. However, above the numbers there is a paragraph that states, in part, ". . . These estimates do not purport to represent actual or expected operations of the investment property for any period in the future."

In other words, this "estimate" is just that—an *imaginary projection* of what might happen. It is not real.

Dear reader, when a RELP gives you numbers upon which to base your investment decision, look out for statements like these. They can be awfully easy to miss, especially when you are scanning the back pages.

Have your CPA look at the prospectus, too. Has the partnership hired a reputable accounting firm to offer an opinion on the tax advantages you will get on interest payments and especially depreciation? Make sure your accountant knows the answer. In addition, ask if you will be subject to any recapture (penalty or payback) due to the IRS in the future.

HOW MUCH DO YOU NEED
TO BUY INTO A RELP?

Public limited partnerships usually allow you to invest a minimum of $2,500. I suggest the beginning investor start with $5,000, provided your income and portfolio allow this amount.

Personally, I think no investor should have more than 20 percent of a real estate investment portfolio in RELPs. As I mentioned at the outset, this is a reasonably risky field.

Keep in mind, however, that at the end of the partnership, in anywhere from seven to twenty years, the properties will be sold. Provided they have gone up in value, you get all your money back, plus as much as 50 percent more. So eventually, you would get your $5,000 plus $2,500 in appreciation, on top of your yearly gains from operating cash flow.

MASTERS—THE AFFORDABLE RELP

Within the public partnership world, there is a special category called Master Limited Partnerships (MLPs). These are the most liquid, and the least expensive, to buy into. Shares are sold daily on public stock exchanges, just as if they were stocks. A typical minimum investment is about $300.

Some well-known examples are American Income Properties (ASE), Burger King Investors Master LP (NYSE), Equitable Real Estate Shopping Center (NYSE), Interstate General (ASE), Standard Pacific (NYSE), and Universal Development (NYSE).

I like MLPs best of all limited partnerships for the unsophisticated investor, since you can sell your shares easily if you need the money.

RESEARCH THE FIELD BEFORE YOU BUY

For more information on specific partnerships—either regular RELPs or MLPs—consult your broker, CPA, financial planner, or the pages of business publications. The *Wall Street Journal* has ads for partnerships.

A publication called *The Stanger Register* is the bible of RELPs. It rates the offerings of partnerships on a regular basis. You should be able to get copies of *The Stanger Register,* which sells for $245 per year, from your broker or financial planner. You can subscribe directly from the publisher, Robert A. Stanger & Co., P.O. Box 7490, Shrewsbury, NJ 07702-4314. Phone: (800) 631-2991 or (201) 389-3600 in New Jersey.

Another source for information is a newsletter called *The Real Estate Securities Review,* published by Barry Vinocur in San Rafael, California.

In addition, you might consult the best book on the subject, *How to Evaluate Real Estate Limited Partnerships,* by Robert A. Stanger and Keith D. Allaire. The Shrewsbury publishing company sells copies for $48.

What if a friend, relative, or business associate says, "I've got a tip on a good partnership?" You cannot lose anything by contacting the general partners. Ask for a prospectus and evaluate it with your CPA. Meanwhile, ask whoever gives you the tip if he gets a commission on a deal he recommends.

BUYING ON THE SECONDARY MARKET

Buying into an established partnership offers you the advantage of knowing which properties it has bought. A study by the *Wall Street Journal* indicates that since the secondary market is so small, and sellers are often distressed, you are likely to pay much less per unit than the original offering price.

A handful of firms are involved in the RELPS secondary market. It is worth a telephone call to find out what they offer. The firms include:

Chicago Partnership Board, Inc. (800) 272-6273
EquityLine Properties, Inc. (800) 327-9990 or (305) 662-4088
Equity Resources Group (617) 876-4800
Florida Income Centers (407) 740-8141
Investors Advantage Corp. (800) 331-9199. In Florida (800) 282-5865
Liquidity Fund Investment Corp. (800) 227-4688
MacKenzie Securities (800) 854-8357. In California (800) 821-4252.
National Partnership Exchange, Inc. (800) 356-2739. In Florida (800) 336-2739
Nationwide Partnership Marketplace (415) 456-8825
Oppenheimer & Bigelow Management, Inc. (800) 431-7811. In New York (212) 599-0697
Partnership Securities Exchange, Inc. (415) 763-5555
Raymond James & Associates, Inc. (800) 237-7591. In Florida (813) 381-3800
Realty Repurchase, Inc. (800) 233-7357. In California (800) 444-7357
Springhill Financial Services, Inc. (800) 255-3264. In California (818) 507-0975

SOME TAX BENEFITS REMAIN

In addition to income and appreciation, limited partnerships do offer you some tax write-offs. As a result of the 1986 Tax Act, however, write-offs passed through to you from partnerships you buy into can now only be deducted against income from other passive investments, not from active income such as salaries or earned fees. That is because a real estate limited partnership is itself a *passive investment,* defined by the IRS as one in which you make none of the decisions about tenants or management.

If you earn income on your limited partnership, but suffer losses on other investments (such as stocks, bonds, or mutual funds), you may be able to balance one against the other on your tax return. This is an area to be explored with your tax advisor.

Basically, you don't have to do much work with a RELP. That is why it is a passive investment. The general partners are putting in their own time and money as well as OPM—Other People's Money—namely yours and that of other investors. Since you are, in essence, investing in people who are supposed to know the field, it pays to learn all you can about them. After all, for the next seven to twenty years, your money will be at their mercy.

17 QUESTIONS TO ASK
BEFORE PUTTING MONEY IN A RELP

1. Who is/are the general partner(s) and how long have they been in business?
2. What other partnerships have they established? What do the performance records of those partnerships tell me?
3. Have they ever been involved in a RELP that failed?
4. What are the partnership's goals? Income? Appreciation? Both?
5. What type of real estate will the partnership invest in?
6. How highly leveraged will the new partnership be?
7. How often will I receive progress reports?
8. What kind of yield is expected annually, and how soon after I invest will I start getting checks?
9. Is there a guaranteed payback? How much?
10. How long will the partnership be in existence?
11. What are the RELP's administrative and acquisition costs? When are they paid?
12. What percentage of the money raised is actually used to purchase property?
13. How much of my investment is actually left over to go into real estate?
14. Who gets paid first and how?
15. Is there a market in which to sell these shares if I want to cash out?
16. What are the tax advantages to me?
17. Are there any tax disadvantages to me and if so, what are they?

19

Private Partnerships —For the Sophisticated and Strong-of-Heart Risk Taker

For the experienced investor, private partnerships can pay off handsomely. These can be deals to buy a single building or a variety of properties, involving as few as a handful of people. They are good investments for people who don't want to be, or don't have time to be, active developers, but who want to cash in on a developer's or syndicator's expertise.

People who put their money into private deals are ones who can afford to lose every cent of their investment. There are usually no guaranteed paybacks, so these deals pose much higher risks than the publicly traded limited partnerships discussed in the previous chapter.

Why, then, take a flier on a private partnership rather than a public one? Because there is a potential for much greater return on your money. Only those stouthearted, sophisticated investors with deep pockets, who can tolerate high risk in return for high rewards, should go into these deals. Some syndications require that investors show a net worth of $1 million or yearly income of $100,000 + before allowing you to buy in.

If you can afford to lose your investment in such a partnership, you can deduct it from your taxes. Right now, you could regain, in tax deductions, 28 to 32 cents of every dollar you lose.

Once upon a time, before tax reform, these partnerships were put together with tax loopholes in mind. Many people with high incomes were wooed as investors on the grounds that they could shelter income from taxation. The trouble was, the deals themselves did not necessarily make a whole lot of sense from an investment standpoint, since they were structured primarily for tax purposes. Now, the emphasis is on generating dollars for deals that work.

Here, however, there are no government regulations, and there is no public authority to turn to for help if you are ripped off.

BETTING ON THE PROS

What you are betting on, most of all, is the expertise of the people who will make the deal happen—whether it involves an apartment house, an office building, a mobile home park, a condominium development, a shopping center, or anything else.

Again, let me emphasize that this is a high risk-high return game. If the deal fails, you lose, period. If you win, you can make a great deal of money. Tax consequences still loom large in this game, although you benefit from laws that shield private partnerships from double taxation: When a private partnership is formed by a group of people, the partnership, and the deal itself, is *not* taxed. All the income, plus all the deductions involved, flow through the partnership to the individual partners, who *are* taxed.

Thus, a private deal has an advantage over a regular "C" corporation, which does pay corporate taxes. Before you receive income from a corporate deal, the corporation is taxed on the profits and then you are taxed personally a second time. Private partnerships avoid the first layer of taxation. The exception to the double taxation corporate problem is the "S" corporation.

If a private deal shows a net loss, partners can use that loss to offset income from other sources. If there is a profit, you pay taxes just once, on your personal gain.

Syndicators have considerable freedom in structuring a private partnership. To use an extreme example, they have absolutely no obligation to make money with the money you give them, or to give the money back.

What if they blow the deal? That's too bad. Some private deal-making partners are willing to sign a personal note to guarantee the deal, but they are few and far between.

PURE PRIVATE PARTNERSHIPS
VERSUS "REGULATION D" DEALS

At the end of this chapter is an example of a *pure private partnership*, which is simply a group of people who get together to do a deal. Others might be more complicated, namely those offered under exemptions that I refer to as *transitional limited partnerships*.

One version of the transitional limited partnership is often called a *Regulation D*. The general partners file with the SEC and receive an exemption from registering the offering. Or they get a letter from an attorney stating that this deal is exempt. This exemption gives you more legal protection than the pure private, unregistered, nonexempt partnership.

A Regulation D might look like a security, but it is not. Instead, it is regulated by "blue sky" laws of various states. If you don't get a detailed prospectus, ask your state attorney general's office if the deal you are considering is exempt from state or federal laws.

There are several reasons for structuring deals as private, rather than public, partnerships. The major reason is that it can take as long as two years to go through all of the registration requirements in a public offering. A private deal can be done almost immediately.

If the deal is small—less than $1 million—most smart deal makers can bring in high rollers as limited partners, who contribute $50,000 to $100,000. Then the general partners don't have to go through the enormous prestart-up expenses of putting together a public partnership.

A private deal might cost the deal makers $25,000 in start-up costs and legal fees, compared to $200,000 to $300,000 needed in the organization of a public one.

Sometimes a deal is a real gamble on long odds—like betting $100 on a 20-to-1 shot at the race track. Such deals won't meet the requirements of a registered public offering. They are typical of the private partnership.

To be fair, many savvy, rich deal makers—the Donald Trumps and Bill Zeckendorfs of the world—got their start by putting together long shot private limited partnerships. They worked very hard to make them pay off, and they made millions of dollars for their investors in the process. Many of their investors were millionaires to begin with, however.

HOW DO PRIVATE PARTNERSHIPS PAY INVESTORS?

Syndicators typically set up compensation systems to pay off limited partners first, while still building in a bonus for the person who gets the deal off the ground.

As a limited partner, you receive a distribution of the money in proportion to your share of the investment. That means if the partnership makes $100,000 one year, and you own 20 percent of it, you get $20,000 worth of the income. This structure can be changed to give you a larger or smaller percentage of the profit. For instance, in some private deals, limited partners may receive all of the cash flow until they have been paid a certain return—8 percent, say—on their investment. This is quite a common arrangement, and a useful one for bringing in wary investors.

In such a case, the general partner who puts the deal together says, "I guarantee that you people will receive all the money that comes in until it amounts to an 8 percent return on your investment." Let us assume you decide to put in $10,000. The first $800 earned via the deal is yours. Only after you are paid does the general partner take his or her cut.

In effect, the IRS says that any private deal you make is okay, provided it is not lopsided in favor of one party. It also has to have what the IRS calls "substantial economic effect." In other words, it must make economic sense, rather than exist solely for tax reasons.

WELCOME TO THE "BREEZEWAY BUILDING" PARTNERSHIP

Let us examine one specific limited partnership.

In this example, the deal is real; only the name and some details have been changed for reasons of privacy. The "Breezeway Building Partnership" is a plan to buy a rental apartment building to be converted into condominiums and then sold to the public one apartment at a time.

The sample documents for this deal, shown at the end of the chapter, are sometimes known as "deal memos" or "partnership agreements." What follows is a relatively brief outline of the proposal:

I will go through the highlights with you. Much of it is *boilerplate*— standard language for such documents. I will tell you what is wrong with various items in the deal, however.

The first document, the Certificate, states that the location of this partnership will be 2100 North Bayshore Drive, Miami. As item 2 states, its business will be to deal in real and personal property in various ways.

In item 4 are the names and addresses of each general partner: John Dollar, Carol Cruz, Harold Bigbucks, and Jane Doe ReMe.

Item 5 refers to the term of the partnership. It begins on the date of the filing of the certificate with the County Clerk of Dade County, Florida.

In item 6, we learn that each general partner will contribute $25,000.

CAUTION SIGN 1! Take special note of item 7. In a typical deal, this item is a major caution sign. Notice that at any point, the other 3 partners could come to you for additional money, with no limit on the amount. This is where people get hurt in partnerships. It is known in real estate circles as the "call" provision.

CAUTION SIGN 2! Item 8, return of contributions, is written in typical partnership language and is much too general. It could lead to problems for a limited partner, since the option to give money to the limited partner is at the mercy of the general partners.

CAUTION SIGN 3! Item 9 deals with the share of profits. At the end of the item, notice that you are totally exposed to the losses of the partnership.

CAUTION SIGN 4! Item 10, the assignment of the partnership interests, is too limiting. If you wish to get out of the deal, this kind of wording makes it awfully difficult to sell your interest to someone else. The normal requirement enables you to assign your interest to someone else, so long as that party is financially able to continue your obligations under the partnership.

CAUTION SIGN 5! In item 11, if additional limited partners are brought in, and you are outvoted by the other 3 general partners, your interest in the property could be diluted.

So much for the "Certificate." Let us now look at the Agreement itself, which, as I mentioned above, is also at the end of this chapter. Most of it is self-explanatory.

WHAT AM I GETTING MYSELF INTO WITH BREEZEWAY?

The contents of a private limited partnership agreement should explain what your group is investing in, where its principal office is, the residence address of the partners, the money involved, and so on.

Normally, there would be a statement called "Schedule C" attached to the papers you receive. It would show a pro forma income and expense statement for the property. So let us assume that such a statement reads as follows:

Pro Forma Income and Expenses
Income

Sale of Condos	2,000,000

Expenses

Purchase Price	500,000
Legal and renovation costs	50,000

Cost of sales commissions, interest, advertising,
and administration   400,000
                            Total costs before taxes   950,000
                            Gross profit before taxes   1,050,000

In other words, the Breezeway Building would cost $500,000, with a down payment of $50,000. The mortgage, therefore, would be $450,000.

The partnership will pay $50,000 in legal, title, and mortgage expenses, plus renovations. This makes the total cost $500,000.

In the Breezeway agreement, item 7, capital contributions, refers to the amount of money each partner puts in. We already know from the Certificate that each contributor is investing $25,000 for a total of $100,000.

The Breezeway partners expect to sell the 40 units in the building as condominiums at $50,000 each. That would bring in a total gross sales revenue of $2 million.

Subtract a sales cost of 20 percent, or $400,000, and the revenue becomes $1.6 million. Now subtract $100,000 purchase and start-up cost and the $450,000 balance on the first mortgage, and the partnership is left with a before-tax profit of $1,050,000.

A MATTER OF FAITH, FRIENDSHIP
. . . AND NUMBERS

Not surprisingly, most investors do not take the time to read a private partnership agreement or memorandum. They tend to put their money into a deal based on trust and friendship with the general partner or deal maker. That is permissible, provided your CPA reviews the memo from the numbers standpoint, and provided your attorney also reviews it in terms of your legal obligations and liability. So long as you go into the deal with your eyes open . . . and with your advisor's okay . . . you do not always need to read every word of a prospectus.

Whether or not you enter into a private joint venture may depend on your personal tax situation. Discuss it with your CPA. Ask your CPA how the passive loss rules affect you, since income earned by limited partners from these deals is considered passive.

The general rule is that if you earn less than $100,000, you can adjust your gross income downwards, by as much as $25,000, from the losses of this kind of investment. If you carry forward unused passive losses, you can offset them with passive gains earned from new partnerships and joint ventures.

An extra word of warning: If you are buying an income-producing partnership, look closely at the unused passive losses that you expect to use to offset passive income. Be sure that the unused losses have not expired.

In some cases, time may have run out, the partnership may have been liquidated, or it may have turned around and become profitable. In such cases, there are no longer any unused losses. You need to ask how many years are left for you personally in unused losses.

Lastly, always watch out for the biggest, most surprising villain of all—"recapture." This refers to paying back to the government money that you deducted from your income tax for depreciation. Ask your tax advisor to protect you against recapture on all your real estate–related investments whereby you have been taking advantage of depreciation.

PHANTOM OF THE INCOME

Private limited partnerships can be good investments for those who hold shares of other partnerships.

For example, some existing deals in which you already have invested may be producing *phantom* income, or losses created by such things as depreciation. Although you don't receive any money, if you do have phantom income or losses, you may be able to use passive income or losses from your new investment to offset them.

A REWARD FOR LEADERSHIP

The general partner in a private deal, as in a public one, is the leader, the quarterback, the organizer. This person can be held personally liable for debts incurred by the partnership. But the general partner also stands to reap the biggest profits if the venture is successful. From a tax standpoint, this person's profits are active, not passive.

In many cases, the general partner receives an additional incentive fee of 10 percent or more from the profits, after all the other partners have received their share. This encourages the general partner to perform to his or her fullest capabilities. If you read through the Breezeway agreement, you will see that the General Partners get 10 percent of gross sales.

As a limited partner, you are not allowed to participate in managing the partnership. The flip side is that you can be held liable for debts only up to the amount of money that you invest.

In many private deals such as the one we have described in this chapter, all the partners are general partners. This means that you have liability for the whole deal. These kinds are the riskiest of the risky.

HOW TO LEARN MORE

"I've got money to risk on these deals and I've got a broad comfort zone that allows me to live with that risk. How do I learn about these private placements?" Is that what your inner voice says after reading this?

Usually the deals come to you via friends, business associates, and relatives. Once you begin investing, you can be sure you will be approached. As a start, ask your financial advisor (if you are thinking about this kind of investment, you undoubtedly have such an advisor) or your CPA. Then talk to your stockbroker, to developers you might know, to real estate brokers, life insurance agents and other professionals.

You can also look in the classified ads under "money wanted" or "business opportunities." You will also come across the names of deal makers in stories in such publications as the *Wall Street Journal, Barron's* and *Business Week.*

SAMPLE CERTIFICATE OF LIMITED PARTNERSHIP: THE BREEZEWAY BUILDING

The undersigned, desiring to form a Limited Partnership under the laws of the State of Florida, do hereby certify as follows:

1. NAME: The name of this Partnership shall be Breezeway Building Partnership.

2. CHARACTER OF BUSINESS: The character of the business of the Partnership shall be to own, build upon, alter, repair, rent, mortgage, borrow, sell, and otherwise deal with real and personal property of any kind or description and to engage in such other activities as may be necessary or desirable in furtherance of the business of the Partnership.

3. LOCATION OF PRINCIPAL PLACE OF BUSINESS: The prin-

cipal office of the Partnership shall be at 2100 North Bayshore Drive, Miami.

4. THE NAME AND ADDRESS OF EACH GENERAL PARTNER: The name and place of residence of each member, General Partners being respectively designated are:

John Dollar, 52 Money Road, Miami
Carol Cruz, 8576 Wealth Avenue, Coconut Grove
Harold Bigbucks, 1 Gold Avenue, Atlanta
Jane Doe ReMe, Palatial Estates, Key Biscayne

5. *TERM OF EXISTENCE:* The term of the Partnership shall commence as of the effective date of the filing of this Certificate with the County Clerk of Dade County, Florida, and publication of notice thereof as required by law, and will continue indefinitely unless sooner terminated as provided in the Limited Partnership Agreement.

6. *CONTRIBUTIONS:* The amount of cash and/or description of the agreed value of property contributed by each General Partner is as follows: Twenty-Five Thousand ($25,000.00) Dollars each.

7. *ADDITIONAL CONTRIBUTIONS:* In the event the General Partners decide that additional capital is required for the needs of the Partnership, the additional capital may be contributed by the existing Limited Partners or new Limited Partners.

8. *RETURN OF CONTRIBUTIONS:* At the option of the General Partners or within a reasonable time after the Partnership's dissolution, any reasoning proceeds from the Partnership activity will be distributed to the Limited Partners on a pro rata basis.

9. *SHARE OF PROFITS:* The net profit of the partnership shall be divided among the PARTNERS and the net losses of the Partnership shall be borne by the PARTNERS pro rata, in the respective percentages of their capital contributions.

10. *ASSIGNMENT OF PARTNERSHIP INTERESTS:* A Limited Partner may not assign his interest without the consent of the General Partner and, if such consent is given, it is not to be effective to substitute the assignee as a Limited Partner unless and until the assignee agrees to become a Limited Partner, and be bound by the terms and conditions of the Limited Partnership Agreement and until the assignee agrees to become a Limited Partner, and be bound by the terms and conditions of the Limited Partnership Agreement and meets other requirements of the General Partner as more fully set forth in the Limited Partnership Agreement.

11. *ADDITIONAL LIMITED PARTNERS:* Additional Limited Partners may be admitted to the Partnership with the consent of the General Partner upon conditions set forth in the Limited Partnership Agreement.

12. *NO RIGHT OF PRIORITY AMONG LIMITED PARTNERS:* There is no right of any Limited Partner to priority over any other Limited Partner as to contributions, income, or otherwise.

13. *RIGHT TO CONTINUE BUSINESS:* There is a right given to the remaining Partners to continue the business of the Partnership as set forth in the Limited Partnership Agreement, on the death, retirement, or insanity of a General Partner.

14. *NO RIGHT TO PROPERTY OTHER THAN CASH:* There is no right given to any Limited Partner to demand and receive property other than cash in return for his contribution.

Signed:

GENERAL PARTNERS: **LIMITED PARTNERS:**

_____   _____

_____   _____

_____

_____

_____

SAMPLE LIMITED PARTNERSHIP AGREEMENT

1. <u>THE BREEZEWAY BUILDING</u>

2. <u>Characters of Business:</u> The Partnership is formed for the purpose of the following:

The Partnership is formed for the purpose of owning, building upon, altering, repairing, renting, mortgaging, borrowing, selling, and otherwise dealing with real and personal property of any kind or description.

3. <u>Principal Office:</u> The principal office of the Partnership shall be located at 2100 North Bayshore Drive, Miami.

4. <u>Certificate of Limited Partnership:</u> Said certificate is to be filed in the office of the Clerk of the County in which the principal place of business of the Partnership is situated, and a certified copy of said certificate is to be filed with the office of the recorder of every county where the real property of the Partnership is situated.

5. <u>Residence Address of Partners:</u> The residence addresses of the Limited Partners are set forth in Schedule ''B'' of this Agreement.

6. <u>Term:</u> The Partnership shall begin as of the date of this Agreement and shall continue until terminated as herein provided.

7. <u>Capital Contributions:</u>

(a) The capital of the Partnership shall consist of the amount shown on Schedule ''C'' of this Agreement. The capital contributions of each of the Limited Partners shall consist of the capital invested by each Limited Partner in the aforementioned Schedule ''C''. An individual capital account by unanimous consent of the general and limited partners, respectively, shall transfer and convey to the Partnership the amount described in Schedule ''C'' of this Agreement. The executed counterpart of this Agreement shall constitute a notice of receipt of the capital contribution.

(b) No original capital contribution shall be made by the General Partners listed in Schedule ''A'' of the Agreement, unless they also be Limited Partners, and then those monies contributed shall be treated as Limited Partner contributions, and for those purposes alone the General Partner shall also be listed in schedules ''B'' and ''C'' of this Agreement, and in no way shall the rights of General Partners be diminished.

8. <u>Excess Capital Contribution and Additional Capital Contribution:</u>

(a) Excess Capital Contribution—In the event that the General Partners determine the requirements of the Partnership are such that the capital contribution of the Limited Partners is more than such needs, such excess shall be distributed on the same basis as distributions, as hereinafter provided in Section 23 of this Agreement.

(b) Additional Capital Contribution—After the Limited Partners have made their original capital contribution as described in Schedule ''C'' of this Agreement, in the event the General Partners decide that additional capital is required for the needs of the Partnership, the additional capital may be contributed by the existing Limited Partners first, and if insufficient capital has been raised after such notification to the Limited Partners, then as the General Partners direct, including, but not limited to, the admission of new Limited Partners.

9. Profits and Losses: The net profit or loss of the partnership shall be divided among the PARTNERS and the net losses of the Partnership shall be borne by the PARTNERS pro rata, in the respective percentages of their capital contributions, as noted in schedule "C" of this Agreement and in accordance to Section 23 of this Agreement.

For the purpose of this Agreement in determining the share of partnership net profits to which each Partner shall be entitled, the partnership profits shall be determined without taking into account any deduction for depreciation.

For income tax purposes all depreciation deductions shall be allocated among the Partner in proportion to their dollar cash capital contributions.

In the event that there shall be any loss after exhausting the capital account of the Partners, there shall be no further liability being limited to their contributed capital only.

The General Partners shall not be liable for the distribution or return of the Limited Partners' capital contributions, or portion thereof. Any such distribution or return of the Limited Partners' capital contributions shall be made from the Partnership's assets.

10. Distributions of Net Cash Flow: There shall be no regular or monthly cash distributions from the funds of the Partnership to the Partners. All distributions will be made to the Partners as herein provided in section 23 of this Agreement, except that regular distributions for the payment of current Partnership obligations and operating expenses, including debt services, taxes, escrow payments, fees, legal, management, operating accounting, and insurance expenses, as well as secretarial, bookkeeping and telephone expenses, subject to retaining sufficient working capital consistent with good fiscal operating policy and management, shall be made.

11. Additional Partners: Except as otherwise provided in paragraph 8(b) of this Agreement, there shall be no right to admit an additional General or Limited Partner, and no such additional Partner shall be admitted without the written consent of all other Partners at the time of such admission.

12. Return of Contribution in Kind: The Limited Partners shall have no right to demand or receive Partnership assets other than cash in return for their contribution except as determined by the General Partner.

13. Powers of General Partner: The General Partners shall have the exclusive control over the business of the Partnership, including but not limited

to, the power to assign duties, to sign all contracts, to assume direction of business operations, full power to purchase, sell, and convey personal and real property on such terms as they may determine, to lease such property or any part thereof on such terms and for such period as they may determine, to borrow money on behalf of the Partnership, and to mortgage personal and real property, whether such mortgage be a first or subordinate mortgage lien, as well as to make any agreement modifying any contract, lease, note or mortgage.

No General Partner shall receive any salary or renumeration for services rendered to the Partnership except as provided in this Agreement.

If there be more than one General Partner, then a unanimity of the General Partners on any such question (excepting, and not including, the determination of the interest or share of any Limited Partner in the capital net profits, or net losses of the Partnership, or the claims of any Partner against the Partnership, or its claims against such Partner) shall be binding on all Partners.

Each General Partner may have other interests and may engage in any business or trade, profession, or employment whatsoever, whether such business, trade, profession, or "exclusive agreement" to sell Partnership assets.

The General Partners may employ mortgage brokers in order to obtain financing sufficient to accomplish the purposes of the Partnership and to pay the origination fee.

The fact that the General Partner, a stockholder or employee thereof, or that a Partner, General or Limited, or any party directly or indirectly interested in or connected with either that corporation or individuals is employed by the Partnership to render or perform a service or that any of the above parties do sell or lease any real or personal property to the Partnership shall not prohibit a General Partner from executing any agreement with or employing such person or firm or otherwise from dealing with him or it and neither the Partnership nor the other Partners as such shall have any rights in or to any income or profits derived therefrom.

Notwithstanding any of the foregoing, in no event shall the General Partner:

(a) Do any act in contravention of the Certificate of Limited Partnership which is to be filed pursuant to the FCA Partnership Law, or any provision of this Agreement;

(b) Do any act which at the time done, is intentionally detrimental to the best interests of the Partnership or which would make it impossible to carry on the ordinary business of the Partnership;

(c) Confess a judgment against the Partnership exceeding one thousand five hundred dollars ($1,500.00) without prior approval of a majority of the Limited Partners, such majority based upon the value of the contributions noted in Schedule "C" of this Agreement.

14. <u>Powers of the Limited Partners</u>: A majority of the Limited Partners may elect to terminate the Partnership upon the occurrence of any of the following:

(a) A General Partner has acted in contravention of the Partnership Law of Florida or in the Certificate of Limited Partnership;

(b) A General Partner has acted in a manner that would make it impossible to carry on the ordinary business of the Partnership;

(c) A General Partner has confessed a judgment against the Partnership exceeding one thousand five hundred dollars ($1,500.00) without prior approval of the Limited Partners;

(d) A General Partner has possession of Partnership property or has assigned rights in specific Partnership property, for other than Partnership purposes;

(e) A General Partner has misapplied money or property of a third person received in his capacity as General Partner;

(f) There has been filed a voluntary or involuntary petition in bankruptcy by or against a General Partner;

(g) There has been an adjudication of insanity or incompetency of a General Partner in a judicial proceeding or a commitment of a General Partner to a mental institution;

(h) There has been a charging order issued against the interest of a General Partner without the removal thereof within six months;

(i) A General Partner has been convicted of a felony;

(j) A General Partner is unable for a continuous period of six (6) months to perform his partnership obligations; and,

(k) A General Partner has done an act which at the time done is intentionally detrimental to the Partnership.

However, none of the abovementioned occurrences shall be so construed so as to permit the Limited Partners to terminate the Partnership, or in any way hold a General Partner liable, upon the unintentional omission of some act, such omission detrimental to the Partnership.

15. <u>Advances</u>: A General Partner may advance money to the Partnership. The amount of any such advance shall not constitute a capital or entitle a General Partner to any increase in his share of the profits or distributions

of the Partnership, but the amount of any such advance, unless such advance is specifically denoted otherwise pursuant to Section 7(b) of this Agreement, shall be a debt of the Partnership to such partner, and, unless otherwise provided and agreed, shall be repaid with interest at a rate not usurious, except that such advance shall be payable or collectible only out of the Partnership assets.

16. Working Capital: In addition to any funds contributed by the Limited Partners to the Partnership pursuant to the provisions of Section 7, working capital for the Partnership may be obtained in the name of, and on behalf of, the Partnership from banks or other lenders, upon such terms and conditions (including the encumbrance of part or all the property) as are satisfactory to and approved by the General Partners. If working capital or other funds are loaned to the Partnership, any interest payable on such loans shall be deducted from the net income of the Partnership as an expense in determining the Partners' distributive shares of net profits or losses, in accordance with Section 9 hereof.

17. Salaries: No salary shall be paid to any Partner by the Partnership. However, the General Partners shall be entitled to receive reimbursement from the Partnership for reasonable expenses evidenced by proper receipts incurred by him or her on behalf of the Partnership, and such reimbursement shall be considered an expense of the Partnership for the purpose of determining profit or loss of the Partnership in accordance with Section 9 hereof. In addition the General Partner shall receive 10% of the gross sales of the units in the building.

18. Books of Account and Records: The Partnership's books and records and the Certificate of Limited Partnership shall be maintained at the principal office of the Partnership, and each Partner shall have access thereto at reasonable hours. The books and records shall be kept in accordance with sound accounting principles and practice, applied in a consistent manner by the Partnership, and shall reflect all Partnership transactions and be appropriate and adequate for the Partnership's business. Further, within a reasonable period after the close of each year, a report shall be transmitted to each Partner indicating his or its share of the Partnership profit and/or loss for such year for federal income and Florida franchise or income tax purposes and his or its share of any other item of income, gain, loss, deduction, or credit of the Partnership required to be set forth separately by federal or Florida laws.

19. Prohibition Against Transfer or Assignment:

    (a) Without the approval of the General Partners, no Partner, whether

General or Limited, shall have the right to sell, to make any assignment— including an assignment for the benefit of his or its creditors or a transfer to a trustee—or receive for the benefit of his or its creditors, to give away, to pledge, to hypothecate, or otherwise to dispose of his or its interest in the Partnership, nor shall such Partner have the right to enter into any agreement as a result of which any person or entity will or could obtain any interest in the Partnership.

(b) Notwithstanding the foregoing, the Partners may assign the right to their share of the income of the Partnership, provided, that the assignee shall not by reason thereof become a partner of this Partnership, nor shall the assignee have any rights given to a Partner in this Agreement.

20. <u>Withdrawal of a Partner</u>: No transfer of partial interest of Partners shall be permitted, except as provided in Section 19(b) of this Agreement; however, should a Partner desire to sell or otherwise transfer all of his Partnership interest, he shall first offer the sale to the other Partners by giving written notice to them by registered mail. The amount of the purchase price to be paid to the Withdrawing Partner shall be based upon the market value of the Withdrawing Partner's interest in the assets, less the liabilities of the Partnership as of the date of such written notice. The Non–Withdrawing Partners shall have the right to purchase all of the Partnership interest of the Withdrawing Partner and shall elect to do so by notifying the withdrawing Partner in writing by registered mail on or before the 15th day following receipt by the Non–Withdrawing Partners of the Withdrawing Partner's offer, and by designating the name of the appraiser to appraise the value of the interest of the Withdrawing Partner, as hereinafter provided.

Within ten (10) days after receipt of said notice, the Withdrawing Partner shall notify the Non–Withdrawing Partner—desiring to purchase its interest—of the name of the appraiser selected by the Withdrawing Partner to appraise its interest in the Partnership and the appraisers selected by the parties shall in turn appoint a third appraiser, and the three appraisers shall determine the market value of the Withdrawing Partner's interest in the Partnership. If the appraisers shall be unable to agree upon a valuation, their valuations shall be totaled and divided by three, and the resulting appraisal shall be the valuation of the interest of the Withdrawing Partner.

If one of the parties fails to select an appraiser within the time provided, the appraiser appointed by the other party shall make the appraisal that shall be the valuation of the interest of the Withdrawing Partner.

The Non–Withdrawing Partner shall pay the purchase price, and the parties shall execute and deliver all documents required to convey the interest of the Withdrawing Partner within fifteen (15) days after the appraisers have rendered their report. The parties shall bear equally the cost of appraisers, even if one party did not select an appraiser.

If the Non–Withdrawing Partners do not exercise their option to purchase, the Withdrawing Partner shall then be free to sell its Partnership interest to an outsider.

Notwithstanding any provision of this Section, the withdrawal of capital contributions shall be prohibited, except as noted in Section 7(a) of this Agreement.

21. Banking: All funds of the Partnership shall be deposited in the name of the Partnership in such bank account or accounts as shall be determined by the General Partners. All withdrawals therefrom shall be made upon checks signed by _____ .

22. Termination and Dissolution of Partnership:

(a) It shall terminate upon the sale of all of the Partnership property;

(b) It shall terminate at the election of the Limited Partners as provided in Section 12 herein.

23. Distribution of Monies: At the option of the General Partners or within a reasonable time after the Partnership's dissolution, the proceeds from Partnership activity will be distributed in accordance with the following order of priority and on a pro rata basis, if applicable, within each class:

(a) The Liabilities and obligations of the Partnership to creditors shall be paid;

(b) Any outstanding loans or advances that shall have been made to the Partnership by one or more of the Partners shall be repaid;

(c) There shall be distributed to the Limited Partners the balance of any contribution made to the Partnership;

(d) There shall be distributed to the General Partners of the proceeds, if any, 10% of the gross sales;

(e) The remaining amounts shall be distributed to the Limited Partners in proportion to their respective interests in the Partnership.

24. Notice: Notice given pursuant to this Agreement must be served personally on the General Partners or may be mailed registered, postage prepaid, return receipt requested addressed to the General Partner to be notified at the address set forth in Section 5 of this Agreement.

25. Successors and Assigns: The provisions of this Agreement, including rights of approval, shall be binding upon and shall inure to the benefit of

the personal representatives, heirs successors, and assigns of all of the parties executing this Agreement; provided, however, that nothing herein contained shall be construed in any way modifying any other provision of this Agreement.

26. Amendment: The Certificate of Limited Partnership of this Partnership shall be amended whenever required by law, and each such amendment shall be recorded.

27. Counterparts: This Agreement may be executed in several counterparts, each of which shall be deemed an original, and said counterparts shall constitute but one and the same instrument, which may be sufficiently evidenced by one counterpart.

28. Headings: The title or section headings of the various provisions hereof are intended solely for convenience or reference and shall not be deemed or construed to explain, modify or place any construction upon any of said provisions.

IN WITNESS WHEREOF, the parties hereto have hereunto set their names, all as of the day and year first written above.

GENERAL PARTNERS: _____

_____

_____

_____

LIMITED PARTNERS: _____

_____

_____

_____

Note: Never sign an agreement such as this until you have reviewed it with your attorney. I wanted you to read this one so you could familiarize yourself with a typical agreement.

20

Making Money Despite Current Tax Laws

Tax reform has created new opportunities—and wiped out some old ones—in real estate investing. An expert on real estate tax regulations, my friend and CPA Paul Kamke, has prepared a series of case studies, showing how you can benefit most from the new tax laws.

As I repeat over and over to real estate investors, a strong team of professionals is a must for anyone seriously interested in making money in this field. On my team, Paul is the accountant whose broad knowledge of accounting procedures, as well as current expertise on tax law, makes him invaluable.

I know that the examples below look like an advanced course in real estate math, but after reading this far, you are educated enough to understand these numbers. Take a few moments to scrutinize these portfolios, and discuss with your own CPA the one that relates most closely to your situation. This exercise will help you to determine how to come out ahead of the tax man, and make the most profit available from safe real estate investing.

ACTIVE, PORTFOLIO, AND PASSIVE INCOME

Under rules set by the 1986 tax act and the 1987 and 1988 revisions, you must assign income each year to one of three categories: active, portfolio, or passive:

1. Active income: This is the money you make from salary or fees in a trade or business. You actively participate in this income.

2. Portfolio income: This is derived from interest, dividends, and security transactions.

3. Passive income: This is produced from any business in which you do not materially participate. Income from rental real estate is also considered passive income. (Income from real estate is active when you are involved in real estate full time and real estate is your trade or business.)

The passive income rules were designed to reduce the ability of taxpayers to offset income from one activity with losses from another. Congress decided that too many investors took unfair advantage of "tax shelters" in real estate and other fields.

Under the new statutes, in most cases, a loss from a passive activity, such as a RELP, may only be used to offset income from some other passive activity. Those losses cannot be used to offset income from salary, stocks and bonds, or any other active or portfolio income source.

Losses that cannot be used in one year, however, can be carried over to future years, when you do earn passive income. Once you sell the RELP or other passive holding, all unused losses associated with that holding may be deducted.

DEDUCTING LOSSES FROM RENTAL INCOME

It still pays to be an active investor in rental property, first because you can reap handsome profits, and second because should you have losses, they may be fully deductible.

The tax rules allow you to offset up to $25,000 each year in active or portfolio income with passive real estate losses, if your adjusted gross income is less than $100,000. The write-off is reduced $1 for each $2 earned over $100,000 up to $150,000. No deduction is allowed for investors whose earnings are above the $150,000 ceiling.

To ensure that you get all the tax benefits you are entitled to, you must keep good, clear records. Start by making sure you can prove you are involved in management decisions to qualify for the active management provision. This means:

1. Approve new tenants in writing.
2. Determine rental terms.
3. Approve all capital repairs and improvements in writing.
4. Maintain files that contain supporting documentation.

Overall, in most cases, you will still be able to shelter your income from taxes each year through your real estate activities. While it's true that losses won't reduce your taxes as much now as before 1986 (since only $25,000 is deductible), real estate investors are way ahead of the game, compared to investors in other kinds of shelters.

BE A CAREFUL RECORD KEEPER

Tax benefits mean nothing if you don't know how to save the proper documentation to support your deductions. As you might have guessed, the key is to have everything in writing.

A few tips on paperwork:

- Save all receipts that you think might be deductible. Many people have more deductions than they think. Hold on to these receipts after you file your returns. The IRS says they must be maintained for 3 years after the due date of the tax return or the date the return was filed, whichever is later.

You are also required to save documents supporting the purchase or improvement of property until the property's disposition.

- Keep a yearly calendar book, detailing your investment activity. Don't forget that travel related to maintaining your investment property is deductible, too.

- Maintain a separate checkbook to be used solely for your rental properties. This makes compiling your real estate transaction activity for tax preparation much simpler, and segregates your investment from personal activities, should you find yourself being audited.

- Finally, don't walk over dollars to pick up pennies. Tax matters are complicated, so consult closely with a good CPA or tax advisor.

JOHN ROSS: INVESTOR WITH ONE RENTAL PROPERTY

Let's start with a single taxpayer, John Ross, who earns $26,000 at his job. Through interest and dividends, his adjusted gross income (AGI) goes up to $27,100. This places him in the 28 percent tax bracket.

Mr. Ross bought a rental property in 1987 and actively participates in managing it. The property produces a taxable loss of $6,000 for the year. With an AGI less than $100,000, all of this loss can be used to offset Mr. Ross's other income. This saves him $1,680 on his current taxes ($6,000 × 28 %).

Here is a look at the details on the rental property:

Rent received:		$13,000
Expenses:		
Utilities	$ 1,100	
Property taxes	2,355	
Telephone	115	

Supplies	375
Mortgage interest	10,550
Depreciation	4,505
Total expenses:	19,000
NET LOSS:	($6,000)

Notice the $4,505 of the loss is the result of depreciation. This deduction does not represent an actual out-of-pocket cost but a paper one. Subtract it from expenses, and it appears that Mr. Ross is only experiencing a negative cash flow of $1,495. Right?

Not quite. His negative cash flow is even less because he is saving $1,680 in taxes during the year, while he must also pay $1,250 annually in mortgage principal payments. Thus, his actual cash loss is a minimal $1,065. ($1,495 − $1,680 + $1,250 = $1,065.)

THE BURTONS: TWO RENTAL PROPERTIES

Now let's look at a couple, Helen and Mark Burton. They both work and have an AGI of $93,000. They are active participants in two rental properties, which they bought in August, 1986.

The properties produced the following results for the year: Property A showed a profit of $8,150, while Property B resulted in a loss of $27,400.

What does this do to the Burtons' tax liability for the current year?

First, they must net the profit and loss of the rentals to see how much is deductible. The result is a loss of $19,250 ($27,400 − $8,150).

Since this amount is less than $25,000, and the Burton's AGI is less than $100,000, the loss is fully deductible.

Mr. and Mrs. Burton are members of a sector of taxpayers in the 33 percent tax bracket. Therefore, they benefit from losses slightly more than John Ross.

For the current year, the Burtons' tax savings are $6,353 ($19,250 × 33%). Again, however, depreciation accounts for a major portion— $16,464—off their loss. Their mortgage principal payments for the year are $3,201. So the Burtons actually have an after-tax positive cash flow of $366.

Here are the details:

Real Estate loss:	($19,250)
Add depreciation deductions	$ 16,464
Add tax savings	6,353
Then subtract mortgage principal	(3,201)

For a total of	<u>19,616</u>
And the after-tax positive cash flow is	$ 366

THE FOSTERS: EIGHT RENTAL PROPERTIES

Now let's look at a couple more heavily involved in rental properties. Paul and Gail Foster started investing in real estate in 1979. They have acquired eight properties since then. Before tax reform, their rental properties generated enough losses to offset much of their other income, thus significantly reducing the taxes they had to pay each year. With tax reform, that has changed.

In 1988, the Fosters had an income from other sources of $125,000. They have three properties with profits totaling $21,564, as well as five properties with losses totaling $97,641.

How do they make out under the current tax law? Netting the profits and losses, the Fosters have a net passive loss of $76,077. Because of tax reform, calculations must be made in order to find out what part of the losses can be used to offset their income.

Since they earn over $100,000 but less than $150,000, they can deduct only $1 out of every $2 over $100,000. The Fosters make $125,000, leaving $25,000 in this 50% category. Thus $12,500 becomes fully deductible as real estate losses.

Here's why: The $25,000 in income over $100,000 causes $12,500 in losses to be nondeductible. This relates to the special $25,000 loss allowance on actively managed rental real estate. Only $12,500 in losses is deductible.

Their losses total $76,077, however. This suggests they have $63,577 in nondeductible losses.

There is some relief for the Fosters, because the phase-in rules of tax reform apply for 1989. Therefore, 20 percent of the otherwise nondeductible losses can indeed be deducted.

Here is where that leaves the Fosters:

Total passive losses	$76,077
Fully deductible loss	<u>12,500</u>
Nondeductible losses	$63,577
Phase-in (1989) at 20%	12,715
Losses carry-forwarded to future years	$50,862

The Fosters have allowable tax losses of $25,215 ($12,500 + $12,715) and nondeductible losses—applicable to offset profits in future years—of

$50,862. They are in the 33 percent tax bracket for 1989, so their tax savings are $8,321 (25,215 × 33%).

Here is their after-tax cash flow:

Real Estate losses	($76,077)
Add depreciation deductions	$75,216
. . . and tax savings	8,321
Then subtract mortgage principal payments	16,545
For AFTER TAX CASH FLOW	($ 9,085)

So the Fosters wind up with a slight negative cash flow. This is well within their budget, considering their yearly income. Additionally, they have $50,862 in losses to offset future profits. That amount could reduce profits in the coming years from their rentals, or reduce capital gains, should they sell any of their properties.

DON'T IGNORE HIDDEN GAINS

At first glance, all the folks in our examples did quite well? But didn't I forget something?

Sure did—mortgage payments, for starters. In each case the cash flow was reduced because of mortgage principal payments. Yet those payments are really money that goes right back into the investors' pockets. Why? Because each dollar of principal paid increases the investors' equity in the property.

If you look at the examples in this light, the results are even more favorable:

	Cash Flow Calculated	+	Principal Payments	=	Actual Return
Ross	(1,065)		$ 1,250		$ 185
Burtons	$ 366		$ 3,201		$3,567
Fosters	(9,085)		$16,545		$7,460

Now, all the investors show positive results in actual return. And I have not considered another potentially positive area—appreciation. If you figure in a very conservative 5 percent annual increase in real estate values, you can picture a smile on the faces of all these people.

Has tax reform taken some of the glitter out of real estate investing by limiting passive write-off? Yes. Is the potential for tax savings and for appreciation still very much available for the majority of Americans who invest in real estate? Absolutely!

NONDEDUCTIBLE LOSSES

You can turn the arithmetic even more in your favor by taking some simple steps to cover nondeductible losses. That means reducing your losses or generating more passive income. There are several ways to accomplish this goal.

First, to reduce passive losses, take out a home equity loan on your primary or secondary residence up to $100,000, as discussed in chapter 3. The interest on such a loan will be fully deductible as home mortgage interest if you have not already taken advantage of this mortgage category.

Use the proceeds from the loan to pay off the mortgage on one of your rental properties. This strategy effectively transfers nondeductible passive interest to fully deductible home mortgage interest.

Second, think about investing in a limited partnership. This will generate passive income instead of portfolio income. For example, if you currently have $2,000 in nondeductible passive losses, you might pursue the following strategy:

Do *not* invest $10,000 in a stock, bond, or mutual fund yielding 10 percent. That would produce $1,000 in fully taxable income. Instead, invest in a good RELP with a projected yield of 10 percent. The $1,000 yield from the RELP would be completely offset by your passive losses, which would be nondeductible otherwise. The net result: no taxes owed on your RELP payout.

STOP READING, START MAKING MONEY!

That's it for the course in real estate tax math. It's high time, don't you think, to put what you have learned into practice!

Now that you have read about 171 ways to make money in real estate, decide which ones among them are best for you. Join the National Association of Real Estate Clubs, and your own local chapter, and start networking.

Don't forget to tune me in on your local radio station, where I keep you posted regularly on deal making, taxes, and other aspect of real estate.

Better yet, if you have a deal you want to bounce off me, or a question to ask on any area of real estate, call me during on-air hours at (800) 356-5566, or off-air hours at (900) 246-4000.

Remember, the only dumb question is the question that has not been asked. See you on the radio.

To receive a free list of radio stations that carry Sonny Bloch's shows, as well as tax updates as they are passed by Congress, send a stamped, self-addressed envelope to Sonny Bloch, Box 420, Tannersville, PA 18372.

REVIEW

171 Ways to Make Money Investing in Real Estate

CHAPTER 1

1. Concentrate on "affordable" housing rather than expensive housing.
2. Make deals only after documents are reviewed by an attorney who specializes in real estate.
3. Use leverage to control 100 percent of a property with as little as 10 percent down.
4. Buy only those properties your analysis indicates will appreciate in value each year.
5. Buy only those properties that will show flat or positive cash flow.
6. Seek motivated sellers with distressed property which they must unload.
7. When interest rates go higher than 12 percent, insist on owner financing.
8. Buy real estate as hedge against inflation once inflation reaches 6 percent a year.
9. Always fill out the 15-minute rental property diagnosis (p. 12) when examining a property.
10. Always buy wholesale—at least 10 percent below market value of an investment property.
11. Take renovation costs, insurance, and taxes into account when analyzing profit potential.

CHAPTER 2

12. Take the comfort zone test (p. 17) to determine whether you will be happier as an active or a passive investor.
13. Devote a certain number of hours each week to your active deals.
14. Invest your own money in real estate when you want to retain a bigger share of a deal.
15. Flip properties—buy and then sell quickly—to generate immediate cash.
16. Hire others to manage your property to give your more time to find new deals.
17. Have your first 500 "real estate investor" business cards printed now, with your photo on them.

CHAPTER 3

18. Borrow against the equity in your home to raise money for the down payment on your first deal.
19. Compare rates on home equity loans to get your funds quickly, for the lowest fees, at the lowest interest rate.
20. Seek out fixed rates, rather than adjustable ones, on your loan.
21. When using adjustable rates, apply for money tied to the least volatile index possible.
22. Seek the smallest possible cap on any adjustable rates.
23. Deduct closing costs on home equity loans from your taxes when that is feasible.
24. Pay a bit extra to lock in a good interest rate.
25. Sell those stocks and bonds that have registered strong gains to raise additional money for real estate deals.
26. Balance your real estate portfolio by investing in raw land and such passive instruments as REITs.
27. Project and prioritize your goals with the wish list (p. 32).

CHAPTER 4

28. Join a real estate club to meet potential partners.
29. Approach friends, relatives, and business or professional associates to be your partners in deals.
30. Advertise in the classified section of your local newspaper for other partners.

31. Have your lawyer draw up an agreement spelling out each partner's responsibilities, and include a clause allowing you to buy out one another.

32. Investigate syndication as a possible arrangement to finance bigger deals.

33. Talk with a potential partner's associates and employer before signing a formal partnership agreement.

34. Run a credit check on potential partners.

35. Be prepared to reveal your own financial picture to potential partners.

36. Have all partners exchange completed personal financial statements (p. 41).

CHAPTER 5

37. Begin your new career with a single family residential property because it is the least complicated real estate investment.

38. Scout properties physically close to home or near regularly visited business or vacation places.

39. Compare crime rate, transportation, commuter systems, and other neighborhood attributes before buying.

40. Scan classified ads regularly to keep abreast of the range of rents and home prices in your area.

41. Keep clippings of ads in a loose-leaf notebook to spot price reductions and to keep track of the length of time properties remain on the market.

42. Distribute your business cards to local buildings, superintendents, postmen, overnight delivery drivers, moving companies, and others.

43. Keep an eye out for "For Sale" signs and houses that apparently have been abandoned

44. Schedule your own "drive-by" tours of potential properties.

45. Fill out property evaluation worksheets (p. 53, 54) for each property you inspect.

46. Place as many aggressively low bids as possible on interesting properties.

47. Project a cash-on-cash return (p. 49) for each property you might be buying.

48. Make as small a down payment as possible to create cash flow.

49. Promote seller financing whenever feasible to speed deals and avoid bottlenecks incurred in financing.

50. Buy a 2-family house and use one residence as your own to get your investing off the ground.

51. Buy a mixed-use property only if rent from the residential unit, not the commercial unit, covers your monthly mortgage payment.

CHAPTER 6

52. Examine existing leases or government controls on rents after acquiring residential property you plan to rent.
53. Shop for a residence as if you were a prospective tenant to become familiar with the rental market conditions prevalent in the area.
54. Set rents on your property so they produce flat or positive cash flow, but are also in line with those in the immediate vicinity.
55. For quick tenants, consult local HUD about housing Section 8 government-supported families.
56. Offer neighboring tenants, concierges, and superintendents a referral fee for finding tenants in a competitive market.
57. Send postcards to neighboring residents asking for tenant referrals.
58. Charge applicants a nonrefundable screening fee to discourage curiosity seekers and bad credit risks.
59. Double check credit references with a credit bureau and applicant's landlord at next-to-last residence.
60. Customize standard lease forms to cover specific do's and don'ts you want to enforce.
61. Collect rent for first and last month at time of lease signing, plus a one-month deposit for security and damages.
62. Encourage prompt rent payments with bonus discount for early payments, penalties for late ones.
63. Permit tenants to pay rents via credit cards.
64. Turn over problem tenants to professionals who handle evictions.

CHAPTER 7

65. Buy raw land and hold it for long-, not short-term appreciation; a good parcel will double in value every ten years.
66. Look for cheapest land in rural areas and best prices at auction.
67. Learn about industrial, commercial, recreational, or demographic changes that will increase the value of certain land.
68. Search for new towns that are outstripping their current boundaries.
69. Buy land in the path of proposed new airports, new highways, or near new interchanges.

70. Pay attention to billboards, classified ads, land directories, and small "For Sale" signs advertising land.
71. Check with Interstate Land Sales Registration office before buying land from a new resort developer.
72. Always inspect raw land in person; don't rely on photos, slides, or videos.
73. Buy only that land which you can get below market value, with the possibility of future development or sale to developers.
74. Pay attention to roads, topography, water, and zoning before signing a contract.
75. Insist on seller financing of land purchases rather than seeking a mortgage.

CHAPTER 8

76. Buy at wholesale a 40-acre parcel with public road frontage, divide into four lots, and sell each with retail markup.
77. Advertise your lots with professionally made signs nailed high on trees.
78. Advertise land as being "For Sale by Owner" with little money down.
79. Take potential buyers on personal tours of "their" land.
80. Accept seller financing with interest.

CHAPTER 9

81. Search for tax sales in tax collector's, assessor's, or treasurer's office in chosen area.
82. Ask to have your name put on a mailing list for announcements of tax and foreclosure sales.
83. Subscribe to a service that compiles weekly or monthly notices of foreclosure sales.
84. Ask local bank officer in charge of nonperforming assets about REOs you might buy.
85. Contact government agencies such as HUD, Fannie Mae, FDIC, and others about foreclosed properties.
86. Buy foreclosure properties only when you are able to agree on a price that is at least 20 percent below market value.
87. Build a 25 percent cushion into eventual market value of a fixer-upper when bidding.

88. Include "jump out" clauses in offer sheet for any foreclosed property.
89. Investigate properties in preforeclosure stage by searching court records or subscribing to listing service.
90. Approach owners of property in preforeclosure stage courteously via mail.

CHAPTER 10

91. Bid at auctions with your head, not with your heart.
92. Discover the least publicized auctions, such as those of foreclosed properties, which will have the best buys.
93. Steer clear of "phony" auctions, such as some conducted by eager developers.
94. Aim for "absolute" sales, where there is no floor on acceptable prices.
95. Bring 3 × 5 index cards with your maximum bid written in bright red ink, and hold it in your hand throughout auction.
96. View properties in person and investigate local prices before attending an auction.
97. Sit in the back so you can watch all the players.
98. Withdraw a winning bid if you are unhappy, using a "buyer's remorse" clause.

CHAPTER 11

99. Examine every quarter the General Service Administration's real property sales list for parcels in your region.
100. Familiarize yourself with surplus property auctions by attending a few without bidding.
101. Be persistent and make as many inquiries as possible on small, affordable sites.
102. Do your standard homework on possible buys by visiting sites in person and checking residential rents in area.
103. Learn about Chapter 7 Bankruptcy Court sales in your area.
104. Contact the local branch of the U. S. Customs office for information on sales of seized property.
105. Get in touch with the nearest National Asset Seizure and Forfeiture Office of the U. S. Marshals Office about their property sales.

106. Investigate SBA sales of property in default that will be auctioned or sold.
107. Be on the lookout for small parcels sold by state transportation agencies.

CHAPTER 12

108. Work with a HUD-affiliated broker to bid on underpriced residences for sale by local HUD offices.
109. Locate especially good values that have not been bought yet on HUD "extended" lists.
110. Select HUD residences with insured government loans that you can assume.
111. For the best deal, buy low-cost HUD properties for cash.
112. Find out about loans available from your local development commission.
113. Start investing by buying a Section 235 home, live in it, then move out and rent it.
114. Work with a broker on buying VA-reposessed homes with guaranteed low-cost financing.
115. Ask if your state waives "first time home buyer" rules on cheap loans for purchases in target areas.

CHAPTER 13

116. Do the numbers on "time cost of managing" (p. 141) before hiring anyone, to make sure management fees still allow you a flat or positive cash flow.
117. Hire a management company only after interviewing several who meet your qualifications.
118. Check a property manager's qualifications with national associations.
119. Request a client list and interview manager's clients at random for opinions.
120. Pay only for those management services you cannot or do not want to perform yourself.
121. Set a limit on the amount a manager can spend for routine repairs without prior approval.
122. Spot-check residences to make sure repairs are made correctly.
123. Even if you have a property manager, qualify for tax deductions by staying "actively" involved in your property.

CHAPTER 14

124. Become an "angel" by making an investor equity participation deal with a relative, friend, or stranger.
125. Use classified ads, attorneys, mortgage companies, and word of mouth to spread your availability in such deals.
126. Set a deadline of no more than ten years for sale of the property you share.
127. Give your partner the option to buy you out before deadline at a profit.
128. Obtain a "deed in lieu of foreclosure" so you can reposess property if necessary with a minimum of trouble.
129. Include a buyout clause if you need money before deadline for sale.
130. Include your name of the mortgage to get additional tax deductions on interest and depreciation.

CHAPTER 15

131. Find out which states pay the highest interest on tax certificates and how long they must be held before being redeemed.
132. Contact your local authority for time, place, and instructions on next tax certificate sale.
133. Obtain list of properties in advance and visit properties you plan to bid on.
134. Be wary of paying too much of a premium on tax certificates in various states.
135. At "open buying," purchase remaining tax certificates once a formal sale is over.
136. Enhance your chances to claim actual property by bidding on certificates that cover vacant land.

CHAPTER 16

137. Use the Sonny Bloch "Golden Rule" (first and second mortgage combined should not exceed 50 percent of market value of property) to buy second mortgages.
138. Look for original owners of properties who have taken back paper and are willing to sell that note for quick cash at a discount.
139. Buy only those second mortgages with five to seven years remaining on them.

140. Find second mortgages by advertising in classified sections and by contacting professional dealers.
141. Accept mortgages (''paper'') at a discount on other properties as payment for your own deals.
142. Make certain you are the loss payee on insurance documents.
143. Restrict your second mortgage purchases to residences; steer clear of churches, bars, or other limited-use facilities.
144. If you are a conservative, hands-off investor, buy REMICs as your entry into the second mortgage market.

CHAPTER 17

145. Invest in Real Estate Investment Trusts for safe, though low, returns.
146. Analyze a REIT prospectus before buying to find out what kind of property or mortgages the company invests in.
147. Look for REITs whose managers have a respectable track record.
148. Buy only those REITs that have consistently had a yield of 8 percent or more.
149. Look for REITs with property in undervalued areas, with cash dividends, and with cash reserves.
150. Use the Cal State Test (p. 190) to grade REITs.

CHAPTER 18

151. Buy public limited partnerships for current income and appreciation, not solely for tax benefits.
152. Look for RELPs with guaranteed annual cash distributions.
153. Choose moderately leveraged RELPs that focus on income-producing properties such as apartment building, office buildings, and shopping centers.
154. Search for ''no load'' partnerships that do not charge a sales commission.
155. Buy only those RELPs whose administrative fees and commission come to less that 20 percent.
156. If you are concerned about selling your shares before the RELP expires, concentrate on Master Limited Partnerships (MLPs).
157. Bet on RELPs whose general partners have verifiably good track records.
158. Make sure the RELP promises to give you frequent reports.

159. Have your CPA go over a RELP prospectus before you invest.
160. Check the small but growing secondary market for RELP shares at a deep discount.

CHAPTER 19

161. Invest in private partnerships only if you are psychologically ready to take a large risk and financially able to absorb a loss of the entire investment.
162. Invest with partners who have an excellent track record.
163. Read the deal memo carefully, with an eye for caution signs that could reduce your potential share of the profits.
164. Have the deal memo cross-checked by your CPA.
165. Watch out for partnerships that can invoke a "call" provision for additional investments from limited partners.
166. Know the tax consequences of investing in a private partnership.

CHAPTER 20

167. Maintain good records and all documentation for tax purposes, including a yearly calendar book.
168. Use a separate checkbook for your real estate rental properties.
169. Use an experienced CPA trained in real estate to do your accounting.
170. Be alert for hidden gains (mortgage payments, appreciation) that are making your investment property more valuable.
171. Reduce nondeductible losses or generate more passive income in order to improve your tax situation.

INDEX